37 $\underline{50}$

1 $\subset$

THE WORLD TRADING SYSTEM

The World Trading System

The Uruguay Round and Beyond

Brian McDonald

First published in Great Britain 1998 by
MACMILLAN PRESS LTD
Houndmills, Basingstoke, Hampshire RG21 6XS and London
Companies and representatives throughout the world

A catalogue record for this book is available from the British Library.

ISBN 0–333–72073–3

First published in the United States of America 1998 by
ST. MARTIN'S PRESS, INC.,
Scholarly and Reference Division,
175 Fifth Avenue, New York, N.Y. 10010

ISBN 0–312–21192–9

Library of Congress Cataloging-in-Publication Data
McDonald, Brian, 1945–
The world trading system : the Uruguay Round and beyond / Brian
McDonald.
p. cm.
Includes bibliographical references and index.
ISBN 0–312–21192–9 (cloth)
1. General Agreement on Tariffs and Trade (Organization)
2. Uruguay Round (1987–1994)   3. World Trade Organization.
4. Tariff.   5. Industrial policy.   6. International trade.
I. Title.
HF1713.M366 1997   97–40581
382'.92—dc21   CIP

This book is printed on paper suitable for recycling and made from fully managed and sustained forest sources.

10   9   8   7   6   5   4   3   2
07 06 05 04 03 02 01 00 99

Printed and bound in Great Britain by
Antony Rowe Ltd, Chippenham, Wiltshire

For my parents,
for
Carol, Gregory, Cliona, and Michael
and in memory of
Padraig Collins

Contents

Preface

I would like to start by thanking my secretaries, who have had the invidious task of typing and correcting the manuscript and have had to adjust it through an endless number of variations and changes. What appeared to me like a search for clarity and accuracy can only have appeared to them as real drudgery, and I am extremely grateful for all their patience. I would like to thank Linda O'Kane and Phyllis Leech, and in particular the latter, who had to carry out the most painful task of getting the final manuscript in order, along with all its footnotes and endless details. My thanks also go to Beverly Must and Winnie Fong.

I would also like to salute Paul Luyten, Roderick Abbott, Jacques Dugimont and Jean-Pierre Derisbourg, with whom I worked in the Commission Delegation to the GATT in the late 1970s during the Tokyo Round, who stimulated my interest in the subject of international trade, and who taught me a great deal about it. I would particularly like to thank Jean-Pierre Derisbourg for all his friendship and support, and for teaching me what I know about trade negotiation. My heartfelt thanks to Angel Vinas for all his advice and help.

In writing this book I have been able to rely on the advice and help of many of my colleagues at the European Commission in Brussels, and I am most grateful to them for their patience. Needless to say I take full responsibility for the result. I am particularly grateful to Jacques Dugimont, Alistair Stewart, Soren Olsen, and Ignacio Garcia-Bercero who helped me with the more difficult parts of the exercise and those chapters where I felt least at ease with the subject matter. I am also very grateful to Graham Vickery of the OECD Secretariat and Alain Franke of the WTO Secretariat for all their help. My thanks also to the European Commission for the use of its resources and some of its time.

I have referred to the European Union throughout this text as this is now the term by which the general public knows the organisation. Strictly speaking, in its economic manifestation it should be referred to as the European Community, but I thought it best to avoid the use of several terms. In the case of the GATT and the WTO, however, this was unavoidable; references to the GATT

concern the life and rules of that organisation up to 1994, when
the WTO came into being, and after 1994 the references are to
the WTO, though the GATT, as a treaty, is still in existence.

BRIAN MCDONALD

The author and publishers are grateful to the following for per-
mission to reproduce copyright material: the United Nations (and
UNCTAD), the World Trade Organisation, the Organisation for
Economic Cooperation and Development and the World Bank. Every
effort has been made to contact all the copyright-holders, but if
any have been inadvertently omitted the publishers will be pleased to
make the necessary arrangement at the earliest opportunity.

The views expressed in this book are the author's own and do not
necessarily represent the views of the European Commission.

List of Abbreviations

AA	Agreement on Agriculture
ATC	Agreement on Textiles and Clothing
ADA	Antidumping Agreement
AMS	Aggregate Measurement of Support
APEC	Asian-Pacific Economic Cooperation Process
AS	Agreement on Safeguards
ASC	Agreement on Subsidies and Countervailing Measures
ATCA	Agreement on Trade in Civil Aircraft
CAFE	Corporate Average Fuel Economy Regulation
CAP	Common Agricultural Policy
CEN/CENELEC	Committee on European Standardisation and the Committee on European Electromechanical Standardisation
CITES	Convention on International Trade in Endangered Species of Wild Fauna and Flora
CSE	Consumer Subsidy Equivalent
DARPA	Defense Research Projects Agency
DBS	Direct Broadcast Satellite
DTH	Direct to Home
EC	European Community
EFTA	European Free Trade Area
EU	European Union
FDI	Foreign direct investment
GATS	General Agreement on Trade in Services
GATT	General Agreement on Tariffs and Trade
GPA	Government procurement agreement
GSP	Generalised system of preferences
IDD	International direct dialling
ILO	International Labour Organisation
IMF	International Monetary Fund
ISO	International Standards Organisation
ITA	Information Technology Agreement
MERCOSUR	Southern Common Market
MFA	Multifibre Arrangement
MFN	Most favoured nation

MSA	Multilateral Steel Agreement
NAFTA	North American Free Trade Area
NTB	Non-tariff barrier
OECD	Organisation for Economic Cooperation and Development
OPEC	Organisation of Petroleum Exporting Countries
PPMs	Process and production methods
PTO	Post and Telegraph office
PSE	Producer subsidy equivalent
QR	Quantitative restriction
R&D	Research and development
SDR	Special Drawing Right
SME	Small and medium-sized enterprises
TAFTA	Trans-Atlantic Free-Trade Area
TBT	Technical barrier to trade
TRIMs	Trade-related investment measures
TRIPs	Trade-related Intellectual Property
UNCTAD	United Nations Conference on Trade and Development
VER	Voluntary export restraint
VRA	Voluntary Restraint Arrangement
WTO	World Trade Organisation

Part I

Development of the Global Trading System

1 Introduction

DEVELOPMENT OF THE WORLD ECONOMY

It is no understatement to say that trade is essential to the prosperity of the world economy and remains one of the main avenues open to us to increase productivity and growth. The history of trade liberalisation has demonstrated this clearly. By opening markets, the most efficient suppliers get a chance to sell while the less efficient are stimulated to be more competitive. Increased specialisation leads to economies of scale and other efficiencies. Some of the figures in Table 1.1 demonstrate this.

Table 1.1 Growth in volume of world GDP and merchandise trade, 1870–1993 (average annual percentage change)

	GDP	Merchandise trade
1870–1900	2.9	3.8
1900–1913	2.5	4.3
1913–1950	2.0	0.6
1950–1973	5.1	8.2
1973–1993	2.6	3.8

Sources: Maddison (1964), OECD (1989), WTO (1995).[1]

While the above figures were based on a selection of countries for earlier periods, those from 1950 onwards relate to all countries and represent the average annual percentage change. The figures show a consistent upward trend in trade and an increase since the Second World War, double that of GDP growth in real terms. The figures show that trade is one of the main motors of increased productivity and efficiency, and an important road to prosperity. The drop in trade growth in the 1913–50 period was due to the depression, partly brought on by protectionist trade policies, and subsequently the war itself. As one can see, there appears to be a strong correlation between trade and GDP growth.

Those countries that have pursued an open trade policy most vigorously, for example the developed countries, the Asian Tigers and some others, can also be demonstrated to have profited very

3

substantially from it and to have grown more quickly than those which did not.[2] The main motor of free trade in the post Second World War era was of course the United States. But it has been imitated by most other developed economies, which have by now attained a level of liberalisation equal to or even surpassing that of the United States.

In the case of the European Union, the free trade orientation has always been very strong and was one of the main objectives of the Treaty of Rome. Through the elaboration of the common market and then the single market, and even the common agricultural policy, the increase in trade within the EU has been extraordinary. This has underpinned a very strong industrial growth rate over the last thirty five years. Contrary to common perceptions of the EU, it has also become the most open trading bloc in the world, and not a 'Fortress Europe' as it is sometimes described. This was achieved through a mutually reinforcing parallel process of internal and external trade liberalisation.

The major industrialised exceptions to the results of the trade liberalisation effort have been Japan and some countries that followed a similar economic model, for example South Korea. The Japanese economy has been strongly export oriented, and while it has participated actively in all the GATT rounds the degree of import penetration in the Japanese market has been very limited. This has given rise to major friction with its trading partners and has created a degree of uncertainty in the operation of the world trading system.

Many of the formal barriers to trade in Japan are low, but the non-tariff barriers have been numerous. The internal structure of the Japanese economy has also tended to favour domestic production over imports. Large industrial and trading conglomerates permeate the economy, including down to the retail level, and have had no incentive to encourage imports. Inward investment has also been controlled in ways that make it difficult to penetrate the domestic market.

Liberalisation of trade in developing economies lagged behind and this had serious results for growth and performance. Some developing countries visibly proved the advantages of an open trade policy, for example Hong Kong and Singapore. Unfortunately, in the past most other developing countries pursued inward-looking, import-substitution economic models, which gave much poorer results for too long. But even they have come around to a more open trade policy, partly under pressure from the IMF and partly because they realised the import substitution model wasn't working. The Communist bloc conducted a virtually autarkic trade policy and was essentially outside the world trading system. Its trade with the West was limited. This situation has been changing fast but while many of the ex-communist countries have become important traders they still retain some of the features of state trading economies.

Inward- and Outward-Looking Economies

An outward-oriented economy is one that maintains a border regime that is basically neutral between imports and exports. An inward-oriented regime maintains a bias in favour of domestic industry and seeks to develop an import-substitution domestic industry behind a protectionist wall. This tends to create two main types of inefficiency.

In the first place, domestic industry is often over-regulated and monopolistic, and does not face competition from either inside or outside the country. The industries seeking protection from outside competition also seem frequently able to assert the need for protection from competition inside the market on the ground that they can only develop in conditions of protection from both outside and inside. The other main problem, which is associated with the first, is that as imports are expensive, so too are the inputs of the exporting industry. This usually prevents them from exporting successfully and reaping the economies of scale and scope that come from access to a wider market.

The difference in economic performance has not just been marginal, it has been dramatic in many cases. Those countries that have pursued an outward-oriented policy have achieved growth rates that are at least two times higher than those of the most inward-oriented countries (Table 1.2). In the case of manufacturing production, the growth rate of outward-oriented economies tends to be even higher, as much as three times that of the inward-oriented economies. It is also the case that apart from trade gains the pressure to compete in an outward-oriented economy tends to be associated with a lot of other efficiencies, such as innovation, higher savings rates and more productive investment.

The import substitution model may not have been entirely the wrong one to adopt, at least in the initial stage of economic development. There are many respectable examples of economies that have grown to maturity behind protective barriers, including the

Table 1.2 Percentage growth rate of GDP and manufactured exports of most outward and inward group or groups of countries

	GDP	Manufactured exports
1963–73		
Most outward group(s)	+ 9.5	14.8 to 16.1
Most inward group(s)	+ 4.1	10.3 to 5.7
1973–85		
Most outward group(s)	+ 7.7	14.2 to 14.5
Most inward group(s)	+ 2.5	8.5 to 3.7

Source: World Bank (1987).[3]

United States and many European economies. Economists in general admit that there is a case for protecting 'infant industries' until they grow to maturity, achieve economies of scale and are able to compete with more established industries.

The levels of protection in the industrialising countries in the nineteenth century were lower on average than those practised by developing countries today. Although industrial countries benefited from higher natural protection before transport costs declined, the average tariff for 12 industrial countries studied by the World Bank ranged from 11 per cent to 32 per cent between 1820 and 1980.[4] Seven of the countries studied had an average tariff of 22 per cent in 1820, the period of the greatest vulnerability or need for infant industry protection. In comparison the average tariff on industrial goods in developing countries was only brought down to 34 per cent by the GATT Uruguay Round and was much higher than that over the last 50 years. (This rate of 34 per cent may however be a little on the low side for some products as it represents an average. On the other hand it is also the rate 'bound' in the framework of the WTO, that is, the level at which a country is obliged to keep its tariff thanks to various rounds of negotiation. Individual applied rates are often lower and the 'applied' average may also be lower.)

The model has too often been pursued beyond the point of maturity of an infant industry or as an end in itself. The result has been too much protection and too little competition, with poor results in terms of growth and welfare.

Some economies, for example Hong Kong and Singapore, have had very open regimes and their growth rates have shown the best record over the last twenty years. Other inward-oriented models, such as those pursued by many countries in Latin America, have tended to show the poorest results. Similar difficulties have arisen in most of the African economies, compounded by the volatility of raw material export prices and by a series of other non-economic factors such as civil and political instability, wars, severe climatic conditions and other structural problems.

For some countries this has meant that they have not been able to diversify successfully away from the production of primary products. This failure has meant an excessive concentration on the export of these products, which are no longer dynamic. There has been a long-term decline in the demand for many commodities due to the substitution of other materials (for example plastics for steel) or increased efficiency (for example reduction in petroleum usage). Even in agriculture, though the world's population is continually increasing, agricultural productivity is increasing even faster, and the long-term relative price of these products is declining.

Various efforts to arrest the decline in commodity prices by means of international agreements of one sort or another (buffer stocks, cartels and so on) have been expensive failures. With one or two exceptions, such as OPEC and some programmes used to stabilise export earnings rather than prices (for example Stabex – an EU scheme), there is little enthusiasm or energy left for such exercises.

In the case of some commodities, prices have held up quite well over time and not everyone has been affected by a long-run price decline, nor have they needed commodity schemes to prop up these prices. But the price of commodities does tend to fluctuate more and they are considered a less reliable base for modern industrial development. The emphasis nowadays is on diversification. In the past many countries have felt that given the decline in commodity prices, an import substitution policy was in order. This perspective has now been generally discarded.

The problem of the long-term decline of many commodity prices has affected Latin American and African countries most. In Asia and some Latin American countries such as Chile, the effort to diversify has been more successful and their exports of industrial products have shown dramatic increases, with the biggest improvement (70 per cent of the total) in the export performance of the Asian dragons.[5]

Since the early 1990s there has been a very substantial reorientation of trade policies in Latin America and a very vigorous attempt to try to move towards a more outward-oriented type of economic policy. This has taken place with more success in some countries than in others, with Chile, Mexico and Argentina on the positive side of the ledger, and some other major economies such as Brazil on the other side, falling short of their potential. But the general change in orientation is clear, and the renewed interest in the establishment of free trade areas within Latin America and the renewed interest of these countries in the WTO itself demonstrate that the corner has been turned. It would seem now that these countries are determined to achieve better economic results through improved economic and trade policies.

UNCERTAINTIES AND DOUBTS

The development of free trade has not come without great uncertainty about its feasibility and the possibility of implementing it. If anything the uncertainties have mounted over the years. Protectionism, which is a permanent threat in the trade field, has become more acute in recent times due to a variety of factors, such as a decline in the economic environment, technological change and the perceived threat from globalisation of the world economy. The fear of globalisation is compounded by the perception that some international trade partners are not playing by the rules.

The Economic Environment

The various structural changes that have become necessary in a modern economy are undermined by poor macroeconomic conditions and recessions. Governments are reluctant to increase trade openness when they are already being subjected to severe criticism on account of high unemployment.

To take an example, the GATT Tokyo Round was put on hold almost the day after it was inaugurated because of the severe oil price rise in 1973. This unsettled trade and employment to the point that it was felt a major market opening move by the GATT partners could not be undertaken immediately. (Ironically the Tokyo Round was completed in 1979, the year of an even bigger oil price hike, but by then these changes were anticipated and the world knew better how to cope with them. Or perhaps the politicians were simply more courageous.)

Governments have also sought to preserve or promote certain industries for strategic reasons, with greater or lesser degrees of success. This has often been a potent inspiration for protectionism. Most studies will tell you that trade liberalisation does not cost that many jobs and if anything tends to increase employment, but it is very difficult to explain this to the man in the street or to the one who is going to have to give up his job and look for a new one. This is the sort of fate that is not usually reserved for those economists who favour free trade.

Technological Change

Technological advances have been rapid and profound and have created severe dislocation, comparable, in the eyes of some, to the 1920s when the last great manufacturing modernisation took place. This was arguably one of the major causes of the Great Depression. We are better able to manage our economic affairs nowadays, but there is still a lot of structural unemployment due to technological change, with jobs for those with skills and few for those without, high wages for some and low wages for others. Our economies have not yet caught up with these technological advances, and investment has so far fallen short of making up the difference between jobs lost and new employment. This has in its turn been made worse by the lack of flexibility in many markets and a lack of adjustment assistance and investment in education and skills.

Globalisation

These uncertainties have been compounded by the fact that the world economy has become globalised in a way we have not seen before and there are more centres of competition. This is due to the more open trading system developed over the last 30 years, but perhaps more importantly investment outside the industrialised countries has become a major factor in this development. This in turn has been largely brought about by the deregulation of capital movements, which has provided the necessary capital to finance an increase in manufacturing capacity in developing countries.

Globalisation poses a different type of problem for the WTO than in the past, insofar as economies with different levels of development and structure now have to be integrated under the global free trade system.

Fifteen years ago the bulk of the trade in manufactured goods was between the developed economies. There was an increasing role for the developing countries but their role was still relatively limited. This is no longer the case and some developing countries are now in the forefront in the export of manufactured goods and services. They are playing an increasingly important role on the world trade scene and there are many consequences to be drawn from this.

Sources of Friction

There are some brilliant examples of economies that have adopted an export-led strategy but have done so from behind substantial import barriers. The main example is of course Japan, and some very successful imitators in Asia, for example South Korea and Taiwan. In Japan's case few overt border measures such as tariffs have remained in place since the Tokyo Round, but the internal structure of the economy and non-tariff barriers make the Japanese market very difficult to penetrate. In the case of South Korea and Taiwan, overt import barriers are still high.

So how have they managed to ensure that their import substitution model was a success compared with the others? This is obviously not an easy question to answer, but they have made extensive use of cartels both to protect the domestic market and to increase prices there. As a result Japanese firms have been able to use the excess returns made domestically to maintain high and continuous employment and to drop their prices on the world market below what the competition can afford. The strategy is geared to high employment and the creation of global market share.[6]

Japanese firms are kept on their toes by having to compete on the world market (if not domestically where they tend to compete on product differentiation rather than price), very often against other Japanese firms (Sony versus Matsushita and so on). This has been combined with a deliberate export strategy (for example low tariffs on inputs, export support, exchange and capital controls), which means they have been in a very good position to compete on world markets. And compete they have! They also have access to cheap finance due to the high Japanese savings rate; this finance is moreover often provided at preferential rates through government intervention or by the banks that are owned by the large conglomerates or cartels that do the exporting.

The Japanese and others have followed a successful import substitution policy by concentrating not only on substituting for imports, but also on creating export markets. This strategy has favoured Japanese producers at the expense of its consumers, and has put producers at a definite advantage compared with producers in other developed economies where the consumer gets a better deal. It is however a strategy that cannot be pursued by everyone at once (see Chapter 3).

The effectiveness of Japanese companies relates to their high productivity and their ability to compete most effectively in upmarket, high tech, high productivity sectors. The problem of other developed countries is that they have fallen behind in some of these areas. It is also the case, however, that the Japanese economy is run on rather mercantilist lines – if not in law, at least in fact – and an enormous trade imbalance has developed between Japan and others. There are some signs of adjustment and increased imports are now helped by the higher yen, but they have come very late and the Japanese trade surpluses are still very large.

The question of whether or not the Japanese market is open is frequently debated. Apart from industry complaints, which are well documented, the trade figures and surpluses speak for themselves. Moreover Japan scores poorly in terms of intraindustry, two-way trade, and well below the level one would expect in a mature developed economy. This means that its imports mainly tend to be products it cannot provide or make itself, for example raw materials, and it imports few of the goods it can produce.[7]

There is no doubt that US and European firms could make a bigger export effort than they sometimes do, and there are many examples of Western firms that have successfully penetrated the Japanese market by dint of sheer hard work. But this does not detract from the overall picture.

Another issue facing the world economy is how to integrate Eastern Europe. This is more of a problem for Europe than it is for other major Western economies and it is certainly going to pose tremendous challenges. Unlike East Germany when it was reunified with West Germany and its wages were artificially inflated, the rest of Central and Eastern Europe is operating at a very low level of wage and remuneration. Once these economies start to develop and export, of course, they are likely to create strains and pressure for adjustment in the West, which we are already beginning to see.

The adjustment will be severe for both Western and East European economies of course. The example of East Germany is instructive. It was completely opened to the West Germany economy overnight and its industry virtually collapsed. Part of the reason for this was that wages were set on a par with those in West Germany through the one-for-one exchange of West and East Deutschmarks. But this was only part of the problem; the main difficulty was the sheer inefficiency, non-market-oriented nature of the East German economy. Imagine what could happen to other less industrialised economies in Eastern European, given that East Germany was supposedly the industrial star! However one can only hope for a breathing space of a few years. When the Eastern economies are restructured and made more competitive the pressure on Western markets could become intense.

Yet another problem that is looming on the horizon is China. Its export potential is almost infinite and what seems like a small volume of exports from China may appear enormous and destructive to individual sectors in other economies. For the moment this export machine is still in its infancy as China only accounts for 2.2 per cent of world trade, but in a few years the situation will no doubt change dramatically.

The other main difficulty lies in the fact that China is not yet a democracy with stable and predictable economic rules, and the way its economy is managed is still very arbitrary. It exports like a capitalist economy but imports like a traditional communist economy with a restrictive and discretionary import regime. While its overall trade surplus is not enormous and has recently been declining, its exports and surpluses are unduly concentrated in a few markets, mainly the United States and the EU. This creates real problems in developing normal trading relations.

Consequences of Globalisation

The lower wages that prevail in developing countries create difficulties for developed countries where wages are high. These differences are due in large part to productivity differences in the sense that developed economies have high rates of skill and productivity, which compensate for the high wages that are paid to individual workers.

However the developing countries can now compete more effectively in terms of both skill and productivity, which is aided by foreign direct investment in machinery, modern management techniques and so on. The developing countries have an edge insofar as they can continue to pay low wages despite the increase in productivity. While there is a tendency for wages to rise in these circumstances, it will be some time before they reach Western standards.

As we have seen, there is an increasing trend in developed economies towards a big differential between those with skills and high wages and those with low skills and low wages. The latter group of workers has to compete directly with the low wage, low skill and sometimes high productivity workers in the developing countries. The increased openness of markets in developed economies therefore poses a more direct threat to this group.

The present industrial transformation has been described as a race to the bottom,[8] with multinationals hurrying to keep up with each other through the implementation of new technologies, the continuous search for lower wages, lower welfare environments and other factors. The main motor has been the electronics and information revolution, which has forced companies continually to upgrade and transform their facilities. While increasing supply they have employed fewer workers, if possible at lower wages, and the result is a shortfall in global demand. This shortfall is compounded by strict monetarist policies and tax structures that fall more heavily on the consuming than the rentier class. This process of creative destruction has left many people on the sidelines and called into question many of the economic and social policies that have served us well in the past.

The claim that globalisation costs jobs is usually overstated[9]. There is little evidence of substantial market penetration by exports from developing countries. Many jobs are also lost in non-traded sectors. The problems suffered by workers in the United States, for example, are more to do with the structural and technological transformation of the US economy, reduced trade union power, and a failure to retrain workers.

However, globalisation is probably having some effect on employment. Certain labour–intensive sectors in particular, for example steel and textiles, have suffered considerable job losses due to competition from developing countries. Moreover, even if market penetration is weak in other sectors, prices set on the world market can affect prices and employment domestically, either because domestic firms have to export to survive or because they have to lower prices to prevent market penetration. But overall the effects are probably much less severe than claimed. For example OECD trade with non-OECD countries has remained in surplus, though there has been some deterioration in the trade balance with Asian countries; this deterioration is confined to sectors such as textiles, clothing and footwear. The rise in imports of manufactures from Asian countries has been largely offset by rising exports to them.[10]

Nor can trade be blamed for the increased pressure on welfare systems in the West. The real difficulties encountered by such systems are demographic and the fact that they are poorly funded. The pressure on younger generations to pay for increasingly older segments of the population has increased the tax burden and no doubt reduced the competitiveness of many Western economies. But the pressure has come from inside these economies and from past government commitments, not from trade.

There is also no doubt that firms in developed countries export capital in increasing quantities and create competing jobs abroad. The motivation isn't usually to benefit from cheap wages abroad, but rather to get closer to growing markets; cheap wages are not the main concern to most firms unless they are in some very labour-intensive activity.

Whatever the motivation, there is no doubt that there has been a substantial increase in flows to developing countries, particularly those in Asia and to a lesser extent Latin America, and it is still increasing. But the amounts are trivial relative both to intra-OECD investment flows and to domestic investment.[11] While this has enabled these countries to export more to developed countries, it has also given them the wherewithal to import more from the latter. One may ask whether investments in developing countries that are based on low wages will generate enough demand to ensure an increase in exports to those countries. But this neglects the fact that growth rates in the more successful developing countries are also very high compared with those in developed countries. This in itself generates a high demand for goods from the developed world. Indeed the developed countries export more to the developing countries than they import from them, and the total economic pie and increase in the global economy has been to everyone's advantage.

The flows of capital have also helped developing countries to grow in a way they were not able to before, caught as they were in a cycle of poverty and poor economic policies, and deprived of some of the capital they needed for rapid development. This capital was not readily available when capital controls were in place. There are still problems of course, which is only to be expected in a period of major adjustment such as this. Some developing countries, for example China, export too much to certain markets, for example the United States and the EU, and import too little, creating major trade tensions.

Another factor that has exacerbated some of the difficulties is the freedom of capital to go where it pleases. Capital movement is good insofar as it leads to productive investment. But just as frequently the flows are highly speculative and unnecessarily disturbing for the international trade and economic system. There is usually nothing in the underlying economic fundamentals to justify the gyrations of the dollar and yen. The collapse of the Mexican peso might have been less severe in the absence of the flight of hot money.

Moreover, while Western trade and exports are going up all the time, the jobs they create tend to be high tech ones that require few but skilled staff. The problem would appear to be the speed of technological transformation and the fact that investment in new facilities, and above all in education and skills, has not caught up with the number of people seeking employment. We are only at the beginning of a major industrial change and it will be some time before it works its way through. The results of this transformation are bound to be largely beneficial in the longer term, but clearly things are going to be difficult in the medium term.

CONCLUSION

Many of the problems described above can be resolved. Displaced workers can be retrained and acquire higher levels of skill. Technology does not necessarily create a permanently unemployed workforce, indeed it can be a creator of jobs and prosperity. The emergence of a global economy does not usually mean less prosperity but more. The problems are more of adjustment and timing. There is no doubt however that we are not adjusting fast enough and that economic growth rates are probably too low to cope with the unemployment created. The result is a climate of uncertainty.

Some developed economies have reacted to the economic pressures of today by downsizing their firms, which affects not only the unskilled but also the managerial class, and there is increasing bitterness in the way this new competitive situation is being handled in the United States. Others, for example many members of the EU, have tried to protect jobs and incomes but have created unemployment instead.

The choices available are not terribly palatable. The European countries can be accused of behaving like King Canute, but the United States can be accused of not caring very much for its employees, and that excessive profits and large executive salaries are being earned on the backs of employees.

At the same time the economic philosophy of the moment is rather hard line and monetarist and this reinforces the short-term difficulties. It is not clear that this economic policy will be sustainable over the longer term if unemployment rates remain at their present level and inequality continues unabated. It is unlikely that society will put up indefinitely with either of these phenomena. Hopefully, however, in the medium term lower deficits and debt and lower interest rates will create more employment provided there is a willingness to invest. More flexible labour markets will also be needed to underpin new investment on the scale required to reduce unemployment.

This is the supply side of the coin, but one should not neglect the demand side. There is evidence in the United States that the regressive tax system in vogue since the 1980s has undermined demand in the economy without increasing investment.[12] The rich get richer, and the incomes of the middle class and poor stagnate or decline. Taxes may have decreased for the rich, but they have increased for the middle class. The rich don't spend much more and the others have less to spend, so overall demand in the economy has been affected. Moreover, despite all the claims of the supply siders, lower taxes have not led to an increase in investment and they are unlikely to do so with relatively stagnant demand. Some rebalancing of the tax burden appears to be in order.

There is also a fair case to be made for some reregulation of capital movements, not to prevent such movement, but to avoid its speculative excess, for example by changing margin requirements, by introducing an exchange tax or other means.[13] What is not good economics, nor something for which politicians have any appetite, is stopping capital movements or erecting barriers to trade. Either of these steps would undermine the necessary process of adjustment. A new consensus is needed to deal with what has become a global issue, but it will have to focus on modulation of the existing structures and the development of international standards. Turning one's back on the natural destination of present trends would only be counterproductive and lead to uncompetitiveness and more unemployment.

The various uncertainties described above have meant that the doctrine of free trade has come in for a certain amount of scrutiny and doubt, and the problems outlined above have tended to shake people's faith in free trade and its benefits. Some developments in economic theory and trade policy have done nothing to allay these uncertainties, and if anything have spilled oil on the flames. These developments are explored further in the next chapter.

2 Trade Theory

INTRODUCTION

The old doctrine of free trade was based on David Ricardo's nineteenth century theory of comparative advantage, whereby countries produced what they were best at producing, and by trading with others they were better off than if all countries sought to produce everything they needed. For example a country with abundant land and a good climate produced agricultural goods, and a capital-rich country with abundant coal and steel produced industrial goods. By trading with each other both stood to gain, and this should occur even if one country was better at both activities: specialisation brought benefits.

The main consequence of the theory was that it created a justification for free trade. Until then, free trade theory had been based on mercantilist notions, whereby a country was considered to be maximising its wealth if it exported more and imported less than others. The theory of comparative advantage demonstrated that this wasn't true. You maximised wealth by exploiting your comparative advantages, not your absolute advantages.

However, like all theories it gave a fairly static picture of the economy and failed to give due weight to the dynamic nature of an economy and of life. It tended to imply that if you were good at activity x you should stick to it and not seek to compete with others who were good at activity y, as your competitive or comparative advantage lay in an endless repetition of activity x. It also assumed a state of perfect competition and did not take account of the fact that many firms operated in a state of imperfect competition. It was closely linked to and based on the article of faith that the market's and Adam Smith's 'hidden hand' knew best. It was associated with the idea that new firms and products would come into existence and change a country's comparative advantage as a natural outcome of market forces. However it frowned on the use of government money to change the situation, as this was not an optimal use of resources.

While the theory itself contained a great deal of truth and laid the foundation for modern free trade, some of the implications drawn from it often lacked common sense. The way it was sometimes interpreted, it was a recipe for not changing or not developing and had an unacceptable semi-colonial ring to it, with developing countries being relegated to specialisation in the production of raw materials for use by the more sophisticated firms in developed economies. In most cases of economic development, the comparative advantage of an economy is often created artificially by policy and nurture. Many comparative advantages do not stem from natural resources alone, or availability of capital, but from the skills of the population, which can be fostered, and the policies adopted or assistance given by governments. Sometimes in a world of imperfect competition comparative advantage can only be exploited by unusual and interventionist measures.

The original version of the theory is still probably an accurate description of what happens between developed and developing countries in trade in certain sectors. This trade is frequently characterised by the comparative advantage of the developing countries in, for example, primary products, and of the developed countries in manufactured products. The comparative advantage of developing countries is also strong in certain manufacturing sectors where the products are relatively undifferentiated (for example raw steel) or where the technology is relatively straightforward and labour costs are an important element in production (for example textiles).

The irony is that reliance on comparative advantage can lead to an impasse or breakdown in trade. The comparative advantage of developing countries is sometimes such that there is a danger that certain imports from them will lead to a total elimination or collapse of the relevant sectors in the developed countries, for example textiles, leaving little scope for survival through specialisation or differentiation. Unable or unwilling to contemplate such a development, nations have tended to protect these sectors. This sort of interindustry trade has not therefore had the happiest history.

This type of conflict has also occurred between developed countries. Trade with Japan has often appeared to have more of the characteristics of interindustry than intraindustry trade. The Japanese have tended to compete across the broad spectrum of an industry rather than in specialised niches of it and have prevented penetration of their home market, thus curtailing the specialisation of others. The Japanese export drive has led to the collapse of certain industries in other developed economies, for example those producing cameras, TVs and video recorders in the United States.

As can be seen from some of the above examples, comparative advantage can lead to the elimination of whole sectors. Some have resisted this sort of development in order to slow down the industrial adjustment of certain sectors, or more positively to ensure a renewal of the industry and its modernisation in order to survive. In the long term few countries are willing to accept the sort of competition created by Japan, where part of the problem is that their firms cannot compete in the Japanese market.

However most developed and some middle-income countries now have roughly the same competitive advantages. A country such as South Korea is capable of producing automobiles almost as effectively as a country such as Germany. What in fact makes the difference between the various developed economies is not that they can't produce the same types of product, but that they produce products that are highly differentiated one from the other within relatively narrow product groups. This specialisation of trade within an industry is what is known as intraindustry trade. Intraindustry trade, where a high degree of specialisation occurs, enables an industry to survive in its particular market segment and allows for the sort of give and take that suits the development of trade. This corresponds to a more refined and specialised version of the notion of comparative advantage.

EXCEPTIONS TO THE THEORY

A number of reasons are commonly put forward for deviating from the pure theory of free trade:

- Economists have long recognised that protection of an infant industry is probably justified and welfare enhancing, provided the protection is removed at the appropriate time, that is, when the industry has grown up and is able to compete with the other big kids on the block. Most Western economies grew to maturity behind a series of protectionist measures such as tariffs.
- It has also been recognised by economists that a dominant producer can control world prices in certain circumstances and it might be in its interest to raise world prices and increase its terms of trade and revenue. For example the United States, which is the dominant producer of soya beans and animal feed, might be able to raise world prices and increase its revenues by imposing

an export tax. Another obvious example is the control exerted by OPEC. This is in the 'national' interest of these producers.

There are other deviations from the theory that in the past have not been well received by the economics profession but are nonetheless common currency:

- Many countries have felt it important to have a strong industrial policy that promotes chosen sectors and spreads this prosperity throughout the economy by maintaining a network of suppliers and boosting exports. This sort of policy has been practised most successfully by Japan, but it has also been successfully used by others, including the United States, where a number of civilian industrial successes have arisen from military programmes.
- A related argument is the need to maintain certain industries that might otherwise be destroyed by severe interindustry competition. This argument is often used in the context of the electronics sector, steel, shipbuilding and even the manufacture of television sets. It is clear that once an industry has been abandoned it is difficult to start it up again. It is important to maintain a rich industrial fabric with good forward and backward linkages. These industries have their own momentum and take a long time to develop, as well as to reach a sufficient position on the learning curve to become technological and competitive leaders. Governments tend to be reluctant to let them go to the wall.
- Finally, it is frequently argued that industries must be protected for national security reasons. This of course applies to industries that are military in nature or related to the military, for example the electronics sector, but it has also been applied to agriculture and food supplies.

These exceptions are in a sense extensions of the infant industry argument, that a sector needs some protection in order to grow to maturity. But of course they take the logic of this beyond the point of protecting a new and vulnerable sector and make a general argument in favour of protection in order to attain certain industrial objectives. This goes way beyond the limited case of infant industry protection.

However these types of industrial policy now have some theoretical support arising out of more modern trade theory (so-called strategic trade policy).[1] Specialisation in modern industrial markets tends to give rise to imperfect competition and oligopolistic behaviour. Economists now concur that a country may produce some welfare gains by promoting an industry that can compete with monopolists or oligopolists from another country in a particular sector. Such promotion allows the industry to capture some of the profits being earned by those firms, and the increased competition also reduces the price level. A good example of this is Airbus, which challenged the duopoly of Boeing and McDonnell Douglas, and the competition led to a substantial reduction in the average price of aircraft throughout the world. Many firms and many industrial sectors nowadays operate under conditions of imperfect competition with assistance of one sort or another from their governments.

While most applications of the theory concern situations of imperfect competition, the theory has been extended to situations where there is no imperfect competition but a government decides that it wants to develop an advantage. The government may want to contribute start-up funds, even if it never recovers its money, either because it thinks the industry is strategic or to create employment. The subsidised programme may only make normal profits, but it may create extensive ancillary employment throughout the economy. The taxpayer is hit and there is no net creation of economic welfare as the subsidies are not recovered in higher than usual monopoly or oligopoly profits. However society as a whole may still be better off with the creation of a new industry and increased employment.

While many countries have been practising a *de facto* strategic trade policy, it is only fairly recently that trade theory has caught up with them and provided a rationale for it. Ironically, some of the academics who propound the new theory are not always confident that it can be practised successfully.[2] They seem to feel that second-guessing the market by the government will not work in the long run. In this respect they are ignoring successful modern economies such as Japan that have risen on the back of a strategic trade policy, and successful programmes run by other countries, (for example NASA in the United States). A fuller discussion is set out in Chapter 3.

3 Trade Policy

The theories described in Chapter 2 have had an influence on policy making, and some of the main types of policy approach are set out here.

FREE TRADE AT ALL COSTS[1]

There is a school of thought that says free trade is good under any circumstances and that no form of protectionism is either useful or suitable. For this school any action to protect an industry – whether to enable it to adjust or even to counter an unfair trade practice of another – is mistaken. If another country wishes to dominate a particular sector it should be allowed to do so if the domestic sector is not able to compete, for the domestic economy will be better off if it switches its efforts and resources to other types of activity. Even trade that is unfair in the sense of dumping or subsidisation is simply considered as a bonus to the consuming country and a negative action on the part of the exporting country. This approach is of course close to the purest form of comparative advantage theory described above.

The unilateral lowering of trade barriers is usually a good thing. A country will have an advantage if it reduces its external trade barriers to help its consumers, reduce inflation or keep its industries competitive. In fact the whole thesis of this book is that countries should reduce their trade barriers when they can. However it also is the view of this author that it may not always be wise to pursue unilateral reductions regardless of the consequences.

This approach to free trade can be overly simplistic and it tries to draw analogies from the notion of a free and fully competitive market. It ignores the fact that very often the trade advantage of a particular country has been deliberately or artificially created by its government.

To take one example, discriminatory pricing, or dumping, which may not be possible for an individual firm in normal open market conditions, is a decidedly feasible option for exporters from a country where imports are kept at a very low or reduced level through import barriers. They can charge what they like at home, and this enables them to dump the product almost indefinitely at a low price in the market to which they are exporting. Moreover their ability to form domestic or export cartels may be condoned by the public authorities. So what may not be feasible for a private competitor on his own, certainly becomes very feasible when his actions are supported by his government. The laws of economics and antitrust that operate at the level of a national market can not be transferred to the international market without qualification.

This type of approach also tends to suggest that any attempt to protect major industries or industries of national importance are misguided. But it seems to neglect the fact that once an industry is gone it is very difficult to build it up again, and consumers may be at the mercy of a successful monopolistic predator who raises prices once the competition is removed. Moreover the adjustment costs of losing an entire industry can be enormous. Many countries prefer to attempt to ensure the survival of major employing industries. Very often they go about it the wrong way, but sometimes they can be successful. A good example of this is the restructuring of the textile industry, which has been fairly successful in Europe. The introduction of labour-saving equipment, increased specialisation and a long tradition of top-class design have meant that the European textile industry has survived and indeed become stronger, though its restructuring efforts are not at an end. It is now able to compete much more effectively with industries in the developing countries. The restructuring of the steel industry has also been conducted with a fair amount of success both in the EU and the United States.

Many economists would argue that this would have been achieved under conditions of free trade anyway, and that delaying the process through government intervention is a costly and ineffective means of achieving the same objective. But governments are frequently obliged to intervene to ensure a slower transition and restructuring for social reasons. The adjustment in terms of employment in the textile and steel industries in the developed countries has been very profound, even with transitional protectionist programmes in place; without them the employment consequences could have been worse. Adjustment programmes also help the firms concerned to finance restructuring.

Governments have been reluctant to abandon whole sectors when they are perceived as strategic from a national or industrial point of view. Some of these programmes have been expensive and costly failures and have gone on too long; but others have had a degree of success.

THE WTO APPROACH

The second school embodies the philosophy of the WTO, which has a strong free trade orientation but also allows for the temporary protection of troubled industries in order to allow for their adjustment. There is also a clear recognition that certain practices, and in particular unfair trade practices, should not be tolerated. Trade is subjected to a series of rules and is 'managed' in this limited sense.

Finally, it encourages negotiated reciprocal reductions in existing protection. The whole exercise of negotiating rounds since the inception of the GATT has been based on the notion that it is easier to get countries to lower their barriers if others are prepared to do likewise. Clearly it is easier for a country to reduce its external trade barriers if its industries have some assurance that what they lose in the domestic market they may be able to pick up in export markets. Few countries are ready to liberalise unilaterally unless others are prepared to do so, and negotiation makes perfect political and indeed economic sense.

The WTO has a mercantilist flavour insofar as it proceeds by negotiation of mutual and balanced concessions. It is not geared to unilateral barrier lowering or liberalisation, and, somewhat defensively, feels that comparative advantage can best be achieved by such mutual negotiations. Once a balance of concessions is struck between the parties however, they must extend these concessions to others (the most favoured nation principle, MFN). The notion of unilateralism is contained in the idea of MFN, but only indirectly as a result of a deal struck among the parties. This is not negligible, but one could hardly say that unilateral barrier lowering has pride of place in the WTO firmament.

It is somewhat difficult to attribute a particular trade philosophy to the WTO. It is really only a negotiating forum in which reciprocal trade negotiations can be given effect. It does not prevent unilateral reductions, and even rewards them if they are brought in as part of a negotiating package. But clearly the mechanism could have been devised somewhat differently and given an even more free trade orientation; insofar as it essentially rests on a system of balanced concessions, by and large it embodies that rather conservative philosophy.

One of the most important features of the WTO is that it is rule-based and has an increasingly powerful dispute settlement procedure. Unilateral trade measures are only allowed in limited and controlled circumstances or require multilateral authorisation. This distinguishes it clearly from the following approaches.

THE CROWBAR SCHOOL – UNILATERAL AND BILATERAL ACTIONS

The third school has frequently been adhered to in recent years by the United States, where unilateral action such as trade sanctions has either been taken or, more often, threatened to pry open a market perceived to be unfairly closed. I call this the crowbar school in honour of the former US trade representative Carla Hills, who threatened to pry open certain markets with a crowbar if she had to – fighting words.

This sort of approach begs many questions. For example, what is unfair? Is it unfair for me or for you? It also ignores the balance of concessions and advantages struck in previous GATT rounds. The United States has argued with some reason that the balance of advantage struck in the WTO is not being respected and that its measures are therefore justified. It is probably closer to the truth that the United States has been plagued in recent years with serious balance of payments difficulties, and balance for the United States will be achieved only when this balance of payments gap is substantially reduced, regardless of whether the balance of concessions in the WTO is being respected.

It is however also the case that some of the issues the United States has sought to resolve in the case of Japan are not covered by the current WTO rules, for example exclusive car dealerships, which prevent imports. Japan is often singled out in this context in the sense that while the developed countries all reduced their trade protection measures under a series of GATT rounds, in the case of Japan this did not lead to a corresponding increase in imports. The uneven situation that has resulted, with extremely large Japanese surpluses and trade imbalances with other Western countries, has led to a great deal of frustration and anxiety about how to deal with these deficits. This school of thought therefore considers that this sort of acute problem, which relates to a relatively limited number of sectors where Japan is strongest or least open, for example cars and electronics, has to be dealt with in more specific terms.

So far the brandishing of trade sanctions has not led to the imposition of them since entry into force of the WTO. However the threat of sanctions has led to a series of bilateral agreements. For example the US–Japan accords on products such as semiconductors, beef and government procurement have led to some opening of the Japanese market. This sort of bilateral agreement has been fairly heavily criticised by free trade experts, but the United States claims there was no alternative way of dealing with these specific issues, and that the bilateral nature of the agreements was only bilateral in terms of negotiation, as the results have been multilateralised.

However, while in many cases there have been positive effects, there have also been negative effects for other trading partners as the agreements benefited narrowly focused US interests and their entry to the Japanese market, which is not always open for dissimilar but competing goods from other countries. In the case of the semiconductor agreement there was only a pretence that this would be based on MFN, and the reality has been much different. US exports to Japan have increased substantially, but nobody else's have.

This type of approach has been adopted with renewed vigour by the Clinton administration, although it appears to think that even these bilateral agreements are not producing adequate results. The administration has therefore taken the further step of insisting that the Japanese government agrees to import fixed quantities of US-made products, for example car parts. This is also referred to with justification as 'managed' trade. It is not just managed according to multilaterally or bilaterally agreed rules; it is truly managed in quantitative terms. It is more than the level playing field on which all compete, with some winners and some losers; it also tries to dictate the outcome of the game.

The Japanese have resisted this sort of quantitative numerical approach, and with reason: one should not be forced to buy products one does not necessarily want. However the crudity of the approach only underlines the intense frustration of the United States (and others) with the inadequate trade relations operated *inter alia* by Japan and China. The danger is that the United States will resort to sanctions as the next step. Resolution of the negotiations between the United States and Japan in 1995 over cars, and the

US – China textile and intellectual property negotiations in 1996–97 did not inspire confidence, as sanctions were only avoided at the last minute. If these agreements do not achieve their objectives, one can expect sanctions to be reimposed with alacrity.

One should emphasise here that the use of unilateral sanctions is a risky and even dangerous business as it can set off a spiral of retaliatory moves. It is, moreover, completely contrary to the WTO rules as trade sanctions generally require multilateral authorisation. Under the Uruguay Round of GATT it was in fact agreed and reaffirmed that in future such multilateral sanctions would not be resorted to. But politics are politics, and there is no guarantee they will not be resorted to again.

The European Union has been a frequent critic of this approach, and in return it has been accused of standing aside and allowing the United States to bear the brunt of the trade liberalisation effort; a sort of free rider, ready only to hold the coats of the protagonists and stand on the sideline, in the words of former US trade representative Mickey Kantor. This is an unjust criticism; the EU is not against a good fight, but feels it should be done within the multilateral rules. Since the reforms of the Uruguay Round these rules have become much more effective, and special attention has been given to avoiding undue delays and blockage in dispute settlement. These rules should be given a chance to operate. Unilateral actions can only undermine this new multilateral system. There has been some recent evidence that, at least in some cases, the United States is prepared to use the multilateral procedures and has strengthened its hand by doing so in conjunction with the EU, for example in a joint approach to the WTO. But clearly the unilateral path still remains an important tool in US eyes.

There is also a potential remedy where the WTO has no rules on a particular subject. A residual clause taken over from the old GATT states that when you have received, for example, tariff concessions on cars from Japan but you still can't sell that product, then the concession is 'nullified or impaired' because a situation exists that renders the concession ineffective. In these circumstances you may call for the situation to be rectified, or ultimately for compensation to be paid.

Admittedly this clause has never been fully tried out, although the EU did initiate a claim of nullification and impairment against Japan in 1982. But the procedure was never completed as a settlement was reached on some of the underlying issues. There is also some doubt whether the WTO will pronounce on, for example, exclusive dealership arrangements (operated by most countries including the United States) in the absence of internationally agreed competition rules to guide it. But it could nonetheless recommend that if a country has nullified certain trade concessions then it should correct the problem even if it is not in strict breach of the WTO regulations; it would have to allow a certain amount of leeway as to how the condemned country chooses to correct the situation.

STRATEGIC TRADE POLICY

A fourth school[2] takes a more ambitious approach with a more industrial type of policy orientation, and has received some justification from new trade theories. The thinking of this school is that substantial assistance must be given to industries that are of a high tech or high productivity nature and constitute the industries of the future, where the Western world hopes to make its living.

The main criterion is probably whether you succeed with your industrial policy or not. This is also where the main doubts creep in. Even enthusiastic advocates of strategic trade policy admit that the choosing of an investment in a particular sector to try to promote an industrial policy goal may simply backfire. You may choose the wrong sector, or invest too much given the returns, or implement the programme incorrectly. There are too many uncertainties in second guessing the market, bureaucracy cannot substitute for the private sector and so on. So while there are arguments to be made in favour of strategic trade policy, the theory of comparative advantage remains the bedrock or rule of thumb for the international trading system.[3]

But of course many highly successful industrial programmes are run by governments in all Western economies and so the question is whether you feel up to taking the risk, and whether you believe in an active role for government in this area or not.

Very few industries are against government subsidies for basic research and development, provided they receive a fair share of the results of this. The participation of industry, including financial participation, will give some guarantee that the programme corresponds to the private sector's wish list. But as with all human endeavour, public or private, there are some successes and some failures. It is impossible to know in advance what these will be.

The government may not be as good at predicting the future as the private sector, but one should not exaggerate the capacity of the private sector either, as it makes plenty of mistakes. The difference probably is that the private sector will recognise its mistakes and cut its losses more quickly. But more importantly, and this is where government financing has an edge, some projects would never get off the ground without strong government backing. The availability of private finance for long-term strategic industrial investments (say, Airbus again) would simply not be forthcoming. Investment in risky futuristic projects will usually not be made by an industry on the scale required.

Apart from the difficulty of picking winners ahead of time, the main problem with the approach is that it could, if pushed to excess, completely undermine the world trading system. Again a good example is Japan, which has been a very successful strategic trade player. It has pursued a very ruthless export strategy based on a rather closed domestic market. It has a strong mercantilist flavour insofar as it treats exports as good but imports as bad, and its successes have come at the cost of others, sometimes to the point of destroying their industries. This can happen under normal competitive conditions, but the difference here is that it is pushed beyond what is reasonable and with the authority and resources of the state behind it. If all governments played the same game on the same scale, there would be an escalation of government competitive subsidisation and protectionism. Only a few governments can play this game at the same time; if all indulged in it the world trading system would collapse, as it did in the 1930s. It is just about tolerable for one country to run up huge surpluses and practice protectionism, but what would happen if all decided to do likewise? Trade would come to an end and it would truly be a zero sum game.

However, less exclusive policies that lead to more specialised intraindustry competition are likely to continue and perhaps increase. These policies have always existed, even in the United States (NASA, DARPA and so on), but they may in the future become the weapons of choice.

Government assistance will probably shift away from overt measures such as tariffs and production subsidies towards measures with less direct impact on trade such as subsidies for precompetitive research and development. The subsidies agreement, which was revised in the Uruguay Round of GATT, allows or 'green lights' subsidies for R & D, regional development and environmental protection

under certain conditions. These subsidies are likely to be less dangerous for the international trade system.

Strategic trade policy has seemed most offensive when it has been
used in conjunction with border measures (tariffs, quotas or cartels with the effect of border measures) or export subsidies. It has
also seemed offensive when combined with production subsidies,
for example Airbus, though somewhat less so than if border measures
had been used, as Boeing still has very substantial access to the
European market. Other measures such as cartel arrangements
(without border measures) are probably more acceptable, and subsidies for precompetitive R & D even more so. There is a sort of
ascending order of acceptability in the instruments used to promote industrial objectives.

In other words there are ways and means of achieving strategic
policy objectives that are more acceptable and WTO-compatible,
and above all that allow for trade and an open market. They are
not exclusionary and allow for competition. But sooner or later
even these measures of support will come under scrutiny and be
subject to attack. One can see this trend already in the Boeing–
Airbus dispute. In the past Boeing has attacked production subsidies for Airbus. This time the shoe is on the other foot, as Airbus
is complaining about NASA preproduction subsidies for research
into and the development of new generations of aircraft and engines. Another sensitive issue is the US federal support for new
generations of semiconductor and high-speed processors.

One can therefore anticipate that while some trade policy instruments are still WTO-compatible and are likely to be used increasingly, sooner or later they may be outlawed too. The next WTO
round will probably have to deal with these problems as and when
they become more acute. More binding rules will have to be adopted
on subsidies and more refinements introduced. Investment rules
will also have to be adopted. In particular a solution will have to
be found to the trade barriers that are caused by anticompetitive
practices, for example by introducing agreed international rules on
competition. This will be a major issue given that it will go to the
heart of how some countries manage their economies.

The WTO will have much to do and its future efforts will have
to be guided consciously or unconsciously by the issues just discussed. Is the future WTO to allow for some strategic trade policies or not? The answer to this question will inform the solutions
that will need to be adopted.

4 The Role of the GATT and the Nature of GATT Negotiations

The opening up of trade during the last forty years has been mainly due to the efforts made in the GATT. There have been seven GATT trade liberalisation rounds in all, including the Dillon, Kennedy and Tokyo Rounds and most recently the Uruguay Round. While this process has been slow and its development rather patchy, the results have nonetheless been impressive. The Uruguay Round was a culmination of all these efforts. The step-by-step approach that has evolved through the GATT has led to the point where the rules and disciplines of the new World Trade Organisation, established by the Uruguay Round, are much more complete and cover nearly everything that is traded.

Table 4.1 illustrates the development of the GATT negotiations over the years. In 1947 only 23 countries participated and negotiated over trade worth $10 billion, but there has been a dramatic increase since the Kennedy Round in the number of countries participating and the amount of trade covered.[1]

Table 4.1 Dates, participation in and coverage of GATT negotiating rounds

Round	Number of countries participating	Value of trade covered
Geneva (1947)	23	$10 billion
Annecy (1949)	33	Data unavailable
Torquay (1950)	34	Data unavailable
Geneva (1956)	22	$2.5 billion
Dillon (1960–1)	45	$4.9 billion
Kennedy (1962–7)	48	$40 billion
Tokyo (1973–9)	99	$155 billion
Uruguay (1986–94)	117	$500 billion

The industrial sector has always been well covered by the GATT negotiations, and indeed it was the sector with which the GATT initiated its work and substantial progress has been made over the years. The rules on agriculture, such as they were, tended more to consolidate existing practices, and until the Uruguay Round little real progress was made on liberalisation. Moreover goods, not services, were covered by the original GATT. This situation was corrected by the Uruguay Round, which laid the groundwork for the liberalisation of agriculture and services, though this is still only in the initial stages.

The GATT laid out a framework for dealing with trade barriers, many of which had become difficult and opaque in the interwar years, had substantially impeded trade and growth, and had precipitated and reinforced the economic depressions of that period.

The instruments of commercial protection can take many forms. The most common is the straightforward tariff or levy (usually expressed as a percentage of the value of imports), which serves both as a means of protection and as a means of raising revenue. Other barriers are called non-tariff barriers (NTBs). These are grouped together as instruments *other than* tariffs because no tariff or duty is levied, rather protection is created by more administrative means. They include a wide range of obstacles that are as varied as the imaginations of the bureaucrats who think them up.

NTBs include instruments that are implemented at borders with regard to imports and exports, and those that are implemented with regard to imports and domestic production; the protection given to domestic producers comes from the fact that the measures are designed to favour them at the expense of importers. Examples of commonly used border measures are quantitative restrictions, which prohibit imports above a certain quantity. Examples of the latter are standards, which apply to all who want to sell in a particular market, but are often designed to take account of the specifics of a domestic product and take little or no account of products made outside the country. Exporters to that market have to make adjustments, often at great cost (sometimes to the extent that two product lines have to be produced, one for the domestic market and the other for export), while domestic producers do not.

The GATT has done its work through a gradual process of negotiating reductions in or establishing rules for various forms of protection. Indeed its mandate for the elimination of tariffs was to achieve this by negotiating mutual and balanced reductions. In the case of some NTBs, for example quantitative restrictions, it contained prohibitions. In other non-tariff barriers the rules were imprecise or non-existent and they had to be developed through negotiation. The result has been a gradual reduction of barriers through negotiation and agreement on mutual concessions and the elaboration of agreed rules.

While the GATT sought to eliminate barriers to trade it also allowed for certain exceptions, such as the right to take protective action to safeguard an industry temporarily, or for balance of payments reasons. It has frowned on unfair trade practices and allowed counter action, such as imposition of a duty, to be taken as and when required.

THE TECHNIQUES OF NEGOTIATION

Tariffs

The original GATT agreement developed a system for *the mutual and balanced reduction of tariffs*, initially on a request offer basis and then, starting with the Dillon Round, by a percentage amount (the various techniques used are described more fully in the section on tariffs). This form of negotiation, known as a 'round', is the traditional form of GATT negotiation and is so called because it involves a round of negotiations between all parties to GATT. The theory behind this is that better progress can be made towards tariff reduction if all do it simultaneously. Countries are reluctant to lower tariffs and expose their industry to foreign competition if they feel that their foreign competitors are not open to competition from them. Some economists, as we have seen, feel that unilateral tariff removal is just as good for an economy as a mutual and balanced reduction. However, for practical political reasons mutual reductions are easier to sell to workforces and industries, which, after all have to bear the brunt of any adjustment that results. In any case the WTO does not prohibit unilateral barrier removal, and between rounds much unilateral tariff reduction actually takes place.

The other advantage of a round of negotiations is that coverage tends to be wider than a simple tariff exchange on the basis of a single industry. The fact that these rounds have covered all parties and a wide range of sectors (indeed most sectors) has meant that a tariff reduction in a particular sector in a particular country, for example steel or textiles, which for the developed countries may lead to major imports but little or no advantage in terms of exports, is easier to accept when that country can gain a competitive export advantage in another sector, for example machinery or cars. A large number of countries, and a wide range of sectors, have tended to improve rather than diminish prospects for a round, by increasing export opportunities for all in as balanced a manner as possible.

Once a negotiation is complete the concessions made are 'bound' at a certain level. If tariffs on for example, chemicals are reduced to 10 per cent, they are then bound at that level and cannot be raised unless affected parties are compensated. The 'binding' of tariffs in this way sets an upper limit on tariffs and it is fairly rare for countries to raise them; if they do, the compensation they are required to give to affected parties by lowering other tariffs can be expensive and damaging to some other domestic industry.

When tariffs are bound the benefit from them is extended to all members of the WTO. This is known as most favoured nation treatment (MFN). A concession extended to one country must be extended to all other members of the WTO. The main proponents of a tariff reduction may be two major industrialised member countries with the most to gain from it, but once granted the benefits are made available to all other trading partners. This provision of the GATT was designed to do away with the multiplicity of bilateral and preferential schemes that grew up in the interwar years, and to ensure that weaker trading partners with little to bargain with are not victimised by the stronger. Similarly, when a concession is withdrawn the main suppliers of the product in question have to be compensated.

Unilateral reductions made between rounds are generally not bound, and countries tend to wait until the next round in order to be credited for the reduction. This means that what is internationally bound in the WTO, and what forms the basis or result of a round, is sometimes different from what is applied in practice often set at a lower, though 'unbound' level.

When tariffs are lowered unilaterally it is rare for them to be raised again (though this is less true in developing countries). Just as a tariff raised to protect an industry can be difficult to reduce due to the political influence of that industry, for example the car industry, so too can a lowered tariff be difficult to raise as certain industries will become very dependent on cheaper imports, for example semiconductors.

Moreover when a product is imported it must be treated in an equivalent way to domestic products. This is essential to avoid a tariff concession being undermined by an internal tax that discriminates in favour of local products. This is the principle of national treatment, which applies to all members of the WTO.

Non-Tariff Barriers

The original GATT also contained certain provisions to prohibit or restrict non-tariff barriers (NTBs). It prohibited the use of quantitative restrictions (QRs), with certain exceptions, and set down certain rules for the use of other NTBs, for example subsidies.

However NTBs, continued to flourish, and indeed the lower that tariffs became, the more interest was shown in NTBs as a last-resort form of protection. The result was that many QRs, which were officially prohibited, continued to exist and other practices, for example subsidies, were not seriously dealt with because the rules were too weak. Moreover mankind's natural inventiveness came into play and many new varieties of NTB were created.

The Tokyo Round was the first to deal seriously with non-tariff barriers and agreement was reached on government procurement, standards, licensing rules, customs valuation and subsidies. In addition a sectoral agreement was reached on tariff and non-tariff problems in the civil aircraft sector.

While these agreements were extensive, in some cases they had limited effects. The Tokyo Round made a valiant effort to tackle the main categories of NTB, for instance standards, procurement, subsidies and so on, but the agreements often reflected disagreement rather than consensus and sometimes fell short of dealing with the issues properly and effectively.

The Uruguay Round, built on the Tokyo Round by revising, updating and completing some of the agreements negotiated on the industrial sector in order to give them more bite.

The negotiating technique used for non-tariff barriers was different from the tariff negotiations. The process was based on rule making, tightening up the existing GATT rules or inventing new rules where none currently existed. The technique was similar to that used for tariffs, however, in that it was based on the system of the negotiating round. The success of the exercise depended on a large number of countries being involved and a sufficiently wide range of issues being covered to attract their interest. It also used the technique of mutual reduction for certain types of NTB in which lists of NTBs were proposed by the various parties, and when a rough balance of commercial interests had been struck, the various NTBs listed were prohibited or disestablished by the parties. This was common where quotas were concerned.

In the Uruguay Round the process was taken a step further. In addition to closing many of the gaps in existing rules and creating new rules, a more sophisticated type of swapping arrangement was arrived at for certain NTBs in the agricultural sector. The earlier arrangement had been a bit crude and measurement of the protective level of the various NTB's in question had led to more arguments than solutions. The answer found in the Uruguay Round was to convert NTBs into tariffs and then reduce these over time. To give an example, a QR on beef might ensure that the domestic product would be sold at a price 30 per cent above the world market price. This would then be converted into a 30 per cent tariff, and the tariff would be phased out progressively. This had the additional advantage of immediately introducing a tariff which is essentially more liberal than a QR. Importers might be able to sell quite a lot in a market protected by a 30 per cent tariff if they have a 30 per cent or even a 15 per cent price advantage, but they can only sell a limited quantity if they are subject to a quantitative restriction.

While MFN is important in dealing with such border measures as QRs, the national treatment provision is more relevant to dealing with other NTBs. Clearly agreements such as that on government procurement would be meaningless if the procurement rules were not applied to national and foreign suppliers alike.

The Tokyo Round agreements on NTBs were made conditional: if countries did not sign up they would receive no advantages. The rights did not accrue as a result of MFN. If a country did not give reciprocity, that is, did not undertake an equivalent level of obligation, it did not benefit from these agreements. For many developing countries this was a big disappointment as they did not feel able to undertake some of the obligations and thus were excluded from the benefits that would normally accrue under the principle of MFN. At the same time, under normal GATT rules they had been allowed special and differential treatment since 1973 (confirmed in the so-called 'Enabling Clause' in 1979). In accordance with this, developing countries were not required fully to uphold GATT obligations and give reciprocity for access to tariff concessions or non-tariff obligations or agreements.

In the Uruguay Round most of these agreements were extended on an MFN basis, and while the developing countries still benefit from special and differential treatment in some situations, these exemptions have been tightened up and made more 'transitional'. Developing countries are therefore increasingly subject to the full range of obligations in the WTO. The general framework of the services agreement is applied to all, but in that context parties are able to request exemptions in connection with both the MFN and national treatment obligations, and a balance of concessions is struck. Needless to say the developing countries have taken out more exemptions than the developed countries, although even the latter have taken out major exemptions in a limited number of cases.

The Tokyo Round agreements on government procurement and civil aircraft were exceptions to this multilateralisation process and remained as plurilateral agreements with obligations confined to a limited number of parties. Developing countries, for the most part, did not join them.

SOME GENERAL RESULTS OF THE URUGUAY ROUND

The Uruguay Round has been a great success insofar as it has made a major and determined effort to close remaining loopholes and put the world trading system back on track. Nowhere has this been more evident than in the industrial sector where, building on earlier rounds, a very high degree of liberalisation now exists. This is less true in developing countries, however, and some tariff peaks still exist in developed countries. While the achievements in agriculture and services are also monumental, they only mark a beginning in many respects. In the industrial sector, however, one can say that the WTO has achieved a high level of maturity and a substantial contribution has been made by all parties to the goal of liberalisation.

Another element of importance in GATT negotiations, and the Uruguay Round in particular, is that by extending GATT coverage they also introduced the prospect of trade sanctions or binding dispute settlement with retaliatory measures as a last resort in areas where they did not exist before. Trade sanctions are a particularly powerful tool for implementing international agreements. In the case of intellectual property protection, numerous international agreements have existed in the past but they have not been well respected. By bringing them within the ambit of the WTO, failure to respect them can lead to fairly immediate and powerful trade sanctions. This will immeasurably improve their implementation.

Another consideration is that the Uruguay Round took the interpretation of trade policy and domestic policy a substantial step further down the road. When the GATT dealt with tariffs it was dealing with border measures, usually seen as external policy measures. But when it tackled NTBs it got much closer to measures at the heart or inner core of domestic policy, for example government procurement. In bringing 'domestic' agricultural policies, as opposed to just border measures, into the international arena it took another major step down that road; likewise in services, where rights of establishment and the migration of personnel are involved. These new elements of the WTO have important implications for domestic policy and have brought the WTO much closer to the heart of national policy making. The distinction between external and domestic policy is an artificial one in the area of trade anyway, and the Uruguay Round gave greater recognition to this than previous rounds. This was a reflection of the increasingly interdependent world in which we live.

The last round was also characterised by much greater participation by the developing countries. Up to and including the Uruguay Round the main players tended to be the developed or industrialised countries. The contribution and concessions offered by the developing countries were not large, partly because many were still following import substitution or protectionist policies. The developed countries were prepared to tolerate this situation in the sometimes vain hope that this would improve their development prospects. They were also prepared to tolerate it because as the main players in the trade field they were in fact making the necessary concessions to ensure a balanced outcome over a wide range of goods of interest to them.

The Uruguay Round was different because the goal of liberalisation was being more extensively practised by developing countries as a means towards economic growth. It is also true that many of them felt that if they did not participate they would not be allowed the concessions that are necessary for their exports to grow. Finally, the developed countries have become less tolerant of those developing countries that have become important exporters getting a free ride in the WTO. The Uruguay Round therefore redefined what is now considered necessary for a negotiating round to be acceptable and equitable in terms of the number of countries and sectors involved (see Chapter 6).

The round also introduced major institutional changes. The GATT came into being after the failure to ratify the Havana Charter. However the early GATT had few of the powers of the international trade organisation foreseen by the Havana Charter. It was merely a treaty between parties with a secretariat, and not an international organisation as such, with a life and powers of its own. The Uruguay Round rectified this situation (see Chapter 5).

No doubt there will be further rounds of negotiation in the future (see Chapter 23). However important elements of the WTO are now more or less permanent negotiating vehicles and future negotiations are already being planned, for example on agriculture and services, or foreseen insofar as most agreements contain a review clause. This gives some guarantee that the liberalisation process will be an ongoing one, with individual sectoral negotiations taking place with separate schedules and requirements. They may be incorporated under the umbrella of a round, but are not strictly dependent on such a round taking place.

5 Institutional Issues[1]

The GATT agreement was the offspring of a much more ambitious attempt in the late 1940s to establish an international trade organisation (ITO) with more substantial powers. This organisation, based on the Havana Charter, was to be the third pillar of the Bretton Woods institutions along with the IMF and the World Bank, but the implementing bill failed to be passed by the United States Senate. The GATT itself was in fact only a treaty or agreement, as its name implies, serviced by a secretariat. It was not a full-blown international organisation in the traditional sense.

The Uruguay Round changed all that. The new World Trade Organisation (WTO), which has emerged from the Uruguay Round, will be a multilateral trade organisation in the fullest sense. But what is meant by 'in the fullest sense'. Instead of being just a framework for exchanging concessions, pretty much *à la carte* and strictly controlled by the parties to it through consensus in practice, it will have a more independent life of its own. It will be more universal in terms of its obligations and membership and it will have more effective and independent dispute settlement provisions. It will also have more political input through more frequent ministerial attendance, and a more visible presence and clout in economic policy in the Bretton Woods Institutions. Finally, it has the possibility of majority voting, which can breathe real life and independence into the organisation. It will not be strictly tied to the apron strings of its creators.

With this new found independence will go new responsibilities, and it is to be hoped that they will be exercised wisely and well. Other multilateral bodies have not acted wisely or have become too political, and in the end they have been largely discredited. It is to be hoped that the WTO will be more successful.

In the first place the new WTO has a single institutional framework encompassing the old GATT but including all the new elements that have been negotiated and developed in the course of the Uruguay Round. The old GATT only concerned itself with trade in goods but the new WTO will also cover trade in services and trade-related intellectual property (TRIPs) and investment issues. Membership of the WTO will require acceptance of all the results

41

of the Uruguay Round, including the agreements on goods, services and intellectual property. Previous waivers and exceptions have been abolished. The Tokyo Round agreements had limited membership and were in part based on conditional MFN status. These have now been extended to all members, but with a few exceptions in some areas, for example government procurement. The WTO also provides for the possibility of cross retaliation: failure to implement one agreement can lead to withdrawal of concessions, or sanctions, in another area.

The result is that it will be more difficult to join the WTO. In the past, provided a country made a reasonable offer on tariffs it could join the GATT and was not obliged to sign on for the various NTB agreements created by the Tokyo Round. This is no longer the case: to join the WTO is to be bound by all the agreements on goods, services, TRIPs and most of the NTB agreements, though there is still room to modulate participation in some agreements by means of limited exemptions (for example services) though a full opt out is not allowed.

Developing countries will still receive special and differential treatment, but their general obligations are still more extensive as the new provisions on special treatment do not allow full exemption, only transitional periods to allow for adaptation. The threshold for joining is thus much higher. The least developed countries, however, will retain much more flexible terms for membership.

The institutional nature of the WTO has been strengthened by the inclusion of a ministerial conference, which is to meet every two years. In the past the GATT was characterised by the absence of ministerial intervention. Ministerial conferences only occurred on the rarest of occasions, either to initiate or to conclude one of the negotiating rounds. This incorporation of a regular ministerial conference will help to give the organisation the necessary political direction, focus and momentum that it will certainly need in the years to come.

The new WTO has also been equipped with a trade policy review mechanism similar to that used by the OECD on economic policy. The idea is that approximately every two years there will be a review of the trade policies of the major players in the trade field. Somewhat less frequently a review will take place of countries whose impact on world trade is not so great, but where it is nonetheless important to seek improvements in trade policy and patterns.

The establishment of this review mechanism should lead to a more coherent and integrated approach to economic policy in general. In other words, the relationship between the IMF, the World Bank and the WTO should be strengthened as a result. It will not be useful for either the IMF or the World Bank to issue trade policy prescriptions without taking account of the results of the WTO trade policy review. The opposite is also true, and the future WTO should also take careful note of what is happening at the IMF and the World Bank. The astonishing thing is that there has been little or no contact between these bodies in the past and they have proceeded with their work if not in ignorance, at least in relative disregard of what was going on in the other institutions. The establishment of the trade policy review mechanism will give the WTO a standing in the economic policy field that the GATT never had.

The other and probably the most important element of the institutional changes created by the Uruguay Round is the strengthening of the dispute settlement procedures. In the past these procedures have tended to rely on consultation, arbitration and mediation and have only moved gradually towards increased use of more binding dispute settlement procedures with the use of so-called panels (of three people, usually trade officials), which held hearings and handed down decisions a bit like a court. In another sense however they were not a court, in that they were not permanently appointed, and were not judges but civil servants, usually drawn from the ranks of trade diplomats in Geneva (a touch introverted one might say).

In the past the panel system was undermined by the lack of deadlines for approving the panel's mandate, for appointing its members, for the panel to take a decision and so on. The result was a very cumbersome procedure that could take years. Member states were therefore hesitant to use it. The Tokyo Round went some distance towards resolving these problems, and since then there has been much more frequent resort to the dispute settlement provisions and panels and much greater acceptance of the judgements and decisions that have been handed down by the latter.

However the Tokyo Round failed to resolve one major difficulty: panel decisions had to be decided by consensus in the Committee of Contracting Parties (parties to the GATT), and the party against which the decision was made could block its adoption. The latter actions became more difficult as time went by, but the problem remained a major one. The Uruguay Round made several improvements with regard to procedures and deadlines, and in ensuring that the selection of panel members is more professional and reliable. It also instituted a system of appeals that should render the process more systematic and judicial in nature. But most important of all, panel decisions are now adopted by majority voting and can only be blocked by the main committee if there is a consensus to do so, which is never likely to happen. This means that the international community is moving towards a more rule – based system rather than one that leans towards negotiated solutions. Whatever one's views of the merits of this, in the end it can only create more pressure to resolve trade conflicts, even if the final resolution is in fact a negotiated one.

These institutional developments have not come overnight. In the course of the Tokyo Round the EU tended to be on the side of those who felt that dispute settlement of a quasi-judicial nature was not a suitable way to deal with trade conflicts and problems. It preferred conciliation and negotiation. Since then, however, the EU's position has evolved to the point where it is closer than the United States to accepting a quasi-judicial procedure. The United States had great difficulty in the latter stages of the Uruguay Round negotiations in accepting strengthened dispute settlement mechanisms, not so much because of what the administration felt about these matters, but rather because of the views of Congress.

The members of both sides of Congress tend to feel that such dispute settlement mechanisms will take some decision-making power away from them. The Democrats fear WTO decisions because of the potential for liberalisation and the likely impact on workers. The Republicans fear them because they dislike any move to reduce the sovereignty of Congress. Their fear mainly concerns the impact of panel decisions, and they insisted on inclusion in the implementing legislation of a clause whereby WTO decisions would be reviewed regularly by the Congress with the possible option of withdrawal by the United States from the WTO. While withdrawal is an unlikely option, this review process puts a certain pressure on WTO panels not to err too far from US interests. This is, to put it mildly, the antithesis of multilateralism, and has the potential to undermine the WTO completely.

The new organisation will therefore have to try to strike the right balance between enforcing the rules and considering the political realities in national parliaments, with one eye continually on a possible adverse reaction from the US Congress. Environmental issues are, for example, likely to be highly sensitive, and WTO decisions that directly overrule the environmental aspirations of certain parties or go too far may well prove counterproductive in the long run. Other examples abound, particularly in relation to health safety and labour standards, and so on, and the future challenge for the WTO will be to try to advance in a manner that will create confidence in its decision-making abilities and its ability to arrive at solutions that take the essential interests of all into account.

A recent issue of great political sensitivity was the US embargo on Cuba and the extension of sanctions to non-US firms dealing with that country. The highly political nature of the matter is a real test for the WTO.

Another issue that has disturbed the Republicans in Congress is majority or qualified majority voting by the main committee of the WTO. The general rule is consensus, but if consensus is not reached after a period of time majority voting can be used. The United States has insisted on diluting the majority rule and having qualified majority voting (and even acceptance by an individual party if an amendment affects his or her rights and obligations).

The Republicans in Congress have an antipathy to majority voting in international bodies and a hostility to the UN that is not always rational. One can add to this the fact that many Western countries have trouble with the idea of turning the WTO into a UN-style body, or reinforcing its existing link, however tenuous, with the UN. The UN is perceived by some, in the words of United States Senator Moynihan, as 'a dangerous place' to be, where the South exacts revenge on a daily basis for the perceived failure of the North to help it, and where even the most banal economic discussion is turned into a political free for all. In a sense it is correct to say that the WTO system looks superficially like that of the UN, consensus in practice but with the ultimate threat of voting hanging over everyone's head. Added to this is the pressure being exercised in certain quarters to make the WTO a specialised agency of the UN.

Despite the fact that it always had some majority voting, the GATT managed to avoid this type of culture, mainly because the South participated little in the main liberalisation business. The new WTO is bound to be different, and the countries of the South are bound to play a more important role in it as they paid a substantial price for participating in the Uruguay Round.

It is also the case that important WTO decisions are subject to highly qualified majority requirements (budgets 2/3 majority, interpretations 3/4 majority, amendments 2/3 majority with important amendments only binding on those members who accept them and a 2/3 majority for their general acceptance).

But it is unlikely that the new WTO will be contaminated by the UN style of doing things because, like the World Bank and the IMF, the work of the WTO is based on real exchange and real economic activity and a strong attachment to consensus. Trade liberalisation is a two-way street, and developing countries have begun to realise that their interests will be best served by mutual concessions and not just unilateral concessions imposed on others. While most exceptions and waivers have been removed, enough of them remain to ensure that most future negotiations will be balanced, and that one side will not be able to dominate at the expense of the others. It is unlikely that the political excesses of the UN will be repeated in the WTO. However only time will tell.

6 Developing Countries

INTRODUCTION

The share of developing countries in world trade or world exports in 1994 was in the region of 40 per cent (including economies in transition),[1] and in the case of manufactured exports about 17 per cent. Manufactured exports in particular have been increasing rapidly, and indeed exports from developing countries have continued to grow by about 12 per cent a year compared with the 4–7 per cent growth of industrial country exports.[2]

Seventy per cent of these exports go to the developed countries, the remaining 30 per cent going to other developing countries and centrally planned economies. Exports have been concentrated in particular product groups such as steel, textiles, clothing, office equipment, telecommunications and other electrical equipment, footwear, toys and leather goods. Engineering products tend to dominate, accounting for 40 per cent of the total, while clothing and textiles account for a further 25 per cent and other consumer goods for 18 per cent.[3]

While the overall outlook appears optimistic, most of the exports especially manufactured exports come from just a handful of developing countries, namely the four dragons of East Asia and China.[4] As pointed out earlier, however, a profound transformation is taking place in the trade and economic policies of developing countries, which are increasingly seeking to become outward and export oriented. This means that one can expect a substantial rise in the amount of exports coming from many more of these countries in the future. However, unlike in the past, one can also expect them to import more as they gradually abandon the import substitution model, which has led to overprotected domestic markets. The developed world will find it easier to accept imports from the developing countries if they can also export to them. The ability of both the developing and the developed world to lower trade barriers depends, in part at least, on their ability to export.

The developing countries as a whole have done well out of the trading system and there are signs of improvement. However the picture is very uneven. Part of the problem, as described earlier, are the policies followed by the developing countries.

The world's trade to GNP ratio has increased by 50 per cent since 1974 and most of this growth has occurred since 1990. The ratio has doubled in Asia and North America, and increased by 50 per cent in Western Europe. The doubling in Asia is mainly accounted for by China, Thailand, Malaysia and Taiwan. The ratio increase in North America was somewhat less. Nor did Africa, the Middle East and Central and Eastern Europe keep pace.[5]

There have, however, been other factors at work that have arguably worked against the developing countries. These were the excessive concentration on primary commodities, the operation of the GATT rules, and restrictions on market access for their main exports.

COMMODITIES

For many developing countries, their main assets and sometimes their only assets have been primary commodities, whether agricultural or mined. These sectors are suffering from a long-term decline in the price of many products due to the substitution of synthetics (for example plastics or composites for steel), efficiency improvements (for example less intensive use of petroleum) or simply a fall in demand.[6]

Attempts to bolster primary commodity prices through commodity agreements (buffer stocks, cartels and so on) have failed, sometimes miserably. This type of solution is no longer considered a real option and the only surviving mechanisms with some viability are those that support income rather than prices. Examples are the EU STABEX scheme and certain IMF schemes designed to provide balance of payments support. Other commodity funds exist not to support the production of commodities, but to diversify away from them (for example the Common Fund in Amsterdam).

THE GATT RULES

The End of Reciprocity

In its original form the GATT allowed just two special provisions for developing countries: less pressure to require tariff concessions (though this was less true for binding of tariffs) and the use of quantitative restrictions to help with balance of payments (BOP) problems. A BOP provision also existed for developed countries, but has not been resorted to since the mid 1970s. However the BOP provision has been used with great frequency by developing countries, and indeed abused. The Uruguay Round made an effort to reinforce the disciplines of Article XVIII (the BOP provision) in order to prevent such abuse in the future.

However the developing countries successfully campaigned in the UNCTAD and eventually in the GATT to secure a major revision of the GATT agreement. They succeeded in securing an exemption from the GATT obligations on the grounds that as developing countries they could not undertake the same obligations as the developed ones, but that they should nonetheless enjoy the benefits of concessions made and obligations undertaken by developed parties on the basis of the MFN principle. In return they would do their best to adhere to the GATT obligations. This major concession was recorded in 1973 on a temporary basis and formalised in the 'Enabling Clause' at the end of the Tokyo Round in 1979.

To give an example of what this meant, all participants in a round of negotiations must make tariff concessions in an exercise that resembles a series of swaps in which one concession is traded off against another. The Enabling Clause allowed developing countries to participate in this exercise without reciprocity and without giving concessions equivalent to those being made by the developed countries.

However it has also had some negative consequences for them. First, negotiations on reciprocal tariff concessions have taken place mainly between the developed countries in connection with products of interest to them. Insofar as these are applied on an MFN basis, the developing countries have also benefited from these concessions but not necessarily with regard to products of interest to them. In conjunction with the import-substitution drive in the developing countries, this has led to poor growth and slow development. Second, with regard to GATT obligations in general the commitments of developing countries have been substantially diluted, with poor consequences for their economies. Third, at the end of the Tokyo Round the developed countries felt it was just not possible to allow a free riding status to be given with regard to the far-reaching obligations of the non-tariff barrier agreements. The obligations had increased too substantially to allow others to avail themselves of them unilaterally and without reciprocity. More generally, it may have led to increasing disrespect for the rules by developed countries and more frequent resort to protectionist measures such as voluntary restraint arrangements (See Chapter 12), which in a sense were a response to what was perceived as an increasingly unbalanced trading system.

Preferential Arrangements

In the light of the let-out for the developing countries, the developed countries were allowed and indeed enjoined not just to grant concessions on tariffs and other border protection measures on an MFN basis, or a similar basis for all, but to grant special and differential or *more favourable* treatment to the developing countries.

The original idea of the UNCTAD secretary general of the time was to introduce a generalised system of preferences (GSP), whereby the developed countries would allow across-the-board, duty-free access to developing countries. The intention was that this would be a single scheme. However the EU, and especially certain members of it, pressed for a set of separate schemes in order to preserve some of the separate preferences that already existed for their ex-colonies.

So instead of a single scheme, the developed countries drew up their own GSP systems for all developing countries (unless excluded for political reasons). The EU also operated regional systems that extended additional preferential margins to some regions. Some of these preferential arrangements were subsequently consolidated in an EU-wide scheme called the Lomé Convention (at the time known as the Yaoundé Agreement – a preferential arrangement that initially embraced some African ex-colonies and was then extended to the Caribbean and the Pacific). Other preferential arrangements, usually of a bilateral nature, were maintained by the EU with individual countries in the Mediterranean.

The United States established a special arrangement for the Caribbean countries (the Caribbean Basin Initiative), which substantially favoured imports from that area and went beyond normal GSP treatment. This proved to be less than an unqualified success, as Congress gutted it of any real significance.

Comparing the GSP schemes, the EU system is a rather inclusive one based on economic considerations, whereas that of the United States is more influenced by foreign policy. The EU system omits some of the tropical products for which the Lomé Convention countries are the principle suppliers, and preference is given to the members of Lomé. There are also exceptions or limitations on certain sensitive industrial items such as textiles, and on temperate agricultural products that are subject to the Common Agricultural Policy.

The impact of GSP and other preferential arrangements on the exports of the beneficiaries have not been as positive as one might have expected given the extensive nature of the preferences. The Lomé countries, particularly those in Africa, have suffered for the last 15–20 years from a collapse in commodity prices, and their overall trade performance with the EU and others has been dragged down by a long-term decline in certain commodity prices. However a significant number of these countries are now beginning to diversify their exports to include processed and industrial products. But there is still a long road to be travelled.

The difficulties encountered by the developing countries have in many cases been due to continued lack of access for certain product categories. In this sense they have failed to obtain the sort of access they might have achieved if they had entered into real, 'reciprocal' negotiations. Their difficulties also stem in large part from their lack of development and competitiveness, which has frequently prevented them from taking advantage of the various preferences they have been granted.[7] Finally, an administrative burden is inherent in such schemes as the exporter has to prove origin, obtain special certificates and so on.

In summary, it is clear that trade preferences are not going to ensure the development of an economy or its trade. These things depend more on the type of economic policy being conducted, the structural problems to be overcome and the general dynamism of an economy and its export sector. For example the Asian tigers and some countries in Latin America are, for the foreseeable future, going to outperform many of the African countries that have special preferences in the EU, regardless of those preferences.

The extension of further tariff concessions under the Uruguay Round on a global basis means that the existing preferential arrangements will become of less value, and some have questioned the need for such preferences. However these preferences are not likely to disappear altogether and do have a certain value for the beneficiaries as a political commitment to their development efforts, by giving them some assurance of duty free access to the developed countries. This access is not *guaranteed* as these preferences are granted on a voluntary, non-binding basis, but the political and contractual character of Lomé, for example, does provide some certainty that access will be maintained and protectionism will be resisted.

THE URUGUAY ROUND

In the Uruguay Round an attempt was made to ensure that developing countries would fulfil more of the GATT obligations. The effect of the various derogations granted in the past was that developing countries more or less exempted themselves from a lot of the obligations and activities of the GATT. As we have seen, in the Tokyo Round non-tariff barrier codes were not automatically applied to the GATT parties, and while this put the developing countries at a disadvantage from an MFN point of view, they did not have to fulfil the obligations of the agreements unless they signed up for them. This situation was not a healthy one and it meant that the developing countries played a less and less active role in GATT. This was particularly noticeable in the Tokyo Round, where the main decisions and focus of discussion lay among the developed countries alone.

The whole emphasis of the Uruguay Round was to ensure that *all* agreements and obligations would be applied *by all*, and that the better-off developing countries should play a bigger role. The general change in attitude towards trade policy and the greater emphasis on outward-oriented economic policies meant that developing countries wished to be credited for the trade liberalising efforts they had made on a unilateral basis, and to secure concessions in return. As a result the developing countries played a much more dynamic role in the context of the Uruguay Round. However, they had serious problems with the inclusion of certain issues, for example services and trade-related intellectual property rights. They were therefore very keen to ensure that if they were obliged to make concessions in these areas, then the developed countries should make real concessions on issues of importance to them, such as textiles and agriculture.

In this they were fairly successful. The Uruguay Round made a valiant effort to meet many of their market access requirements. These were substantial in the case of tropical products and textiles, and to an extent in temperate agriculture products. On the industrial side in general, there was a major increase in zero-duty tariff lines, a major reduction in tariff peaks, and a very substantial reduction in average tariffs and tariff escalation. In addition the non-tariff agreements were reincorporated in the WTO and subjected to MFN (with the exception of procurement). The market access negotiations must be considered a major success for the developing countries, though of course for some products, for example textiles, they will have to wait till the end of the transition period to receive the full benefits.

The sort of balance of concessions struck in the Uruguay Round was indeed quite different from that forged in previous rounds. The package developed in the Tokyo Round covered areas that were mainly, though not exclusively, of concern to the developed countries, for example government procurement, subsidies, antidumping and civil aircraft, and reflected problems that had become issues in bilateral disputes between them. With some exceptions, subsidies in developing countries tended not to be as large, and their use as a tool of industrial policy was far less than in developed countries if only because they could afford them less. Antidumping actions were most often taken by developed countries, and of course an agreement on civil aircraft was born out of a deal made initially between the United States and the EU. Tariff concessions also tended to be concentrated on goods in trade between developed countries.

In the case of the Uruguay Round however, substantial tariff concessions were made to and by developing countries, and concessions were made in sectors of great export interest to them, for example textiles, steel, tropical products and, to a certain extent, agriculture. In return, developing countries were asked to open up their service markets, to protect intellectual property (most abuses occur in developing, not developed, countries) and to fall into line with the more traditional agreements on subsidies, anti dumping and so on, which many of them had not signed in the Tokyo Round. They were also expected to increase their tariff bindings across the board.

What they have put back in terms of access to their markets has however been very uneven. While they reluctantly agreed to the inclusion of services and intellectual property rights in the overall package, access to their service markets has remained limited and future negotiations will have to tackle this. On the question of tariff reductions, their performance has been relatively good. They have bound a lot more tariffs, though tariff reductions are still inadequate in many cases.

The general movement of the developing countries towards WTO was encouraged by the fact that they had been getting less access to GATT advantages in the tariff field than they would have liked, very much less access to non-tariff agreements, and less control over non-tariff measures of importance to their exports, such as voluntary restraint arrangements. While they managed to have these arrangements and measures reintegrated into the normal MFN context, it cost them the special and differential treatment they used to enjoy. Though formally the Enabling Clause remains in effect its significance is much less. They are now obliged to adhere fully to WTO obligations, with a let-out only for limited transitional periods or if they fall into the category of least developed country.

Moreover many of them will no doubt feel dissatisfied about textile barriers remaining relatively high for the immediate future, and they will certainly have hoped for better access for their agricultural products. But it was very difficult to achieve some of the market openings they sought in the Uruguay Round, and there will be considerable and painful adjustment for many developed countries. More importantly perhaps, some of these negotiations will continue in the future irrespective of whether there is a new round, as automatic review clauses are built into many of the agreements, for example those on agriculture. The existing advantages have some guarantee of being extended, to the benefit of the developing countries among others.

In a sense the WTO has come full circle for some of the developing countries. The attempt to live outside the GATT rules or in derogation from them has brought relatively few benefits. Preferential arrangements have not led to the advances or benefits expected of them. While they are still important for some countries, particularly the least developed, they are no longer perceived as the ultimate panacea. Developing countries have realised that they are better off living by the rules. Opening their markets has enabled them to secure concessions from the developed economies that were not available before, as well as to become more efficient and to benefit from cost and price reductions.

While one should not overemphasise this point, it is clear that the new WTO is on a more even keel and the threat of its being split into two camps or circles (inner and outer) has receded. It has been a salutary development in that most WTO members now seem to understand and accept that participation and contribution are more likely to pay off in the longer run. Anything less can only lead to instability and recrimination within the trading system.

No doubt there are some who feel that the Uruguay Round was a disappointment, that it didn't meet all their export needs and that it didn't go far enough, fast enough. But it is clear that in the context of uncertainty described in earlier chapters, the achievement of the Uruguay Round was a major one. It was attained at a time when high unemployment and recession were plaguing the world economy. Moreover the Round made a valiant attempt to deal with nearly all the salient problems in the world trading environment of the past twenty years.

7 Regional Arrangements

An issue that is of increasing importance in the development of the trading system is the existence of regional trade arrangements. These have often been criticised as distorting the world trading system because of the preferences they create for those inside them. The European Union is of course the prime example of such a regional arrangement. Others are the North American Free Trade Area (NAFTA – the United States, Canada and Mexico); the free trade area between Australia and New Zealand; Mercosur (Brazil, Argentina, Paraguay and Uruguay); the Andean Group (Colombia, Chile, Ecuador, Peru and Venezuela); and in Asia the ASEAN free trade area and APEC (18 countries in the Pacific Basin).

The WTO allows such regional customs unions and free trade areas to exist, and indeed encourages them. It has formally embraced some of these arrangements (art XXIV) and tolerated others. It requires only that they do not raise barriers to trade against those outside the arrangement, that they embrace all trade, and that they quickly move towards a free trade area or customs union. The rationale for the provision on protection is clear enough. The other provisions are designed to avoid partial arrangements: parties to them must be genuinely pursuing a full free trade arrangement and not a preferential deal for some individual sectors. If an exemption to the GATT rules is to be allowed, it carries a price tag, that is, that the free trade arrangement must be an extensive one.

The danger that economists sometimes see in these regional arrangements is that they may be more trade-diverting than trade – creating. That is, exports to the region might be reduced and trade might be diverted to producers within the free trade area. These may, incidentally, be less efficient producers with an overall economic loss to the region's economy. This may occur despite external barriers remaining the same, as the removal of internal barriers could create a preference or advantage for those inside the arrangement.

In the case of the EU, while there has been very substantial trade creation within the EU itself, this has also led to very substantial trade creation with outside partners. This is due to several factors. For example the common external tariff has generally been lower than many existing national tariffs and there has been a net overall lowering of external trade barriers at each enlargement. Moreover the effect of the increase in trade within the arrangement has led to a substantial growth in the economies of the member states, which in turn has led to an increase in the volume of imports to the countries in question.

Trade in Western Europe has developed more rapidly than trade with the rest of the world due mainly to the impact of the EU. Intraregional trade increased from 52.8 per cent of total trade in 1958 (at the inception of the Common Market) to 69.9 per cent in 1993. Expressed as a percentage of output, total trade went from 33 per cent to 45 per cent of GDP between 1958 and 1990. Extraregional trade went from 15.8 per cent in 1958 to 16.1 per cent in 1979 and 12.8 per cent in 1990. Trade with the outside world has increased in absolute terms, probably more than it would have done in the absence of the EU, but decreased as a percentage of overall EU trade (taking extra- and intra-EU trade together). It has however remained stable as a percentage of EU GNP, ranging from 12.2–16.1 per cent in the period 1958–90.[1]

Lifting barriers in the EU is estimated to have increased trade volumes between member states by 20–30 per cent in manufactured products. Manufactured imports from outside the EU increased their share of consumption from 12 per cent to 14 per cent between 1980 and 1993. The impact of the introduction of the Single Market in the EU on trade flows has been estimated at an average loss of 4.2 per cent in domestic market shares in the 15 sectors studied, with the gains divided almost equally between EU and non-EU imports, while for all manufacturing the loss of domestic market share was 2.3 per cent, with most of the gains going to non-EU members. The competitive price-cutting response of home firms should to some extent restore the loss of market share caused by the direct effect of the single market programme. There is little evidence of any substantial diversion of non-EU trade.[2] Table 7.1 sets out some useful figures.

It is also interesting to note that the EU has the highest import penetration rate of all developed trading partners or trading blocs: 14.97 per cent compared with 12.29 per cent for the United States and Canada and 9.52 per cent for Japan (1990–91 figures).[4] So much for Fortress Europe.

The creation of the European single market is an interesting example of the dynamics and momentum a customs union can

Table 7.1   Trade in goods and services, 1994

	Goods ($ billion)	(%)	Services ($ billion)	(%)	Total ($ billion)	(%)
EU (12)	2997.5	34	829.3	38	4184.0	39
EU (12) extra	1297.0	15	331.7	15	1628.7	15
US	1201.7	14	298.9	13	1500.6	14
Japan	672.2	7	166.4	7	838.6	7
World	8548		2160		10708	

Source: WTO (1995).[3]

achieve. It facilitates exports to the single market, by developing common standards, allowing commercial establishment throughout the single market, for example in the banking sector, by the liberalisation of internal frontiers and elimination of all internal quotas. It also tends to have the effect of reducing the overall level of the common external trade regime.

To take one of the more sensitive examples, the case of cars, import quota arrangements for non-EU cars, which have existed in some member states for more than twenty years, will be progressively eliminated as a result of decisions taken on the finalisation of the single market in 1992. In addition, by the turn of the century the voluntary restraint arrangements into which they have been merged will have been progressively eliminated. This provision has also been embodied in the results of the Uruguay Round. In other words the liberalising elements in the EU prevailed and the impetus towards a lower external regime has been maintained. The external measures of the less liberal countries have been aligned with those of the more liberal, not the other way around.

It is also true that in the case of the EU, at each step of its development and accession by new member states negotiations took place in the context of the GATT. This allowed for general external liberalisation to take effect at the same time as the internal liberalisation measures were being put in place. Moreover the EU has always maintained a very extensive series of free trade arrangements with its neighbours in Europe and the Mediterranean, as well as an extensive set of preferential arrangements with other developing countries (see Chapter 6).

Moreover if the individual national customs tariffs are raised on certain products in the course of creation of a customs union, there is an obligation to compensate trading partners with tariff concessions on other products. At each enlargement of the EU compensation has been extended when other parties have suffered trade losses, even though they may have benefited overall from the result. Internal liberalisation made it easier to agree to global liberalisation, while pressure to liberalise from outside the EU in the context of a GATT Round made it easier to create a single community market; a virtuous circle of sorts.

The importance of these types of arrangement is that they permit a very substantial trade liberalising effort to take place among countries that are prepared to do so and have economies that are compatible both from a geographical and an economic point of view. This ensures that the world doesn't stand still and waste time because it is looking for the perfect solution to all its problems. Global negotiations in relation to trade take time and enormous effort and involve many partners whose economies are simply not compatible and whose interests are not commensurate, and involves countries that are not at the same level of development. The global approach is essential, but by its very nature it cannot move as far or as fast as regional arrangements such as the EU.

Those who argue against regional arrangements often assume that there is a clear and feasible choice between regional and multilateral trade. The reality is that multilateral liberalisation is usually much more difficult to achieve than regional free trade and is usually more shallow. Some of the potential disadvantages of regional arrangements could be reduced by unilateral disarmament of trade barriers by the regional blocs (so-called open regionalism), but it has yet to be demonstrated that this is politically feasible (see the remarks on APEC below).

It is also important to understand that this sort of regional effort puts the members of these arrangements in a much better position to make the concessions that are necessary for successful global discussions. In other words they are often in the nature of a dress rehearsal for a more extensive world-wide effort and they often point the way to solutions to global problems. The experience gained within the EU has without doubt made a very important contribution to ensuring that European industries can stand up to the competition that is implicit in global liberalisation.

The arrangement signed in 1992 in Washington between the countries of North America (NAFTA) is also of major significance and should substantially increase trade and prosperity on that continent. It is unusual and difficult in the sense that it involves free trade between two highly developed partners and one that is less so, with the disparities in income levels that this entails. In the EU, while there are definite disparities between wage levels in certain member states, for example Ireland, Greece and Portugal, compared with others, these disparities have never been as large nor are the economies in question potentially as large as the Mexican economy could become (although at the moment Mexican GNP only represents 5 per cent of US GNP it has a population of 100 million and could become an economic powerhouse). There is also political uncertainty and concern in the United States about the allegedly low social and environmental standards in Mexico, which make for real uncertainty as to the future workings of the agreement and its possible impact on the US economy.

On the other hand the US debate on NAFTA, because it has concentrated on NAFTA's impact on the United States, has distracted everyone from the potential effect of the agreement on Mexico, which has potential as a competitor but also shows many signs of weakness. In the EU weaker adherents are strongly supported by a series of special funds to help them adjust to the pressures of free trade in the EU. There is no corresponding mechanism in NAFTA.

In the initial stages of NAFTA the trade balance seems to have swung massively in favour of the United States and Canada, and the 'giant sucking sound' of jobs going south of the border, made famous by Ross Perot, is now only a whisper. The collapse of the peso may put this situation into reverse. From adversity, is the Mexican economy going to develop into an exporting tiger? Or are these gyrations a sign of a fundamental instability in the agreement? Only time will tell.

The EU has sought to develop a series of free trade arrangements with those Central and East European countries that aspire to join the EU in the future. Again the disparity in income levels and industrial development will make these agreements relatively tricky and potentially difficult to operate. The problems that will emerge will probably take some time to do so in that the economic and export capacity of the Central and East European countries is still relatively low. But the EU is already beginning to sense some of the difficulties that lie in store for it, for example in connection with dumped aluminium and steel products, and of course the agricultural systems in the EU and Central and Eastern Europe are largely incompatible and very expensive to harmonise. These agreements will require careful monitoring and management over the years to ensure that they succeed. However they are essential agreements and absolutely vital to ensuring that democracy and economic stabilisation become a fact of life in the eastern part of Europe. Other developed countries have not so far undertaken similar arrangements with Central and Eastern Europe in order to improve the prospects both of their development and of global security. The United States and other OECD partners, in particular Japan, have been very slow to do anything along these lines, though this may change with accession of these countries to WTO.

APEC is also an interesting development, grouping as it does a whole range of countries from the most sophisticated to some that are still in the process of developing. It is pursuing free trade for the developed countries by 2010 and the developing countries by 2020, and is based on the concept of 'open' regionalism. Free trade will be created among the partners as in any free trade area or customs union, but these advantages will be extended to all on an MFN basis. This is good in theory, but there is doubt whether some partners in APEC will actually go down the path of trade concessions without reciprocity. It is hard to envisage the United States doing so, given its problems with Japan and China. In any case this may be a relatively moot point in a few years as further progress is made in the WTO; the APEC schedule for liberalisation by the years 2010 and 2020 may be superseded by the Uruguay Round follow-up, or in the new round that is likely to start by 2000.

Are there limits to the creation of free trade areas? Looking at the economic record the answer is probably no: these mechanisms generally create more trade rather than less. But there may be some political limits to them. Those who are left outside such regional arrangements tend to resent them, rightly or wrongly. If a transatlantic free trade area (TAFTA) were created, APEC, NAFTA and TAFTA together would represent 80 per cent of world trade. One might wonder about the scope and purpose of the WTO in those circumstances, and the WTO might be perceived as weakened by such extensive arrangements, though I have argued that these arrangements will strengthen rather than weaken the multilateral system.

There has also been a certain amount of soul-searching as to other effects of such arrangements. A recent World Bank report on Mercosur[4] was fairly critical of its trade-diverting consequences. Another recent study[5] was critical of the international rules on regional trade arrangements.

Whatever the truth of these studies, it is clear that care will have to be taken to ensure that regional arrangements do not become introverted. Contrary to some common perceptions, a regional arrangement does not become suspect if the trade inside it increases more rapidly than trade with partners outside; that is the nature of the beast and one should probably only begin to worry if trade with the rest of the world declines as a percentage of GDP.

But it is also clear that the best safeguard against trade diversion is vigorously to pursue multilateral trade liberalisation, and to ensure that the current WTO rules are respected and perhaps strengthened. The WTO is currently involved in an examination of these rules with a view to improving the definition of an acceptable arrangement.

Part II

Tariff Matters

8 Tariffs

INTRODUCTION

GATT's primary focus in the early years was on the reduction of tariffs, as tariffs were probably the most common or at least the most visible form of protection in use. A tariff is an import tax that is levied at the border. Unlike many other types of protection, tariffs have the advantage of providing revenue as well as protection. Indeed in many developing countries it is one of the few secure sources of tax revenue.

Tariffs have a further advantage in that they are considered one of the least protectionist types of border measure. Quotas and other NTBs limit imports to a predetermined amount or exclude them altogether. Moreover domestic producers are encouraged to charge what they can, given that they face no price competition from outside the domestic market. Tariffs give only limited protection, for example a tariff of 10 per cent will not protect domestic producers if importers can sell at a price 15 per cent below theirs. Of course tariffs of 80 per cent or 50 per cent are probably prohibitive and may be just as protectionist, if not more so, than a quota in that they may exclude imports altogether. But at moderate levels tariffs tend to promote competition and trade and ensure that domestic prices are not free to rise unduly.

Tariffs can take many forms. A tariff may be specific, that is, a flat rate on a particular product, or it may be a variable levy that changes to take account of differences between domestic and world prices: this was the mechanism used in EU agricultural policy. For the most part however, nowadays tariffs are *ad valorem*, that is, calculated as a percentage of the price of the imported product. (How that price is calculated is discussed in Chapter 9).

Most countries now use a common or harmonised customs nomenclature in which products are listed in accordance with a common terminology and definitions developed by the Brussels-based Customs Cooperation Council. Tariffs are then ascribed to these various products or product categories. This basic or nominal set of tariffs constitutes the foundation of the tariff. A tariff structure will however often contain exceptions of one sort or another, depending on circumstances. Some tariffs may be temporarily suspended because of short supply, or set at preferential rates, that is, lower rates may be granted to certain developing countries to assist their development. A distinction therefore has to be made between the basic or nominal tariff and the rates actually applied.

In practice a tariff will have a certain inertia, as its industrial/ political proponents will tend to prefer a certain level of protection or lack of it. A protected industry will continue to seek that protection. Alternately an industry that imports, for example, microchips at zero duty will want to continue to do so in order to remain competitive in the computer market. However tariffs are free to move up and down and in practice they often do, with all the resultant uncertainty that this can create for trade.

The main effort of the GATT has therefore been twofold: to reduce the average level of tariffs, and to ensure that they are fixed or 'bound' at the new reduced level and cannot be raised again without a cost being incurred. For example if a country raises a 'bound' tariff on a particular product it must compensate the principal suppliers of that product with equivalent tariff reductions on other products or face sanctions, that is, the withdrawal of tariff concessions by the affected party.

When the WTO negotiations reduce tariffs by a certain percentage, this is calculated by reference to the average tariffs prevailing in a prior period, usually the three years prior to the start of the negotiations. The agreed tariff reduction is then phased in according to an agreed schedule. Under the Uruguay Round this is due to take place over a period of five to ten years, depending on the product. However, while the agreed average reduction may be 30 per cent, the actual reduction on a particular product may be less or more. Within the overall reduction average there may therefore be substantial variations on individual products.

It is an important principle of the GATT that the tariffs thus lowered are lowered for everybody (the most favoured nation or MFN principle). Concessions made bilaterally between the EU and the United States were lowered not only for those two countries, but also for all other members of the GATT. The tariffs may only concern products of major interest for the bilateral partners, but more often than not they are of export interest to others too. This principle of the GATT was designed to rectify the prewar situation in which preferential tariffs were used to carve out spheres of influence by the more powerful countries by dint of economic power or leverage, often at the expense of weak or developing countries.

Even with this principle in place, developing countries have complained that earlier GATT rounds did not take sufficient account of their exporting needs, though this has been increasingly rectified by the most recent rounds. This was largely due to the fact that in earlier rounds, developing countries did not participate very actively and made few tariff concessions themselves. However in later rounds, and in particular in the Uruguay Round, they were much more active and made real concessions. In return they have received a better deal. The more advanced countries have come to realise that if they make concessions on binding they will be submitted to more and better bound concessions in the developed countries; they will have to rely less on unbound concessions by the latter, such as they get under the generalised system of preferences.

RESULTS OF THE URUGUAY ROUND

Judging whether a negotiating round has been successful depends on a number of factors. The following list is general and not exhaustive: individual countries will assess the advantages they have drawn from a round in more detailed terms and in relation to their own export capacities. Some criteria for assessing a round are:

– Has it lowered tariffs overall and by how much?
– Has it reduced tariff peaks?
– Has it led to an increase in bindings?
– Has it led to a reduction of tariff escalation?

Reduction of Tariffs

General reduction formulas

The various negotiating rounds described earlier tackled the task of reduction and binding through an elaborate system of exchange of concessions on an item-by-item basis, or in later rounds by applying an across-the-board average reduction.

The average reduction in the Tokyo Round, for example, was in the order of 30 per cent, coupled with a formula to ensure a greater than average reduction of higher tariffs, so-called tariff peaks (defined as tariffs above 15 per cent). Negotiation was also conducted on the basis of trade weighting. Greater value was given to a reduction of a tariff where the product involved was heavily traded than to one where there was little trade. It is true that reducing a tariff where there is little trade may, if the reduction is substantial, lead to the creation of a new market. But greater value is nonetheless attributed to tariff reductions on products where the possibility for trade is already proven to exist.

The attempt to introduce a harmonisation formula in the Uruguay Round did not work however. The main reason was that the United States was unwilling to reduce some of its tariff peaks, especially in sensitive sectors such as textiles. At the same time it wanted duty free access for entire product sectors that were of export interest to the United States. It was therefore keen to have a request and offer, sector by sector approach to certain products.

On the other hand the EU, which had a relatively flat tariff regime with fewer peaks, was aiming for a reduction in US tariff peaks in areas of export importance to the EU, such as textiles, chemicals, ceramics, glass and so on. Textiles were of particular significance for the EU given the need to compensate by exports to the U. S. in the higher end of the market for the increased access to the EU due to be given to developing countries, on the middle and lower end of it. This was due to occur as a result of textiles being brought back under GATT rules (see Chapter 15).

Degree of reduction

The final compromise led to a reduction of tariffs to zero by the EU, the United States and some others (plus the elimination of non-tariff barriers) on a series of products: steel, construction materials, medical equipment, agricultural equipment, pharmaceuticals, most furniture, beer and spirits. Tariffs in the chemicals sector were harmonised at low levels (maximum 6.5 per cent). These concessions were adhered to in part by other countries.

Duties above 15 per cent were halved, which satisfied most aspirations. The United States, however, retained its peaks on textiles and the EU on trucks, despite requests that these be reduced. A tariff reduction of 33 per cent was applied to all other products.

The final reduction on industrial goods amounted to an overall average of 37–38 per cent and an average of 40 per cent among developed countries. This translated into the following percentage reductions by developed countries:[1] US, 35 per cent; EU, 37 per cent; Japan, 56 per cent; Canada, 47 per cent; Australia, 39 per cent; New Zealand, 53 per cent. These are averages however, and individual reductions read differently. The result for the EU was, for example, a reduction of almost 50 per cent on US tariffs for EU exports compared with the overall US reduction of 35 per cent. In all, close to 40 per cent of EU exports now benefit from zero duty in the United States, and for developed countries as a whole industrial imports benefiting from zero duty will jump from 20 per cent to 44 per cent of trade.[2]

The overall average reduction was improved by important offers made by developing countries. The reduction effort of some countries – for example India (55 per cent), Korea (50 per cent), Thailand (20 per cent), Chile and Brazil (25–30 per cent) – was greater than that of others, for example Hong Kong and Singapore, which already had very low tariffs. Singapore's tariff is bound at 10 per cent, and 100 per cent of Hong Kong tariffs are zero, though their rate of bindings is less satisfactory. The result was to bring the tariffs in many of these countries down to levels that, though still high, are much closer to what is reasonable given their degree of competitiveness and development.[3]

While tariffs of around 100 per cent have not been unusual in Asia, these now average 9–28 per cent in Malaysia and Thailand, 37 per cent in India, 37 per cent in Indonesia to 22 per cent in the Philippines. The top rates in the Latin American countries range from 25–35 per cent.[4]

The volume of industrial imports entering developing countries duty free has risen from 39 per cent to 42 per cent, a performance comparable to that of the developed countries, though these figures are skewed somewhat due to the low-duty or duty-free regimes of Singapore and Hong Kong.

When GATT came into being in 1947 the level of tariffs for industrialised countries averaged 40 per cent or more. After the Tokyo Round this fell to an average of 6.3 per cent, and as a result of the Uruguay Round it will fall to 3.8 per cent. Table 8.1 lists the average tariffs resulting from the above reductions for a series of key countries.

Tariffication

Another technique used for the first time in the Uruguay Round was 'tariffication'. This method was developed to eliminate, as far as possible, the rather large number of non-tariff barriers (NTBs)

Table 8.1   Average tariff offered (trade weighted, excluding petroleum)

Country	Per cent	Country	Per cent
EU	3.6	Mexico	33.7
US	3.5	India	32.4
Japan	1.7	Korea	8.3
Canada	4.8	Singapore	5.1
Australia	12.2	Malaysia	9.1
New Zealand	11.3	Thailand	28.0
Chile	24.9	Indonesia	36.9
Brazil	27.0		

Source: GATT (1994).[5]

that still existed or had recently come into being in the agricultural sector. The idea was to convert these NTBs into tariffs, which are inherently less trade restrictive, and then to reduce these tariffs over time. It affected about one third of agricultural tariff lines where NTBs also existed.

This solution was born out of frustration with the proliferation of NTBs and the relative failure of GATT to do anything about them. In the past, efforts had been made to exchange concessions on various NTBs that were considered major obstacles to trade. The difficulty of calculating whether equivalent concessions were actually being given, however, tended to undermine the process. By converting NTBs into tariffs it became easier to compare like with like and to reach a mutually satisfactory deal.

The impact of NTBs on trade was calculated on the basis of the difference between the domestic and the world price. A quota on beef for example, which raised prices 20 per cent above the world price, was considered to have a tariff equivalent of 20 per cent. The NTB in question was then converted to that level of tariff and subjected to a tariff reduction process. The tariff reduction here was based only on average tariff reductions, that is, it was not designed to reduce tariff peaks and was not trade weighted. The reduction was 36 per cent overall with a minimum reduction of 15 per cent for each tariff.

This sometimes produced very high tariffs that would effectively exclude imports altogether (at least under quotas some access is guaranteed). Some of the new tariffs were as high as they were because of the high level of protection afforded by the NTBs they replaced. Others were the subject of so-called 'dirty tariffication', and higher tariff levels than were strictly warranted were demanded in exchange for giving up certain important NTBs.

The overall effect of the tariffication, however, is positive. Rigid NTBs have been replaced by what are in principle less restrictive tariffs that are bound and will be reduced over time. Moreover, as a percentage of the overall tariffication exercise the number of high tariffs resulting are relatively few though they do relate, not surprisingly, to some sensitive sectors, for example meat and dairy products.

To deal with this situation it was agreed that, for products subject to tariffication, current access opportunities would be maintained on terms at least equivalent to those existing prior to the tariffication process. In addition, where little or no access existed because of the restrictive nature of the previous regime, a minimum access was guaranteed of 3–5 per cent at tariff rates designed to ensure such access. (The tariffication rate would be reintroduced when imports exceeded the 3–5 per cent level.)

The new tariffs resulting from the tariffication process, and the other normal tariffs on agricultural products, are to be reduced by a simple average of 36 per cent in six years for the developed countries and 24 per cent in ten years for the developing countries, with initial minimum reductions of 15 per cent and 10 per cent. Bindings have reached 100 per cent in the case of all participants. However, a special safeguard provision exists to allow duties additional to the bound rates to be reintroduced if certain conditions such as import surges or dramatic declines in import prices occur.

In some respects, therefore, liberalisation in the agricultural sector was more effective in that 100 per cent of bindings were attained and NTBs were eliminated. The resulting average tariff levels, however, are likely to be substantially higher, though complete figures are not available as the tariffication process produced a large number of specific duties, the *ad valorem* equivalents of which have not yet been calculated.

Distribution of tariffs

Within the broad averages referred to are many variations in tariffs on individual products (tariff lines). The distribution of these lines in terms of the level of duties charged is set out in Table 8.2.

Table 8.2 indicates clearly the percentage of tariff lines bearing zero duties, and various levels of duty up to and above 35 per cent.

Table 8.2   Pre- and Post-Uruguay Round tariff profiles for industrial products (excluding petroleum)

	Tariff lines		Imports from all sources	
	Pre-UR	*Post-UR*	*Pre-UR*	*Post-UR*
Developed economies:				
Total	100	100	100	100
Duty free	21	32	20	44
0.1–5.0%	24	25	41	32
5.1–10.0%	22	20	24	15
10.1–15.0%	10	9	7	5
15.1–35.0%	16	13	6	4
Over 35%	7	2	1	1
Developing economies:				
Total	100	100	100	100
Duty Free	11	10	39	42
0.1–5.0%	6	5	6	5
5.1–10.0%	7	5	8	10
10.1–15.0%	5	5	4	5
15.1–35.0%	30	55	28	30
Over 35%	42	20	15	8

Source: GATT (1994).[6]

It also sets out the percentage of imports that will be entering at the various levels of duty. In the developed countries there has been a major reduction in duty at all levels. Furthermore there has been a substantial increase in the amount of trade covered by duty free rates in developed countries (from 20 per cent to 44 per cent) and 91 per cent of imports now enter at tariffs of less than 10 per cent.

The developing countries have also made a substantial effort – the number of tariff lines in each category remain roughly similar, but there has been a substantial reduction in the number of tariffs above 35 per cent and a corresponding bunching of tariffs in the 15–35 per cent category. While the number of tariff lines at zero is about a third the number for the developed countries, they cover roughly the same percentage of imports. In summary, the situation on zero tariffs is satisfactory though somewhat skewed by the performance of Singapore and Hong Kong, and there has been a substantial flattening of the tariffs at the highest levels. After zero duty categories, the next largest percentage of trade is in the 15–35 per cent tariff category.

Table 8.3 Tariff reductions on industrial products (excluding petroleum) by developed countries, selected groups of countries

| Imports | Import value ($ billion) | Trade-weighted tariff average | | |
		Pre-UR (%)	Post-UR (%)	Percentage reduction
All industrial products:				
All sources	736.9	6.3	3.8	40
Middle-income countries	165.8	6.8	4.3	37
Least developed economies	3.9	6.8	5.1	25
Excluding textiles and clothing, fish and fish products:				
All sources	652.1	5.4	2.9	46
Middle income countries	123.7	4.8	2.4	50
Least developed economies	2.1	1.8	0.7	61

Source: GATT (1994).[7]

Have the tariff offers of developed countries favoured other developed countries more than developing countries? If all products are taken together, the reduction of duties has favoured the other developed countries more. However if textiles and clothing, and fish and fish products are excluded the picture is the exact opposite, and the developing countries are in a substantially better position (Table 8.3). Textiles in particular have been subject to a special regime that has most affected exports from developing countries (see Chapter 15).

Bindings

The tariff used as a reference point for reductions is the basic tariff, not the 'applied' or 'preferential' rate. This can sometimes lead to what appear to be strange results. A tariff can be reduced from a nominal rate of 20 per cent to 10 per cent and bound in GATT at the lower level. This 'bound' level might still be higher than the actual 'applied' rate, which might only be 5 per cent. Or again a country might raise its basic rate from 20 per cent to 25 per cent but bind it at that higher level. Other countries might accept this in exchange for the certainty they are getting from the 'binding' at the new rate. A country that bound its tariff at 25 per cent might well continue to apply a rate of 20 per cent in practice.

All of this is just to explain that, while the GATT system is geared to reducing tariffs, the issue of 'binding' and certainty is so important it is accepted that the rates bound in the GATT are sometimes at higher rather than lower levels. At the same time the rates actually applied in practice can often be different and lower from those that are 'bound' in GATT. The bindings represent the internationally agreed tariff level, not necessarily what is applied in practice.

The degree of binding among industrialised countries was already high before the Uruguay Round. In the case of the EU, the United States and Canada, close to 100 per cent of industrial imports were covered by bound tariffs. For Japan it was 81 per cent. However there were some laggards among the industrialised countries, for example Australia (only 35 per cent bound) and New Zealand (58 per cent bound).

Among the developing countries many had few or zero bindings; even liberal trade regimes such as Hong Kong and Singapore had few or no bound tariffs. There is however an explanation for this: as these economies were already operating very low or zero tariffs, the only bargaining chip they had was the possibility of offering bindings. Even in the Uruguay Round, therefore, they held back on the level of bindings in order to preserve some bargaining power for the next round. This was more true for Hong Kong than Singapore, which made a respectable effort in the latest negotiations.

The Uruguay Round led to a substantial improvement. New Zealand bound 100 per cent binding of its tariff lines (up from 58 per cent) and Australia's 35 per cent rose to 84 per cent. There was also a dramatic improvement in the case of the developing countries (though this represented somewhat less in trade weighted terms). The overall result is shown in Table 8.4.

Tariff escalation

Another element of importance in assessing a round is the question of tariff escalation. Many tariff structures contain low tariffs on the raw materials used by domestic producers, but higher tariffs on the product that is processed, depending on the degree of processing. This creates problems for developing countries that are trying to diversify out of the production and export of raw materials into processed goods. The higher tariff on processed goods can also

Table 8.4   Scope of tariff bindings (percentage of imports covered
excluding petroleum)

Country	Per cent	Country	Per cent
Indonesia	92	Brazil	100
Thailand	70	Chile	100
Malaysia	79	New Zealand	100
Singapore	73	Australia	84
Hong Kong	23	Canada	100
Korea	89	Japan	81
India	68	USA	100
Mexico	100	EU	100

Sources: GATT (1994), European Commission (1994).[8]

give a higher or more effective level of protection than would appear at first glance from the level of the tariff itself.

To take an example, the world market price for a particular product, for example a pair of shoes, may be $10, with $5 for the leather and another $5 for the value added by labour and machinery. A 25 per cent tariff on a pair of shoes will set the import price at $12.50. Assuming that a domestic manufacturer can obtain the raw material duty free, the effective protection of the 25 per cent tariff on imported shoes is 50 per cent, and the company can now spend up to $7.50 on its input or increase its profits. The irony is that this effective protection increases as the value added or amount of processing of the exporter increases. This can undermine the efforts of developing countries to move upstream. They tend to develop industries that involve the light processing of raw materials, for example textiles, footwear and so on. These products face greater effective protection as a result of the operation of the tariff where the value added in the export market is less important.

The pattern of tariff escalation according to the level of processing has remained since the Uruguay Round. Tariffs in developed countries are still higher on more-processed goods, as can be seen in Table 8.5, which divides goods into three product groups and distinguishes between raw materials, semiprocessed manufactures and finished products.

However the tariffs on the various stages of processing have been heavily reduced in most cases, and flattened to the point where the remaining tariffs are very low in the developed countries. The biggest tariff escalation now lies between finished industrial products and the raw materials that go into them, at 4.5 per cent. On

Table 8.5 Imports and tariffs of developed economies by stages of processing (weighted average and percentages)

Product group	All sources		Developing economies	
	Pre-UR per cent	Offer	Pre-UR per cent	Offer
All industrial products				
Raw materials	1.8	0.8	2.1	1.0
Semiprocessed manufactures	5.3	2.8	5.3	2.9
Finished products	7.4	4.8	9.1	6.4
Total tariff escalation	6.4	4.0	6.8	4.5
Industrial tropical products				
Raw materials	0.4	0.1	0.1	0.0
Semiprocessed manufactures	4.1	2.1	6.3	3.0
Finished products	6.3	2.9	6.6	2.7
Total tariff escalation	4.2	1.9	4.2	1.8
Natural-resource-based products				
Raw materials	2.2	1.7	3.1	2.3
Semiprocessed manufactures	2.9	1.5	3.5	1.7
Finished products	7.7	4.8	7.9	5.6
Total tariff escalation	3.2	2.0	4.0	2.6

Source: GATT (1993).[9]

industrial tropical products and natural-resource-based products the escalation between raw materials and finished products is 1.8 per cent and 2.6 per cent respectively.

This is also the case with individual products, with one or two exceptions, for example tobacco, where tariffs are higher and there has been a substantial reduction of tariff escalation. As for semi-processed manufactures and finished goods, the degree of reduction has been greater on finished industrial goods than on intermediate products; the reverse is true in the case of natural-resource-based products. Tariff escalation has also remained high for textiles, but this is a special case. There is still a slight bias against imports from developing countries compared with imports from all sources.

One can not conclude that tariff escalation in developed countries has ceased to be an important issue as a result of the Uruguay Round, but there has been a substantial improvement. One should also recall that preferential tariff arrangements exist for many products of export interest to developing countries, and in practice these exports often enter duty free or at very low rates. Escalation has even less meaning in this context.

9 Tariff-Related Issues

Tariff concessions can be undermined by a series of other obstacles erected behind a tariff wall. Even if tariffs were to be reduced from 10 per cent to 5 per cent, this would be to no avail if a border tax were to be introduced under another name, for example an import charge, a stamp duty and so on. This type of charge is subject to a 'standstill' under the WTO, provided the tariff on the product is bound.[1] The Uruguay Round has improved transparency and control over them by requiring that they be included in the schedules when tariffs on the same products are listed and bound at certain levels, and can give rise to claims for compensation if they are raised or new ones are introduced.

The GATT also forbids the use of taxes in a manner that discriminates between foreign and domestic goods, whether this discrimination is obvious (that is, taxes levied at different rates), or non-discriminatory on the face of it but discriminatory in effect (for example higher taxes on large vehicles affected US exports). Such tax differences applied domestically could undermine or nullify tariff concessions. This would be against the principle of national treatment.

Another example of the sort of difficulty that can befall an importer and effectively nullify any tariff concessions is valuation by the customs services. When *ad valorem* duties are applied, someone has to evaluate the product to decide how much duty should be paid.

One cannot accept any value being attributed to a product by an importer who is trying to reduce his or her tariff bill. Nor can one accept arbitrary evaluations by a customs service that bear no relation to the real price of the product. The United States, for example, used to apply the American selling price (ASP) to imports of chemical products. This was based on the selling price of equivalent US chemical products and disregarded the actual lower values of imported goods. This situation has been put on a firmer footing since the Tokyo Round, where an agreement on customs valuation was reached, and further refined in the Uruguay Round. The agreement includes the basic and rather obvious principle that valuation should be based on the actual transaction cost (the real sale price).

There are refinements of these rules to determine the exact transaction cost, taking account of exchange rate movements, the ancillary costs of the importer and so on.

Another important influence on the choice of measure to apply
– tariff, quantitative restriction, antidumping duty and so on – are
the rules of origin. When applying a tariff for example, the customs authorities have to determine where a product comes from,
as different tariffs apply to different countries in certain circumstances. The product is usually deemed to come from a particular
country only if a substantial transformation or a major part of the
manufacturing process was carried out there. These decisions are
not always easy, and different countries use different rules. The
EU, for example, uses a lower threshold of transformation for products coming from countries with which it has preferential arrangements or free trade areas, than those with which it does not. These
differences not only lead to confusion, they also breed resentment.
Those to whom different rules of origin are applied may not only
be paying higher duties, but the different rules of origin may further reduce their competitiveness; they have to prove that their
product has been subject to greater transformation than others.

The Uruguay Round produced an agreement on rules of origin
containing certain rules on transparency, non-discrimination and
so on. It also set up a programme of work to harmonise rules of
origin, to be completed by 1997. The ultimate goal is that all members
of the WTO will apply the same set of rules. The rules of origin
that are applied to preferential arrangements will continue to be
treated differently, however.

Rules were also negotiated in the Tokyo Round to ensure that
licenses are administered in a manner that does not distort trade.
These were contained in the agreement on import licensing procedures, which was revised in the Uruguay Round. Many licenses
are required, simply to have some understanding of trade flows,
for statistical purposes and so on. These are supposed to be available automatically.

Other licenses are issued to control imports when a legitimate
trade barrier is in place, for example when safeguard measures have
been instituted. There again, however, there are rules to ensure
that such licenses are not exercised in an abusive manner and are
tailored to strict non-discriminatory implementation of the measure
in question.

It is a common practice of governments nowadays to use private firms to carry out an inspection, usually of the invoice price, before products leave their home port. This practice cuts out some types of fraud, cheating on exchange costs and so on. In the course of the Uruguay Round an agreement on preshipment inspection was negotiated. This sets out some rules on non-discrimination, against excessive delays and other difficulties.

Part III

Non-Tariff Matters

10 Antidumping

INTRODUCTION

There has been much discussion in recent years of the rationale and need for antidumping rules, and there has also been much criticism, whether justified or not, of the rules used to implement antidumping actions with regard both to the rules of measurement of dumping or injury and to the rules of procedure.[1] This chapter will focus on both these aspects.

THE RATIONALE FOR ANTIDUMPING RULES

Under the rules of the GATT, dumping occurs and antidumping duties may be levied by an importing country when producers sell their goods in that market at a price below that which they are sold in the home market (price discrimination), or below the cost of production (normal value). Price discrimination is considered to be unfair and to lead to distortions of trade, which need to be corrected. The duties are designed to offset the injurious effect of the dumping margin in the importing country. When sales are made below cost in the domestic market they are not considered to be sold at 'normal value', and a calculation is made of what the selling price would normally be in the domestic market, based on the producer's costs of production. This is then compared with the export price to determine if there is a dumping margin.

If sellers have no sales or no normal market value sales in their domestic market, a domestic sales price or normal value may be 'constructed', that is, composed according to what the goods would normally cost if they were sold in the domestic market. In these circumstances normal value may also be based on export price to third countries. Again, if the sellers are operating in a non-market economy, for example China, where there are no reliable prices or costs in market terms, analogue prices are used, that is, domestic sales prices in the market economy of another country at a similar level of development.

Sales below cost, or price discrimination, can occur in a number of situations and it is frequently contested that these are 'normal' aspects of competition among firms and not in any sense 'unfair'. This argument tends to ignore the fact that international trade is not taking place in a perfectly free manner, or in one that resembles the normal operation of a single or national market. The international playing field is not level, and this can frequently give rise to distortions and the unfair or unacceptable practice of dumping. The various situations in which this may arise are as follows.

Sales Below Cost

First, suppliers may have rational reasons to want to sell below cost. For example, they may have invested at a certain point in time and the prices in the market may have dropped below the original estimate. This is a relatively rare case and the business is unlikely to be sustainable for long.

Second, a firm may have a dominant position or monopoly and may wish to undermine its competitors by sales below cost. It can only do this if it has deep pockets. Within national boundaries this practice, which is disallowed by most competition authorities, relates to the situation where a monopolist or a near monopolist is trying either to maintain a monopoly or to establish one. In order to do so the price is reduced to below variable costs in an effort to drive out competitors. When the monopoly has been achieved or reinstated the price is raised again. This practice is known as predatory pricing.

The losses associated with predation can only be borne by a firm that is making excess profits and it has accumulated a war chest for this sort of action. Usually the excess profits come from another product it is making, and these profits counterbalance the drop in price on the product in question. A good example is Boeing, which uses its monopoly profits on jumbo jets to lower the price of its other models, for example the Boeing 777, and to compete more aggressively.

In domestic markets this is considered an unusual practice and one that is difficult to establish. The assumption is that most firms do not have the resources to indulge in prolonged selling below cost. Furthermore when a monopolist puts its price back up it is likely that other producers will reenter the market. The main exception to this might be where the reentry costs are excessively high, or where a new firm in the market will require a considerable amount of time to become competitive (for example semiconductors, large aircraft).

Given that most firms are unlikely to indulge in this sort of high-risk, high-cost adventure, most economists are sceptical of the existence of the sort of predatory intent needed and the willingness to suffer prolonged losses with such an uncertain outcome. Prosecutions for predatory pricing are therefore rare, and have become even rarer in recent years, for example in the United States where most monopolies are considered contestable. If a monopoly is contestable, new entrants will prevent price gouging and the budding monopolist won't even try to predate.

Third, the competition rules do not usually address the issue of non-dominant firms using similar tactics. It is assumed that they can not do so and remain viable. If normal profits made on other products made by an industrial group are used to undercut competitors on another product, the whole group will either make a loss or very little profit. It is only the existence of monopoly profits or a dominant position, and the assumption that these profits might be sufficient to eliminate a competitor or frighten off new entrants, that allow a reasonable case to be made for the competition authorities to intervene.

Fourth, the argument has also been made that when a single firm sells below costs in order to increase market share, this is reasonable and normal. It will do so if, by increasing production, it can recover its costs through economies of scale. The firm calculates that if it can sell more at a lower price it will ultimately become profitable.

As we have seen, the sale of goods below cost is not rational as competitors will do likewise; the modern view of predation suggests that this is unlikely even when a monopolist is at work. A non-dominant competitor who is selling below cost is therefore likely to have some important advantage that allows it to do so. A producer's control of the home market will give it an edge over competitors in open markets elsewhere, and allow it to do so for a considerable period of time. It can sell below cost if the home market is captive and allows it to achieve some economics of scale; the key is that the producer's competitors will be at a disadvantage and will have less economies of scale if they cannot compete in its market. The producer may also have a protected home market for other goods it sells, which permits it to cross-subsidise goods sold abroad. Finally, it may be charging high prices in its captive home market which permit it to sell at a loss abroad (but this really falls under the heading of price discrimination – see next section).

Price Discrimination

A typical example of sales below cost arises where a firm's production at home has reached the point that it has covered its fixed costs. It will then be in a position to sell additional production at a much lower price that covers only its variable costs and a profit.

This situation can only really arise when a market is protected in some way, for example by a tariff. If it is not, then goods sold abroad at a lower price will return and undermine the prices being charged at home (so-called 'parallel imports'). In an open market such as Hong Kong, for example, the market for goods sold at $10 at home will be undermined by the same goods being sold abroad at $5; they will be reimported into Hong Kong and sold for $6. If a producer is simply offloading products it can't sell at home, it may not care about parallel imports, but in that case it is probably about to go out of business, at least with regard to that product. At most the offloading will only be a temporary and unsustained phenomenon.

This gives one a clue to the 'unfair' or 'pernicious' aspect of dumping. A producer is using the unfair advantage of a protected home market to charge higher prices and make higher profits. It then uses this advantage to charge lower prices abroad than would otherwise be possible, carve out an improved market share and squeeze competitors, or even get rid of them.

Whatever the motivation, the key to the ability to dump lies in the level of protection of the home market and the ability to leverage this into a form of subsidy for more aggressive action in a foreign market.

These actions may be conscious moves on the part of a state to improve the international position of its industry. A government may use measures to encourage the strategic development of an industry in a way that enables a firm to dump more easily and in a prolonged manner. A typical example, of which the Japanese are frequently accused, is the protection of the home market and the exclusion of foreign competitors by diverse means, and its cartelisation in such a way as to permit a firm or a group of firms to sell at high prices domestically. Sales in the home market at a higher profit enable the firms to sell at an unusually low price in export markets. This enables them to build up market share globally, to increase their economies of scale and thus to become real global competitors at the expense of others. Moreover they can achieve this without having a monopoly or dominant position. Protection of the home market, not a monopoly, provides the necessary finance to carry out the operation.

This can make eminent economic sense for the dumper, even if it does not have monopoly power and may have more limited objectives than the elimination of a competitor. It may be carried out in pursuit of more tactical goals, such as gaining a foothold in a new market and offsetting high initial startup costs, or simply to off-load products that are in excess supply.

Price discrimination of this sort has frequently been condemned by competition authorities, though usually the complaints are brought by those who are paying higher rather than lower prices. The US Robinson Patman Act was designed to deal with all forms of price discrimination. Similar rules exist in EU law where there is an abuse of a dominant position. However the Robinson Patman Act is not frequently invoked these days because it is rare that a producer can divide a national market sufficiently to make price discrimination pay.

While it is difficult to divide national markets, this is not true internationally. A country could have created obstacles to market access that would enable a firm to have one price in its home market and another outside it. Moreover a dumping action could result in losses in the export market, without losses overall, as they could be recouped in the home market. At the same time these losses can be incurred almost indefinitely as long as there is a degree of protection of the home market.

Summary

Antidumping provisions do not exist in a national market, or in a 'single' market such as the European Union or the United States. In these markets, which in principle are open, competition would do away with any dumping margin and strenuous efforts are made to ensure that there is such competition. The EU, for example, has always made an enormous effort to avoid any carving up of markets and to ensure that parallel imports within the single market are not in any way impeded. The United States has made a similar effort under the interstate commerce clause.

Residual anticompetitive actions within national or single markets are dealt with by the competition laws on predation, price discrimination and so on. In the absence of international competition rules,

dumping laws control the anticompetitive actions internationally
The procedures are in many cases more rapid and effective than
competition laws, and carry the sanction of trade measures. This
reflects the fact that there is an absence of international rules and
a level playing field.

In the end, economic arguments for and against price discrimination or dumping depend in part at least upon what view is taken
of the functioning of the market. One important consideration is
that competitive or even 'unfair' behaviour in a truly open market
is easier to tolerate. However if a firm is benefiting from the artificial advantage created for it by its own government through, for
example, tariffs, then this is a matter of reasonable concern for
competing firms in another country.

Another point is that how economists come down on the issue
of dumping really depends on their overall trade philosophy. In
Chapter 3 it was pointed out that some feel that the interests of
consumers should be paramount, and that dumping serves this interest (they obtain cheaper goods). Some economists argue that an
importing country should welcome the cheaper goods as they en-
hance overall welfare and release resources for more productive
uses in the economy.

This is a perfectly reasonable intellectual standpoint, but one this
author doesn't completely share, as it neglects the importance of
maintaining industries in vital sectors and takes too little account
of the overall strategic needs of an economy. It also neglects the
unacceptable nature of the protected base from which the dumping emanates. Arguably the United States lost its consumer electronics industry through foreign dumping practices and its vehicle
industry was damaged (though in the latter case some of the increased competition was clearly good for it and it might have occurred without dumping margins anyway, as the Japanese had simply
become more efficient at making cars). But one of the reasons it
lost world market share was that it could not fight back in the
closed Japanese market.

In the long run it might be possible to abolish antidumping rules,
but this would only be possible in a more open trading system where
common competition rules and effective enforcement exist. The
Singapore Ministerial Declaration gave an initial impetus to talks
on these issues. A working group has now been set up in the WTO
to analyse the need for global competition rules.[2] This will no doubt
include some discussion of dumping and other anticompetitive

practices. However, in the absence of a strong agreement internationally on competition rules, and more open markets, it is unlikely that one will be able to do without antidumping rules.

MEASUREMENT OF DUMPING AND INJURY – THE RULES AND CHANGES MADE DURING THE URUGUAY ROUND

While the rationale for dumping actions is quite clear and has long been recognised by the WTO rules, implementation of the rules has left something to be desired. The Uruguay Round went a considerable distance towards rectifying that situation.[3]

The main problem with identifying dumping activities is one of measurement. The goods sold for export have a particular price, which must be compared with that of the same product being sold in the producer's home market to see if in fact they are being sold at a lesser price. This seems straightforward enough, but in some cases the producer is not selling in the home market. To find some equivalent measure to the home market price or 'normal value', therefore, it is necessary to know the price of products being sold in third markets. But if this is not happening, the value of the home market price, or 'normal value', has to be made up or 'constructed' on the basis of production costs. An additional complication is raised by state trading economies, where accounting practices are such that it is impossible to establish or construct a home market price or 'normal value'. In such cases another country is selected and the home market price or 'normal value' is based on prices in that market of producers who manufacture, preferably by the same process, and sell, under competitive conditions, the product concerned on its home market. This is the so-called analogue price.

One can see that in these cases the problem of measurement is considerable and that the method used to arrive at a home market price or 'normal value' is in some ways artificial.

There have been problems in the United States with the method for constructing a home market price.[4] In addition to the basic costs, 10 per cent is added for overheads (this is within a reasonable range) and 8 per cent is added for profits. The 8 per cent can sometimes be unreasonable given that profits are often squeezed by a depressed market and different margins can be expected in different product sectors. It is unnecessarily artificial to construct a

price at that level when average profits may have fallen throughout the industry. Again this type of artificial measurement serves
to increase the dumping margin.

There is now a general standard of 'fair comparison' that is likely
to settle on a fairer set of calculations. Some are already spelled
out; for example the new agreement recognises that sales below
cost that occur during start-up operations do not always represent
an exporter's true costs.[5] It also allows 20 per cent sales below cost
to be taken into account.[6] The Japanese proposal to allow forward
pricing was not agreed however (forward pricing means dropping
prices in order to achieve economies of scale and ultimately profitability). Constructed value should now be based on actual data,
not on artificial calculations. There is some discretion however when
actual data is not available.

Similar problems arise in the calculation of dumping margins.
The following are some examples from former US practice. In the
normal course of events one would use the average price over six
months in the home market and in the export market. However
this does not happen and while the price for the home market is
based on an average price, it is an artificial average as it makes no
allowance for discounting, and this tends to drive up the average
price in the home market. On the other hand, in the case of the
price in the export market no average is taken, and the price is
based on a comparison of individual prices on a transaction-by-
transaction basis. This could be compensated by charging higher
prices on other contracts, but they are not taken into account in
calculating an 'average' price. This of course drives down the price
for the purposes of assessment. It can be argued that the dumping
margin is artificially created or enlarged through an unfair measurement technique. Another example is the decision of some authorities to ignore currency fluctuations, which can easily create a dumping
margin that is clearly outside the control of the exporter.

There is now a provision in the antidumping agreement that requires an averaging of the domestic and export prices, or a trans-
action-by-transaction comparison.[7] There is still a margin of discretion
in certain conditions however. Some allowance is also made for
currency fluctuations, but after 60 days the exporter is deemed to
have adjusted his or her prices.[8] It is also likely that the new test
will deal with other problems of asymmetry, for example inclusion
of certain overheads in the domestic price but not in the export
price.[9]

In the case of dumping, as in the case of subsidies, it has to be shown that the behaviour has caused material injury to a domestic industry.[10] The injury test is a fairly strict one that considers all the circumstances of the case, including such matters as loss of market share, price undercutting, loss of profitability and so on.[11] Above all it has to be demonstrated that it was the dumping that had actually caused the injury[12] and not some other factor, such as the complainant's products going out of fashion (for example a consumer preference for small cars instead of large ones), that the industry as a whole was suffering from a recession, or some other factor that would indicate the operation of greater forces.

It also requires that the margin of dumping be taken into account:[13] if it is small there is less chance of it being the cause of injury. On the other hand it is now possible to cumulate dumped exports from various sources for the purpose of a determination of injury.[14] At the same time it allows exemption for *de minimis* suppliers (less than 3 per cent of imports, unless suppliers with less than 3 per cent together amount to more than 7 per cent overall). A dumping margin of less than 2 per cent is also considered *de minimis*.[15]

The agreement does not however contain an explicit requirement to take consumer as opposed to producer interests into account. Such a clause would of course substantially weaken the antidumping remedy, whose main purpose is to protect industry against unfair trade practices. The consumer's interest is nearly always to receive cheaper albeit dumped goods. Nor does it require that a party reserve some discretion allowing it not to impose duties in pursuit of some wider national or economic interest, though some countries do have such a clause in practice.

Two of the most contentious issues in the negotiations covered circumvention and country hopping. Circumvention relates to the practice of firms hit by antidumping duties moving their operations to another country or to the country of export. In either case the firms frequently use the same inputs and the new operations are mere 'screwdriver' or minimal assembly operations. Both the EU and the United States apply antidumping duties to the imports when this happens. No solution was found to this question during the Uruguay Round; it was not condemned, nor was it condoned. The issue will no doubt be the subject of difficulties in the years ahead.

'Country hopping' is a term used to describe the same circumstances but where a new investigation has taken place. The United States succeeded in having a provision included that would allow retroactive duties when the investigation concluded there was dumping in this situation.

A related issue is the use of rules of origin. If a firm hit by dumping moves to another country but its assembly operations don't qualify it for a new origin, it continues to be subjected to the original antidumping duties. However some countries have continued to apply the antidumping duties even when a new origin can be established by the degree of assembly in the new country, as the imports were still 'dumped' goods. This was another unresolved issue.

There have been some procedural improvements:

- Provisional duties may only be levied after a preliminary determination of dumping and injury, and not at the start of an investigation as has been the practice of some. Imposition of the provisional duties must not exceed six or, in exceptional cases, nine months.[16]
- Price undertakings, that is, to raise export prices, are now given somewhat more encouragement, though it is still at governments' discretion as to whether to accept them.[17] In the United States, for example, there has always been reluctance to accept undertakings because of their possible anticompetitive effects.
- There are some new rules on the calculation of duties and retroactivity.[18]
- There is provision for a 'sunset' clause on duties imposed, unless a review demonstrates the need to continue them.[19] There was no sunset clause before, and duties could continue indefinitely.

The procedural rules on complaints considerably strengthen the requirement to establish a good *prima facie* case.[20] They also require the complainant to represent at least 25 per cent of producers of a like product and have the tacit support of 50 per cent.[21] Employees can also have standing, but there is no rule on how their interests can be reconciled with their management if views diverge.

The dispute settlement procedures for antidumping were improved significantly, as they were throughout the WTO. The procedures were also speeded up somewhat and the conciliation steps removed to arrive more rapidly at multilateral resolutions. However resort to the WTO procedures cannot take place until provisional duties are in place;[22] some had wanted to be able to appeal to the WTO when investigations were initiated.

The role of panels was substantially restricted in that a new standard of review was established.[23] If a country's has properly established the facts and evaluation of them is unbiased and objective, a panel cannot overturn them even if it reaches a different conclusion. Nor can new facts be considered. The panel must also accept the interpretation of a provision if it is one of several possible ones. It is clear that this provision is designed to ensure that panels do not easily overturn antidumping decisions; but panels may have their own views of what is unbiased or what interpretations the provisions of the agreement will bear.

CONCLUSION

While antidumping activity once tended to be a priestly art practised by a handful of developed countries, now everyone wants to get in on the act, and many more countries are establishing antidumping authorities and legislation, including, for the first time, many developing countries. The number of investigations by developed countries has stabilised and in some cases fallen. However the existence of an investigation can be trade-inhibiting.

However one should not exaggerate the impact of these measures. In the EU, for example, the percentage of imports covered by antidumping duties in 1995 was only 1.2 per cent. If China is included this figure climbs to 1.4 per cent. The United States has some 306 duties in place, the EU about 157, Australia 85 and Canada 83, out of a reported total of 710 on 30 June 1995. In the case of the EU, for example, its exports face some 100 duties and investigations at the time of writing. The total on 30 June 1994 was 662, so the 1995 figures represent an increase, but there is a decreasing trend of investigations.[24]

To a large extent the increased use of antidumping measures is due to increased liberalisation around the globe, and countries in the cold wind of competition feel more secure if they have some trade weapons up their sleeve to be used as a last resort. In a sense it is the price one has to pay for free trade. However, as one can see from the statistics above, while there has been an increase in measures taken, these can not be deemed significant or out of control. We do not seem to be on the slippery slope of aggravated protectionism.

What is more difficult is the question of how to treat the old state trading economies, which are now in transition. They bear many of the features of open economies but frequently retain elements of the old. This is true in Eastern Europe, but perhaps more importantly in China. According to the World Bank some 60 per cent of China's economy is liberalised, but the problem is distinguishing those firms that are truly operating according to market principles and those which have some state ownership or subsidy. One way of dealing with this is through individual inspection of firms, but this has certain limits given the bureaucratic burden it can pose.

The next round of WTO negotiations, which is likely to deal with competition rules, will probably look at the issue of antidumping as well. The recent Singapore ministerial meeting of the WTO agreed that competition and trade should be discussed.[25]

11 Subsidies and Countervailing Duties

INTRODUCTION

Almost all countries subsidise various sectors of the economy, be these in agriculture, industry or services. They do this through a variety of measures, including direct grants, loans and equity participation through tax expenditure or relief. Many firms that are involved in both military and civilian production receive substantial subsidies on the military side, which then spill over on to the civilian side. Another important source of subsidy can be procurement, in particular in the military field.

The extent of subsidisation varies from economy to economy, but one should be aware that some of the figures on subsidisation do not necessarily reflect the whole picture. Military subsidies do not appear clearly in national expenditure statistics though they are often extremely important. The definition of a subsidy is not something upon which everyone can agree, and there are few studies of government funding that can give a realistic picture of what is going on. Some studies do exist, and I will try to draw some lessons from them below, but at best they are incomplete. These are the most recent OECD report on Public Support to Industry (1996)[1] and the Fourth Survey on State Aid in the European Union (1995).[2] This chapter will concentrate on manufacturing subsidies and the WTO agreement on subsidies and countervailing duties. Subsidies to agriculture are now subject to a different set of rules and are dealt with in Chapter 19.

You will see from Table 11.1 that the European states tend to subsidise more than, for example, Japan and the United States. However these are only elements of an overall picture that is not well drawn in the literature. In the case of the United States for example, little account is taken of the importance of military expenditure, and no account of the breakdown between agriculture and manufacturing. The result is therefore very uncertain if one is to draw lessons about manufacturing, which is the purpose of this chapter. Table 11.1 gives only very broad indications.

Table 11.1   Subsidies shown in national account statistics as a percentage of GDP

	1968	1972	1976	1980	1984	1988	1992	1994
Italy	1.91	2.11	2.92	3.44	3.80	3.05	2.64	2.63
France	2.67	2.01	2.46	2.55	3.06	2.51	2.20	2.37
Canada	0.90	0.92	1.87	2.68	2.77	1.87	1.95	1.47
United Kingdom	2.05	1.80	2.88	2.50	2.36	1.33	1.16	1.10
Germany	2.43	1.91	1.98	2.08	2.07	2.28	1.56	1.65
Japan	1.11	1.15	1.31	1.50	1.27	0.92	0.71	0.88
United States	0.48	0.58	0.32	0.39	0.60	0.64	0.54	0.50

Source: OECD (1960–94).[3]

During the 1970s public support programmes for manufacturing were intensified, mainly because of the difficult structural problems being encountered, the oil crisis and so on. In the 1980s there was a realisation that these subsidies were becoming too expensive and that an effort would have to be made to reduce and redirect them. There was a growing understanding that many, though not all, subsidies to crisis sectors such as steel, textiles and shipbuilding were wasteful and that it would be more sensible to concentrate on R & D and future technologies, or at the least on general non-sectoral subsidies such as general investment incentives, retraining, regional aid and so on.

Increasing attention to budgetary austerity and deficit reduction has also meant that less money is available for such support. Nowadays governments tend to prefer to invest either in basic infrastructure or in programmes that will support new industries, such as R and D. The private sector has been called on to manage itself better and to rely less on government handouts. At the same time, with the reduction of government deficits, private companies are now in a better position to find their own finance at more reasonable cost.

While manufacturing subsidies in the OECD appeared to be declining in the mid to late 1980s, they increased again in the period 1989–93. In real terms they went from $39 billion in 1989 to $48.4 billion in 1991, but declined to $40.1 billion in 1993. This represents a support rate of 1.15 per cent in 1989 and 1.23 per cent for manufacturing activity in 1993.[4]

Figures for the EU show a decline of about 25 per cent overall since 1988 (44 billion ECU), but relative stability if 1989 (33.5 billion ECU) is compared with 1992 (34 billion ECU). The figures for the

Table 11.2   Subsidies in the OECD as a percentage of overall manufacturing subsidisation, and in order of importance 1993

	1989 per cent	1993 per cent
Regional	21.8	31.2
R & D	16.3	17.6
Export and trade	17.6	17.0
Small and medium sized enterprises (SMEs)	13.9	7.6
Sectoral	11.4	6.9
Crisis	4.2	6.5
Investment	7.6	5.3
Labour	5.3	4.5
Energy	1.1	2.9
Environment	0.6	0.7

Source: OECD (1996).[6]

EU and the OECD are not directly comparable, given the substantial differences in methodology and coverage.[5]

The data in Table 11.2 show a very substantial increase in subsidies for regions, and energy subsidies more than doubled between 1993 and 1989. The subsidies for R & D and exports were high and stable, but there was a considerable decline for small and medium sized enterprises (SMEs) and to a lesser extent for investment incentives, labour retraining and so on. The figures for sectoral aid show an encouraging downward trend, but there was a sharp increase in crisis assistance.

The picture for the EU in 1992 was similar, with regional aid out in front (50 per cent), followed by sectoral aid (12 per cent), R & D (10 per cent), SMEs (9 per cent), exports (9 per cent), energy (2 per cent) and the environment (1 per cent). The EU spends less on average on R & D and more on sectoral aid; in the case of some member states subsidies are much higher or lower.[7]

While subsidies will probably always be with us, one can tentatively draw some conclusions from these trends:

– Subsidies in general show volatility around a longer-term stable or even declining trend, but this is hard to be sure of given the cyclical nature of some of the figures.
– Sectoral subsidies are in general decreasing, but particular crises or adjustment problems can reignite them.

– More horizontal adjustment subsidies for investment, retraining and SMEs tend to vary with the politics of the moment, and while fashionable for a while, seem to be becoming less so.
– R & D and trade subsidies have reached quite high levels but have stabilised at those levels.
– There have been some major increases in environment-related subsidies for energy saving.
– The subsidy effort today is concentrating on regional subsidies, which have increased dramatically.

With some important exceptions, the general trend appears to be towards subsidies that are less distorting and more general or horizontal.[8] This picture is at least partly reflected in the subsidies agreement renegotiated under the Uruguay Round. This agreement, which is discussed in detail in the next section, condones certain subsidies for R & D, the environment and regions but forbids export or trade subsidies, though important exceptions exist in this area. Its biggest innovation is to try to tackle domestic subsidies more effectively. Domestic subsidies not directly linked to exports but directed at certain firms or industries are deemed more distorting than general subsidies given to all firms.

These domestic subsidies, which are not made generally available but are specific to certain sectors or firms, are now more clearly actionable in the WTO if adverse effects can be shown. Hence sectoral and crisis subsidies are probably actionable insofar as they are specific and not general, though adverse trade effects must be proved. It may be difficult to show adverse trade effects while a sector is in crisis, as it may not be very competitive, though the subsidies may have important import displacing effects. Domestic subsidies are one area where one cannot be sure of a decline in the volume of subsidies, particularly where crisis subsidies are concerned, and this may give rise to substantial conflicts in the future.

One should not forget the importance of indirect subsidies granted through procurement. The amounts are very large for OECD countries as a whole, for example $207 billion in defence procurement and another $6.38 billion in space agency procurement, (OECD, 1993 figures).[9] By dint of their sheer volume these measures can have an important subsidising effect. In comparison, total manufacturing subsidies in the EU in 1991 were only 34 billion ECU. However these contracts are less a matter for the subsidies agreement than for the procurement agreement. For these reasons the procurement agreement is also of considerable importance in this context.

SUBSIDIES IN INTERNATIONAL TRADE[10]

While the general trend of subsidisation therefore appears to be decreasing, it is still substantial and individual subsidies to individual industries can create tensions and set off trade conflicts. A well-known case is the battle that has been taking place between Boeing and Airbus Industries. Boeing claims that Airbus is heavily subsidised by direct production subsidies from the European governments involved. Airbus replies that these subsidies are perfectly reasonable given the need for long-term finance, which is not available from the banking system. Moreover these subsidies are ultimately repaid, and are sometimes in the form of equity participation. They point to the various advantages Boeing receives through a series of federal and local tax rebates and through the military business that is given to Boeing. Furthermore, some planes, for instance the jumbo jet, were originally developed as military cargo planes with substantial government finance. The vigorous competition from Airbus, both on price and technology, has been good for the consumer, and aeroplanes nowadays cost much less and are much more efficient.

One line of argument has been that if a country decides to subsidise its exports, the importing country can only benefit. Unless the exporter is trying to eliminate all competition and monopolise the market, what is the harm? The opposite argument is of course that certain companies can be profoundly affected by a subsidy given to its competitor (Boeing versus Airbus). Secondly, subsidies tend to perpetuate themselves and can become a way of life. This can ultimately lead to a general siege mentality and protectionism in managing the economy. Sooner or later this is bound to create generalised trade friction.

One can see that there is no end to the creativity of the arguments that can be made on either side. But a more profound question is whether subsidies as a whole really have much effect on trade and whether they really need to be controlled by such a body as the WTO. They may, after all, be beneficial. Indeed subsidies are so prevalent and so much a part of common fiscal behaviour that there was a certain reluctance in the GATT to come firmly to grips with it.

Clearly one has to distinguish between subsidies that are harmful and those that are not. Regional subsidies, for example, aim to correct for serious economic disadvantages, and far from making firms operating in that region supercompetitive in the world market, they simply ensure that they can operate at all in an environment that is essentially hostile to economic development.

Again, many so-called domestic subsidies, which benefit both producers for the home and the export market, are of such a general nature that they do not give those firms any particular advantage in the world market or form part and parcel of a government's economic preferences for society and its ideology. One cannot be expected to include in a company's competitive advantage the infrastructure supplied by the government or the level of corporate taxation, which may be lower in one country than another, though competing levels of taxation are becoming an issue in the context of the EU single market.

On the other hand export subsidies, geared to the export market as such, tend to be the most likely to cause injury to foreign competitors, as they tend to be focused precisely on giving exporting firms a competitive edge in the global market.

Between these two extremes are some domestic subsidies that can also injure competitors or give an unfair advantage. Some domestic subsidies come close to operating like export subsidies in that they are specific and not generally available. Subsidies to a specific industry may give it an unfair edge insofar as it is competing with foreign firms in a highly traded sector, and indeed this is often the intent of such subsidies.

This distinction between general and specific subsidies can be a bit artificial, as specific subsidies may be no more distorting than those that are generally available. There is an underlying assumption however that they are, probably based on the idea that a government can give more effective assistance and a larger subsidy if it concentrates its resources on a specific industry or group of firms.

GATT therefore tended to deal with export subsidies as a matter of priority and the Uruguay Round confirmed GATT's prohibition of these subsidies as a matter of principle. It also sought to come to grips with domestic subsidies that have adverse effects on others; while not prohibiting them outright, it made them actionable in certain circumstances. It also decided to clarify the situation with regard to subsidies that are not harmful and declared them non-actionable.

THE ROLE OF THE WTO

Before dealing with these details however, a word of explanation is in order. The WTO agreement deals with the issue of subsidies in two ways. A complaining party can take up the matter with the WTO dispute settlement arm as a question of principle, or it can take countervailing measures against such subsidies. The latter course involves the imposition of duties on a subsidised import, to offset or countervail the amount of the subsidy.

The choice between these two approaches is based on different considerations. A government will attack a subsidy as a matter of principle if it wants to have the practice eliminated. If it is a prohibited export subsidy it doesn't have to prove that the practice is causing injury to its domestic industry. If the subsidy is an actionable domestic subsidy it can attack it provided it is causing 'adverse effects'. This can be established by showing, for example, a loss of market share, price undercutting or a nullification of a tariff concession. It is equally available whether these adverse effects are in its domestic market or on its exports to third markets, including the market of the subsidising country. If the adverse effects are not eliminated the complaining government can take countermeasures. These procedures are open only to governments, and not individuals.

The second option, countervailing measures, can be taken by governments usually following a complaint from the domestic industry, and requires proof that a like (that is, identical or very similar) product is benefiting from a margin of subsidy that is causing injury to the domestic industry in its home market. The result will be the imposition of a duty to remove the injurious effects of the subsidised imports of that product, but the subsidy or its more general effects are likely to remain in existence in the absence of condemnation by the WTO. The advantage of the procedure is that it does not require a complaint before the WTO; a government may take action autonomously in accordance with WTO rules (if it fails to follow the rules its actions can be challenged in the WTO). On the other hand it only applies in connection with injury in the home market and not in any other.

It is also important to note that even if a general attack on a subsidy fails, for example, adverse effects are not shown, subsidies on a particular product can still be countervailed if the existence of a subsidy and injury in the domestic market can be shown.

However these remedies can not be used at the same time with regard to injury in the domestic market. It should also be noted that in some respects antidumping and countervailing duties are interchangeable. Antidumping duties can cancel the price differences or below cost sales of subsidised products without having to prove the existence of a subsidy; only proof of a dumping margin and injury are required (see Chapter 10). A safeguard measure may also be used against a sudden flow of imports causing injury, whether the product in question is subsidised or not (see Chapter 12). These are sometimes easier remedies as they don't require proof of subsidy. The United States has been one of the main users of countervail remedies, given its hostility to subsidies, at least rhetorically. The EU has rarely used them as it has not wanted to provoke a counter-reaction to its own subsidy programmes, though this situation has changed somewhat.

Having a particular subsidy outlawed or its adverse effects declared illicit under GATT has never been easy, mainly because there was no clear definition of what constituted an actionable subsidy or injury to another party. Article XVI of GATT only prohibited export subsidies because these were deemed most likely to affect other parties (and that only since 1962). In the case of other subsidies, such as domestic subsidies given regardless of export performance, parties were enjoined 'to seek to avoid them' insofar as they could be shown to have negative effects on other partners' industries or trade. This was not exactly an enforceable obligation.

Moreover under the GATT, in the countervailing duty context, it is required that duties only be imposed where injury or a threat of injury exist. However, this is couched in fairly imprecise terms and does not spell out clearly the need for the subsidy to be the actual cause of the injury. Furthermore these provisions on how countervailing measures can be taken have not always been well observed in the implementing legislation of certain major partners, for example injury tests were only introduced in the United States after the Tokyo Round ended in 1979.

The weakness of definition has led to abuses. It is difficult to have a measure generally outlawed and eliminated, so governments have abused the countervail provisions and have taken many actions in their name that can only be considered protectionist as they were not based on any real injury or threat of it.

THE URUGUAY ROUND

The Tokyo Round went a certain distance towards dealing with some of these issues, particularly in the context of countervailing duties. However the Uruguay Round went a good deal further, especially with regard to the question of general discipline. It set out with more clarity what is meant by a subsidy, and set up three categories in the red, amber and green structure of prohibited, actionable and permitted subsidies. The new rules are contained in the agreement on subsidies and countervailing measures.

What is a Subsidy?

The definition of subsidy is broad[11] and covers any financial contribution by a public body whereby a benefit is conferred. It gives some examples, for instance grants, loans, equity infusions, loan guarantees (potential contribution), fiscal expenditure and provision of goods and services (other than infrastructural). It covers price or income supports (which may not involve a direct transfer or contribution). It also covers private bodies acting on behalf of the government. It is also made clear that such contributions as loans, guarantees, equity infusion and provision of goods are only subsidies if they confer a benefit, that is, are provided at rates that are better than those available on the market.

These definitions are a distinct improvement on the original GATT and subsequent Tokyo Round provisions, though they are still somewhat incomplete. They do not resolve such knotty questions as whether one is dealing with gross or net subsidies. It is sometimes argued that a steel industry whose prices are regulated and kept artificially low, but which benefits from certain subsidies, is not a net recipient of a subsidy and should not be countervailed or held in breach of the agreement if the cost to it of price regulation outweighs the subsidy given. However, it seems that negotiators wanted to include such things as upstream subsidies, that is, when a producer benefits from subsidies given to a supplier of inputs that results in cheaper raw material prices for the producer.

It can be assumed that the dispute settlement mechanisms will resolve these issues in a way that favours undistorted trade. In this case the steel producer will probably not be able to argue its net negative subsidy successfully, nor will a recipient of upstream subsidies be allowed to argue that it is not in receipt of a benefit.

Similar arguments are made in the case of regional aid, which may or may not outweigh the cost of doing business in a less developed region. In the case of regional subsidies however, the agreement has skirted around the problem by treating them as non-actionable if certain conditions are fulfilled (see below).

It should also be noted that there is a separate and different treatment of agriculture subsidies, which are dealt with in the agreement on agriculture. The subsidies on civil aircraft are dealt with in both the subsidies agreement and the agreement on civil aircraft. Both sectors have been the subject of lengthy and difficult negotiations and constitute a separate story (see Chapters 21 and 16 respectively). Suffice it to say here that civil aircraft are subject to some different rules; agriculture is subject to a completely different set of rules.

Export Subsidies[12]

Under the 'red' or prohibited category are export subsidies of course, but also any subsidies made contingent upon the use of domestic over imported goods. These subsidies are also subject to new expedited dispute settlement procedures and expedited enforcement procedures. These subsidies are simply banned and there is no need to prove adverse effects, as in actionable domestic subsidies, or injury, as in countervailing cases.

However there is a set of rules to define what is an export subsidy and more importantly what is not covered by the term. Essentially they are defined as subsidies contingent on export performance or on purchasing domestic rather than foreign goods. A long illustrative list of export subsidies is included in Annex I of the agreement.

What is not included in this definition, or exempted from it, are a series of individual export incentives. Chief among these are the rebate of indirect taxes and duty clawbacks, provided they are not excessive (that is, no greater than the original tax or duty). Anyone who has travelled in Europe will be familiar with the procedure whereby one can claim an indirect tax rebate upon export of a product when one is returning home. These rebates are exempted on the principle of destination, to the effect that taxes should only be paid where the product is consumed or at its destination, and not in the country of origin. The principle of origin was however retained for direct taxes, for example those on income and profits, and no rebate was allowed for these when a product was exported.

This compromise, which appeared practical and even fair (indirect taxes were supposedly shifted to consumers but not direct taxes) when the GATT was founded, has since given rise to loud complaints from some countries, for example the United States, where there are more direct than indirect taxes, unlike in Europe, where there is a heavy indirect tax incidence. The United States sought to compensate its own exporters with a tax deferral system called a Domestic International Sales Corporation (DISC). This allowed exporting companies to receive tax deferral for the proportion of direct taxes corresponding to its exports if it constituted itself as a DISC. This was struck down by GATT[13] as it did not allow direct tax rebates, and as the deferral was considered indefinite, in effect it constituted a rebate. In the end an alternative solution was reached whereby direct taxes are rebated when the exports in question are channelled through a foreign subsidiary (a so-called foreign sales corporation – this is a derogation from the usual US taxation system, which taxes on worldwide sales and normally catches these sales even though channelled through an offshore corporation). These are currently being challenged.

Duty clawbacks are allowed when a firm imports raw materials that are subsequently incorporated into goods for export. The rules on incorporation were set out more clearly in the Uruguay Round.

Other examples of what do not constitute export subsidies are those on primary goods, including agricultural goods. These have benefited from the long-standing exemptions for agricultural goods in the GATT as a whole. We will see in Chapter 21 on agriculture that there now exists a 'peace clause' that limits attacks on them, but may only last while export subsidies on agricultural goods are reduced in accordance with an agreed schedule.

Another case is export credits, managed in the context of the OECD, where the rules on what is permissible are somewhat more flexible than the WTO allows in principle. In the OECD the emphasis is not so much on eliminating such subsidies but on controlling their levels and imposing certain conditions on their operation. We have seen that trade or export subsidies are still an important item in government budgets, but in some cases probably fall within the exceptions just mentioned.

Actionable Subsidies[14]

The second, 'amber' category contains so called 'actionable subsidies', that is, subsidies that are not forbidden *per se*, but which may be attacked under certain circumstances. These are so-called domestic subsidies that are not explicitly geared to the export market or export performance, and to be actionable they must at least be specific and not general. A subsidy is general if it is generally available, automatically and as a whole, in accordance with published criteria. It fails this test if it is earmarked for certain industries or enterprises, or if eligibility is not automatic. It could also fail the test, and be considered specific and actionable, if despite its objective aim the money nonetheless repeatedly finds its way to certain enterprises. In the agreement this is termed 'disproportionate use'.

To be actionable a subsidy must also adversely affect the interests of other signatories. Adverse effects are defined as: (1) injury, which is based on an examination of such facts as price undercutting, decline in domestic output, market share and so on – above all the subsidiser has to prove that this deteriorating situation is not being caused by the subsidised imports, for example by showing that it is being caused by a change in consumer taste; (2) nullification or impairment of concessions made in the WTO, that is, if a tariff reduction of 20 per cent is being nullified by a subsidy for domestic producers; or (3) serious prejudice, that is, displacement by competing products at home or in a third market, an increase in world market share of the subsidised product or price undercutting.

Serious prejudice is also deemed to exist and the burden of proof is reversed if the subsidy exceeds 5 per cent of the product value, if it is designed to cover operating losses continuously (that is, not one-time, non-recurrent losses to allow for long-term solutions and to avoid serial losses) or if it is in the form of forgiveness of government debt or a grant to cover debt repayment. If these conditions do not exist the burden of proof is not reversed. (For convenience let us call the former 'dark' and the latter 'light' amber).

The novelty here is that for the dark amber subsidies the burden of proof is on the subsidising country to show that the subsidies in question are not adversely affecting the complaining party. This requires proof that certain subsidies are not injurious, which is much more difficult. It obliges those granting the subsidies to explain how they operate. It is also likely substantially to increase the number of such subsidies that will be struck down. In the case of the light amber subsidies there is a normal burden of proof.

The dispute settlement procedure takes about twice as long as that for export subsidies, but as with export subsidies it is based on a panel finding. Rejection of a panel finding requires consensus, and it can not be blocked, as in the past, by the subsidising party.

The further development of a category of actionable domestic subsidies is a very far-reaching development in GATT, but it is still necessary to establish the existence of a subsidy and its adverse effects. A whole string of new subsidies have been confirmed as actionable. Perhaps some examples will illustrate how extensive the impact could be. The so-called practice of 'targeting' industries by a series of measures such as procurement, cheap credit, R & D finance, a protected home market or other measures to encourage the penetration of markets abroad is probably subject to remedial action now. This type of strategy is hard to prove, but if it is, the selective nature of it, which its name implies, could make it actionable.

Another example is the common practice of giving tax, investment, training and other incentives to attract foreign investment and factories. If these incentives are not open to all in accordance with some objective criteria, they too might be actionable. More often than not, such incentive packages are geared to individual investments and are not repeatable, if only because they are so expensive. There is a fine line to be walked in such a case.

The new rules will probably also affect sectoral and crisis subsidies, which as we have seen are still very much present in government subsidy programmes. They may not create adverse effects however, as firms receiving such subsidies are not usually very competitive.

Non-Actionable Subsidies[15]

The third, 'green' category involves non-actionable subsidies. If a subsidy is non-specific and general, as defined above, it is considered non-actionable. Even if a subsidy is specific it will be considered non-actionable if it is devoted to certain purposes, for example industrial research and precompetitive development activity, assistance to disadvantaged regions, or certain types of assistance for adapting existing facilities to new environmental requirements. These categories of non-actionable subsidy are strictly defined.

While the ruling that such specific subsidies are in the green category is useful in terms of clarifying that these subsidies are not harmful, it is nonetheless left open to a party that feels it has suffered serious adverse effects from such a subsidy to seek a determination or recommendation to that effect. In this sense these subsidies are merely semi-permitted and are still open to remedy, though there is a very strong presumption that they are not harmful.

The burden of proof here is of course on the complainant, and in view of the low *pro rata* impact of such subsidies on individual products, it is very difficult to demonstrate adverse effects.

These 'safe harbour' provisions also reflect the growing trend we have seen to use these types of subsidy. Regional and environmental subsidies have increased very substantially and R & D subsidies are a significant element in the overall picture.

Countervailing Action[16]

The Uruguay Round introduced a new set of rules on the use of countervailing measures. It set out disciplines on the initiation of cases and rules of evidence to ensure greater transparency, improve the possibility of parties presenting their cases and ensure that complaints are well founded. It also set out disciplines on the calculation of a subsidy as the basis for determining injury to a domestic industry. The agreement requires that all relevant economic factors be taken into account when assessing the state of an industry and that a causal link be established between the subsidised imports and the alleged injury. It makes provision for the termination of cases where the subsidy is *de minimis* and establishes a cut-off date for the conclusion of cases (eighteen months) and the duration of countervailing duties (five years), subject to an expiry review. It also contains certain *de minimis* rules, whereby a product cannot be countervailed if its subsidisation is less than 1 per cent.

Developing Countries and Economies in Transition[17]

The least developed countries, and some others no longer classified as least developed but whose per capita annual income has not yet reached $1000, are not bound by the provision forbidding export subsidies. Other developing countries have a derogation for eight years, after which they must phase them out. They must not increase their level and must phase them out earlier if they are inconsistent with their development needs. They can ask for a derogation to be extended.

However they lose their derogations if they attain export competitiveness (3.5 per cent of world trade for two consecutive years) in a particular product. In that case they must phase out the export subsidy on that product within two years.

Subsidies contingent on the use of domestic products should be phased out by developing countries in five years, and by the least developed in eight. Again a longer derogation may be sought.

In the meantime export subsidies, as well as other domestic subsidies granted by developing countries, are treated as if they were in the amber category, but in this case there is no presumption of serious prejudice as regards the so-called 'dark amber' category of subsidies, and debt forgiveness on social subsidies in the case of a privatisation programme is not subject to dispute settlement if properly notified.

In the case of economies in transition, both export subsidies and subsidies contingent on the use of domestic products should be phased out in seven years. Debt forgiveness measures are also exempted from the provisions on actionable subsidies (though not stated, this is to assist these economies in their move toward privatisation). However, prohibited subsidies must be notified if they are to be exempted from dispute settlement provisions, and they remain subject to countervailing duties.

12 Safeguards

INTRODUCTION

The GATT agreement has as its main objective the liberalisation of trade, and for that purpose it contains a set of rules and disciplines designed to lower barriers to trade, be these tariffs or non-tariff barriers, and to eliminate them progressively. However the agreement recognises that sudden surges in imports may be very disruptive and create serious injury to a particular industry, or threaten to do so. Consequently Article XIX of GATT allows an importing country to impose border controls of a temporary nature. These controls can be imposed irrespective of whether the imports in question are being dumped, subsidised or are in some other way unfair. The imports might in fact not be being dumped, subsidised or in any sense falling foul of the other provisions of GATT against unfair trade practices. It is simply that a sudden surge of imports, whether legitimate or not, and injury to a domestic industry entitles the importing country to introduce temporary controls.

The safeguard procedure of Article XIX of GATT was taken over by the WTO and reinforced by the agreement on safeguards negotiated during the Uruguay Round. The advantage of the safeguard clause is that it makes it easier for parties to the WTO to undertake its obligations. The safeguard clause acts as a sort of safety valve; it also allows time for an industry to adjust and become more competitive.

There are, however, some limitations on the use of the clause. The surge of imports must cause serious injury to the domestic industry or a threat thereof. Serious injury is defined by the WTO and is set at a level higher than material injury, which is the criterion used for unfairly dumped or subsidised goods. The burden of proving injury against the latter is set somewhat lower given that the imports are unfair to begin with. There was no definition, however, of what was meant by a 'temporary' safeguard measure.

Most importing countries only want to control imports that are subject to a sudden surge, and not those coming from all sources. But the WTO requires that the safeguard measure be applied to all such imports from all sources. This may be unfair on other exporters who have not increased their exports to the market in question and may even be losing market share. They nonetheless have to pay for the surge in exports from another country.

However this application of the most favoured nation clause to safeguard measures is also an obstacle to its use. Affected countries can retaliate by suspending equivalent concessions and raising tariffs on the exports of the country taking the measure. Most importing countries are reluctant to take such generalised measures and face general retaliation. So the principle of applying the measure to all, in fact works in favour of the exporting countries.

This was of course the deliberate intention of the GATT agreement. The idea was to make it difficult, and not easy, for parties to take such measures. The greater the retaliation a country faced, the less likelihood that it would act. Perversely the result was that many countries adopted such measures outside the GATT rules. These so-called 'grey area' measures take a multitude of forms, whether voluntary restraint arrangements (VRAs), orderly marketing arrangements, or other. The idea behind these measures is that the exporting country voluntarily exercises an export restraint, though the reality is that it has been given no alternative. In some cases they are compulsory (compulsory import cartels), though even in the case of a compulsory cartel the fiction of 'agreement' may be maintained. In this way these measures are not considered to be overtly inconsistent with Article XIX. However it is clear that they are in conflict with the spirit of Article XIX, which requires that such measures be taken on an MFN basis for a temporary period. The grey area measures are selective and for the most part have been in place for lengthy periods.

The importance of these voluntary arrangements can not be understated. They covered up to 8 per cent of imports of developed countries' imports. VRAs alone accounted for a substantial part of this in as much as they were the instrument of choice in such major sectors as vehicles and steel. Prior to the Uruguay Round there were 200 such arrangements in existence. Some of these arrangements accounted for a vast amount of trade as they covered many steel imports and imports of Japanese cars.[1]

The smart way to introduce a safeguard measure is to apply a tariff. VRAs have generally taken the form of a quota. This reduces the quantity sold, but the product is sold for more. Another crucial difference is that the exporter pockets the difference, and not the government of the importing country. In the United States

Table 12.1   Incidence and duration of GATT safeguard measures

Duration	Number
Less than one year	34
1–4 years	54
4–8 years	43
8–12 years	9
12–16 years	6
16–20 years	2
20–24 years	1
24–36	2
Total	151

Source: UNCTAD (1994).[2]

the VRA on Japanese cars has been in existence since the Reagan era, and is partly responsible for the massive profits made by Japanese producers. They made more money on the more limited number of cars they sold, and this stimulated them to go upmarket and sell more higher-priced cars (Lexus, Infiniti and so on). The result has been a large, self-inflicted economic wound to the US car industry. The result of these grey area measures can thus be very perverse.

Another difficulty that occurred in the context of Article XIX was that the notion of a 'temporary' measure was not defined. The result was that measures introduced to protect an industry threatened with serious injury tended to perpetuate themselves and be not temporary but permanent fixtures of the trade scene. Table 12.1 shows the duration of the 151 safeguard measures taken in accordance with Article XIX of GATT since 1950.

While relatively few measures last longer than eight years, they are frequently in sensitive sectors such as agriculture and textiles. For other important sectors such as steel and cars the instrument of choice seems to have been VRAs, though these have also been used for agricultural and textile products.

THE WTO

In the course of the Tokyo Round the main effort made by the EU and others was to change the rules of Article XIX and to allow measures to be imposed selectively on those countries that were creating the difficulties. This negotiation proved long and arduous, and in the end did not bear fruit.

In the course of that Round, those in favour of selective application of the clause tried to win around the smaller or less dynamic exporters by pointing out that they would not be hit by selective measures. The credibility of this argument was somewhat undermined, however, when the United States and Canada, which ironically were opposed to selectivity, imposed voluntary restraint arrangements on even the smallest exporters in the context of the Multi-Fibre Arrangement (MFA).

The Uruguay Round made a major step in terms of reintroducing the original GATT discipline. It established a prohibition against the so-called grey area measures.[3] (Some of the grey area measures are not covered however, as they are interindustry agreements, and while governments are required not to encourage these, they are not required by the WTO to stamp them out. Though of course their own anticartel laws may require it, or at least enable them to do so.)

Existing grey area measures are to be eliminated by 1 January 1999.[4] There is one exception: until 1 January 2000 one specific grey area measure may be maintained by each importing member, subject to mutual agreement with the exporting party directly concerned, allowing a slightly longer phase-out period.[5] This exception was essentially designed to cater for the restraint arrangement which was negotiated by the EU with Japan on cars.

The WTO agreement on safeguards requires that Article XIX actions existing when the agreement came into force be eliminated within eight years of their introduction or five years after the agreement is applied.[6] It also contains a clause that requires future safeguard measures to be eliminated after four years, but they can be renewed for another four.[7] This clears up the question of what is meant by a temporary measure: it is clear that 'temporary' means no more than eight years in all (ten for developing countries). After the first year of application, the measure must be progressively liberalised.

A safeguard measure previously applied to a particular product cannot be reapplied to that product until a certain time has elapsed. Moreover safeguard measures may not be taken against a developing country with less than 3 per cent of the market share or to developing countries with less than 9 per cent of the market. How-

ever, in critical circumstances a party may take a provisional safeguard measure based only on a preliminary determination of injury for a period of 200 days.[8] The agreement does not define what
types of measure can be used, which implies that a party is free to
use whatever measure it likes, for example tariffs, quotas or even
subsidies) to compensate for damage done to an industry (this may
constitute another exception to the subsidies agreement).

The agreement also provides for the possibility of some selectivity.[9] According to Article XIX, quota shares should be allocated
on the basis of imports in a previous representative period. However this allocation amongst suppliers can be modified in certain
circumstances and the importer with the largest recent surge in
imports given proportionately less, though in that case the measure cannot last longer than four years and cannot be taken where
there is only a threat of injury. This allows for a degree of selectivity, but only with the use of a four-year quota, which is somewhat restrictive. This measure of selectivity can only take the form
of a quota: tariffs cannot be used as this was felt to be too obvious
a retreat from the principle of MFN.

Another element is that customs unions such as the European
Union may introduce safeguard measures for just one or a number
of its member states if the main damage is being done to them.
This reduces the scope of the measure taken, and the possibility of
retaliation or compensation for it.

The agreement also requires a state to provide compensation. If
it fails to provide full or adequate compensation the affected state
may withdraw concessions on its side. It may not do this, however,
within the first three years of application of the measure.[10] This is
a major innovation.

CONCLUSION

The Uruguay Round managed to tie up a lot of the loose ends
that were not dealt with by the Tokyo Round and introduced much
stricter discipline in the operation of the safeguard clause. It also
provided the necessary flexibility to bring an end to the grey area
measures; without some degree of selectivity and without the sus-
pension of compensation for the initial period of three years it is
hard to see how this could have been brought about.

One should however be aware of one limitation: while the new

WTO agreement covers 80 per cent of world trade it does not cover textiles and agriculture under certain conditions. Forty-seven per cent of Article XIX actions have related to these products (70 of the 151 measures taken since 1950.)[11] In the case of the EU, 50 per cent of its grey area measures, and in the case of the United States, 13 of 24 such measures related to these products in the period 1991–92.[12] The agriculture agreement provides for the elimination of non-tariff measures by turning them into tariffs. It allows safeguards in limited conditions to deal with major exchange rate fluctuations and large import surges (see Chapter 21). Safeguards may also be used if a party fails to apply the rules on reduction of support. Textile restraints are to be phased out gradually by 2004. A more discretionary safeguard clause will be maintained until then, given the sensitivity of this sector (see Chapter 15).

13 Technical Barriers to Trade

The agreement on technical barriers to trade, reached in the Uruguay Round, is a revised and improved version of the agreement established by the Tokyo Round. The WTO agreement on this subject uses the word 'standard' to refer to voluntary standards. Mandatory standards imposed by law are referred to as 'technical regulations'. For simplicity's sake this text will refer to standards throughout as a generic term covering both.

The agreement covers the standards that are applied to industrial and agricultural products in order to ensure a level of quality or safety for the consumer. It does not cover subjects falling within the new agreement on sanitary and phytosanitary measures. It does however cover standards drafted as process or production methods if product related, unlike the earlier agreement, which only covered standards drafted as product characteristics (see Chapter 23 for the environmental implications of this change).

Standards can create major obstacles to trade. A standard that is designed to deal with a locally made product, and incorporates the design of that product in the standard, can effectively exclude imports from other countries where the design is different. In order to comply a foreign producer may have either to change his production line completely or to create a second production line for export to that particular market. In many cases the producer in question will simply decide not to bother exporting to that market.

Mandatory standards clearly oblige producers seeking to sell in a particular market to conform. If they do not they may face sanctions in the form of seizure, fines or even imprisonment. By definition, voluntary standards do not carry the same consequences and in theory at least producers can ignore them. On the other hand, if they do, they may find it very difficult to sell their products to other industrialists or consumers because they may not match commonly used systems, for example light bulbs with the wrong attachment, or because it may be considered that their products are not the best. Moreover insurance companies usually insist that certain voluntary standards are complied with when insurance is being sought.

116

With tariffs and other forms of protection being lowered to the point where they have become fairly negligible, standards have sometimes become the preferred weapon of protection. Add to this the fact that countries often require that a product not only adhere to a standard, but that it be certified as being in conformity with that standard. This means that the product has to be tested by a recognised laboratory. This procedure is also an attractive way of creating obstacles to trade through administrative delays, refusal of access to a laboratory, the difficulty of carrying out the procedures in a foreign country and so on.

STANDARDS AS OBSTACLES

The WTO has tried to deal with these problems in a number of ways.[1] It has insisted on the need for full national and MFN treatment for imported products; in this sense at least importers are assured that the same standards or equivalent treatment will be applied to them as to domestic producers and imports from other countries.

There is also a key provision that a standard should not create an 'unnecessary obstacle to trade'. While the agreement recognises that standards perform an important function in protecting health, safety and the environment, these standards should not go beyond what is necessary to achieve their purposes. This allows foreign importers who feel that the local standards are excessive to argue for a different, more efficient standard, or one that is confined in its scope to the strict purpose for which it was designed.

An example of this, which is referred to in the agreement, is that standards should be drafted in terms of performance rather than design. The key issue in terms of protecting the safety of the consumer with regard to a car, for example, is whether the brakes will work and not how the brakes are designed. Sometimes of course a design will indicate a weakness in the system, but the real test is the efficacy and durability of the product.

A standard may also fail by this criterion if it is not based on a legitimate objective. Legitimate objectives include objectives such as health, safety, public order, the environment.

NOTIFICATION AND COOPERATION

Another method used to try to avoid obstacles to trade is the requirement that governments notify each other of standards in the course of preparation, and, except in emergencies, consult other parties to the agreement about any problems they may have.[2] There is no obligation to agree with a complaining party, but this mechanism at least allows for a better understanding of the trade implications of a new standard, and where there is political will solutions can be found.

INTERNATIONAL STANDARDS

While a national standard may not create unnecessary obstacles to trade, it may still create difficulties for exporters by virtue of being different. The agreement therefore encourages states to adhere to international standards where possible.[3] Insofar as these standards have been developed by international agreement and consensus, they represent a guarantee of some sort that most producers' concerns have been addressed and free trade will be facilitated. Unfortunately international standardisation has not been one of the great successes of the international arena. While international standardising bodies exist like the International Standards Organisation (ISO) in Geneva, they have not made as much progress as had been hoped, and in the ISO, for example, certain sectors have tended to attract the interest of the United States (for example aeronautics, telecoms, electronics, films), while others have attracted the Europeans more (for example electrical equipment, mechanical engineering). The result is that these international standards have tended to be biased either towards a US or a European perspective, depending on the sector. Greater activity and participation by other partners should ensure that this body becomes truly international and a useful adjunct to the WTO agreement.

MUTUAL RECOGNITION

Another idea that was included in the Uruguay Round review of the agreement is that states should seek to accept the standards of other states and act accordingly.[4] This is now one of the main principles of the EU single market. The member states of the EU are considered to have arrived at a sufficiently similar level of development to ensure that standards in country X are likely to be just as secure or safe as in country Y. In order to avoid the very laborious process of trying to harmonise all those diverse standards, mutual recognition has become the rule rather than the exception. Harmonisation of key provisions still has to take place where real differences in approach to safety occur, but the burden of proof is now on those who say that harmonisation is necessary.

The extent to which this principle can be applied to all the members of the WTO, however, is a different matter. The WTO countries have a very varied level of development and very profound differences in their approach to safety, the environment and so on. However the establishment of this principle should ensure that, at least in the case of the more comparable developed economies, a more general acceptance of each others' standards will occur.

CERTIFICATION

In order to demonstrate or ensure compliance with a standard, a product may need certification by a recognised laboratory.[5] This may be mandatory or voluntary, but either way producers may have difficulty selling their products if they cannot obtain the necessary certificate of conformity.

This can give rise to various types of obstacle. The laboratory may for example have been set up by a competing domestic industry and may actively discriminate against outsiders by delaying approval, charging extravagant testing fees and so on. Alternatively it may give advantages to domestic producers, allowing them on-site inspections or even delegating the testing to them, for example self-certification, but refusing such concessions to foreign producers.

The WTO agreement tackles the problem at source by insisting, at a minimum, that foreign producers have access to the conformity assessment procedures. It also requires that this access should be granted on the same conditions as for national producers in a comparable situation. The phrase 'in a comparable situation' must be interpreted in a trade liberal manner. A laboratory may charge higher fees to foreign producers compared with national producers if additional expenses are involved, such as travel, but these fees must not be excessive and must reflect real costs. The laboratory must also produce the certificate of conformity within similar time limits and subject to similar conditions as for domestic producers.

Another element in conformity certification that is extremely important from a convenience point of view is to allow manufacturers to certify their own products. This may happen either through the national laboratory delegating its inspectors to the factory floor (fairly common in the automobile industry) or by allowing manufacturers to certify their products themselves (in such cases the penalty for failure to certify properly ensures that the certification is carried out properly). The importance of on-site inspection is that it saves time and avoids unnecessary administrative delays. The revision of the agreement in the Uruguay Round ensures that if such procedures are available for some manufacturers they should be available for all. This should facilitate a major improvement in relations with Japan, where some foreign car manufacturers have negotiated the right to carry out on-site inspection themselves, as indeed the Japanese manufacturers themselves do. In the past Japan has been an enthusiastic user of certification to impede imports of cars. This should now be available to all car manufacturers, or indeed manufacturers of any product.

The next-best solution to self-certification or on-site inspection is that national laboratories should endeavour to recognise tests carried out by laboratories in other countries. Insofar as on-site inspection is not allowed to foreign or domestic producers, this is an important provision. Countries are encouraged to negotiate agreements whereby they mutually recognise the tests carried out by their respective laboratories. While this will mainly be of advantage for the developed countries, developing countries should also be able to participate. Developing countries may have lower safety or environmental standards for economic reasons, but there is no reason why they cannot set up a well-functioning laboratory to test a product in accordance with the standards applicable in the country to which the product is exported. Several mutual recognition agreements are already in existence.

ACTIVITIES OF LOCAL AUTHORITIES

The other main issue that the WTO agreement has tried to grapple with is the question of who should be bound by the rules of the agreement. Clearly national governments are, as well as the national laboratories under their control. The problem is however that many standards activities are carried out at the local level.

Given the constitutional situation of many federal states, it has been difficult for them to ensure that local or state authorities will comply with the rules of the agreement. The agreement therefore contains a provision requiring them 'to take all reasonable measures' to ensure compliance by local authorities.[6] This has been supplemented by a new provision saying that governments shall 'formulate and implement positive measures and mechanisms' to ensure compliance. Central governments are also required to avoid any actions that will ensure that local authorities do not comply with the rules.

In the Tokyo Round, with great difficulty a provision was negotiated that makes the central government responsible if a state, local or municipal authority fails to comply with the rules. This was considered essential to ensure that a federal authority really does make all the necessary efforts to ensure compliance by local or state authorities. If it does not ensure that compliance, then its partners in the WTO are entitled to withdraw concessions in order to compensate themselves for the nullification or impairment by the local authority of concessions granted to it by the central or federal authority.

This provision at least ensures that subcentral entities in federal systems are brought into the international trade system. With some exceptions, such as where the federal authorities have real powers over the subcentral entities (for example Germany), the subcentral authorities have frequently had a free ride and ignored international trade rules as they saw fit. This situation had become increasingly intolerable. Some subcentral entities are extremely powerful and control economies of global significance – one only has to think of California, which has frequently taken the lead in important standardising issues such as exhaust emissions.

Federal authorities have frequently complained that they do not have the necessary authority over their local entities, but in practice this is not true. It just requires a greater effort to ensure compliance through court cases or other political pressure, for example withholding finance (so-called 'positive' measures). One has to admit however that the politics of this are sometimes difficult, though not always as difficult or unusual as it has sometimes been stated. In the United States, for example, the Department of Justice routinely takes states to court for measures that impede commerce (the interstate commerce clause). It is a small step from enforcing internal trade rules to enforcing international trade rules if they are backed up by internal US legislation.

PRIVATE STANDARDISING BODIES

The Uruguay Round introduced a novelty in the form of guidelines for standard-making bodies.[7] This is called the 'Code of Good Practice for the Preparation, Adoption and Application of Standards'. This is open to all standardising bodies (governmental or not, national or regional).

Non-governmental bodies are defined as any body other than a central or local government body, and clearly covers any private institution or organisation. The sort of body envisaged here is fairly common. One only has to think of the many industrial associations that develop standards for their own industry and frequently establish laboratories to carry out conformity assessment procedures. Many of these bodies are not above devising standards in such a way as to award themselves a fair measure of protection.

These guidelines reproduce the basic obligations of the agreement such as MFN, national treatment, adherence to international standards and so on, and add a few on transparency and consultation.

The provisions of the code apply automatically to all governmental standardising bodies. Moreover governments are expected to take all reasonable measures to ensure that other standardising bodies in their territories comply with the provisions of the code. Governments will be liable under dispute settlement procedures for a failure of bodies under their control to comply with the obligations of the agreement.

The rules in the code on transparency and consultation addressed inter alia the United States' desire to have more say in the important standard-making activities of bodies such as (known by their initials in the French language the Committee on European Standardisation and the Committee on European Electrotechnical Standardisation CEN/CENELEC). These organisations, which are the main standardising bodies for electrical equipment, are involved in a very major overhaul of nearly all EU standards, with a view to harmonising them and creating a true basis for the completion of the single market in Europe. However the United States can now gain access to the documents produced by these bodies at an early stage and be fully informed and make its views known. The code requires publication of a half-yearly report on standards under preparation. European firms also have access to US standardising bodies, though of course these are not conducting the same fundamental reappraisal of standards as the EU. Moreover the US standards tend to be less closely adhered to by the electrical industry; European standards have a more legislative and binding impact on the entire industry.

This innovation is very important in terms of improving international cooperation in the voluntary standards field, and will provide a solid basis and motivation for the development of truly international standards.

These provisions do not however cover individual firms. IBM has been accused in the past of setting its own standards and imposing them on the industry. This arose out of its quasimonopoly position in the computer industry. Rightly or wrongly, this type of problem has been left to the antitrust laws and has not been dealt with by the agreement, but arguably are covered by the code.

INTERNATIONAL AND REGIONAL STANDARDISING BODIES

In the case of international and regional standardising bodies, all parties to the agreement are expected to take reasonable measures to ensure that these organisations comply with the agreement.[8] Clearly an individual government cannot be held responsible if it is outvoted in one of these bodies, but it is expected to block consensus if that is the rule of procedure. There is also provision that individual governments do not have to observe the decisions of such international or regional bodies if they do not conform with the rules of the agreement.

14 Government Procurement

Government procurement was not covered by the original GATT agreement. Indeed Article III, which contained the national treatment principle, explicitly stated that procurement was an exception to that principle. In other words a government could discriminate in favour of domestic suppliers against foreign suppliers.

This type of discrimination has been common. One only has to think of the Buy America provisions in federal and state legislation in the United States. Under EU law there is also a degree of discrimination against non-EU suppliers. However in the EU it is sufficient if a product is in free circulation, that is, if it has been imported into the EU, for it to qualify for non-discriminatory treatment.

As well as being deeply embedded in legislation, the use of procurement as a form of industrial policy is even more profound. Nearly all governments use their public money to direct and develop industry. This phenomenon is most obvious in defence and research. Governments are strongly committed to promoting their defence establishments (the so-called military – industrial complex) and nowadays there is even greater pressure to help advance industry's technological base through expenditure on research and development. Add to this the need most governments feel to spend government money to create employment. Domestic employment is not fostered by spending money outside the country on imported goods, however cheap they may be. The instinct to reserve government procurement for domestic purchases, though diminishing in this age of budgetary austerity, is still very deep rooted and strong.

THE TOKYO ROUND

It was decided to attempt to tackle this difficult issue in the Tokyo Round. The result was the first agreement on government procurement. The main purpose of the agreement was to bring procurement under GATT, including Article III thereof (national treatment).

The economic purpose was to render procurement more efficient and ensure that governments received value for money. In effect governments were being asked to act in accordance with their interests as consumers and as the guardians of financial austerity, rather than as makers of industrial policy and creators of employment.

The government procurement agreement that was established under the Tokyo Round was designed to ensure full transparency and fairness of procurement procedures. In this sense it was a very complete and exhaustive agreement, though in fact some refinement and improvement was undertaken during the Uruguay Round in the light of experience. The purpose of these provisions was to ensure that foreign bidders would be aware of the opportunity to bid, would have sufficient time in which to bid, would have fair access to the bidding procedures and would not be discriminated against when they did submit a bid.

The coverage of the agreement was quite substantial. However, while it covered all central government entities and most of their procurement activities, it did not cover the procurement of services (unless they were ancillary to the procurement of goods), construction and some of the sectors that constitute the largest part of government procurement, items such as electrical generating equipment, mass transit equipment and telecommunications. Not did it cover the purchase of military equipment, although some civilian procurement by defence departments was covered, for example desks, pencils and computers to administer the payroll.

It also failed to cover, in federal systems, subfederal units such as states and *Länder*, and in unitary systems local authorities and cities. Nor did it cover private entities that followed government procurement guidelines and rules, for example the Post Office in the United States. There were various reasons for this, but essentially the problem was one of timing and substance. Some of these exempted entities constituted the core of government industrial policy and to permit foreign competition in these sectors was more than governments were prepared to allow at the time of the negotiation of the Tokyo Round.

The scope of the agreement was also limited by the number of signatories (only 23), mainly developed countries.[1] Furthermore the rules of the agreement only applied to contracts above a certain threshold (130,000 special drawing rights or SDRs, an IMF unit of measurement with equivalent values in each currency). Nor did the agreement apply where development aid was involved. Finally the agreement did not do away with the normal elements of a border regime. A particular contract might be subject to the procurement agreement but the product in question might be subject to a tariff of 20 per cent as it would still be subject to the existing border regime.

To understand the importance of procurement in the world economy one should realise that it accounts for approximately 10–15 per cent of world GDP, or approximately $1000–1500 billion. At a rough guess, if all this procurement was opened up to international bidding one might see economies from increased trade and efficiency on the scale of about 10 per cent of those figures, or $100–150 billion. This is clearly a prize worth striving for. The Tokyo and Uruguay Round agreements have only covered a fraction of this overall amount. But the Uruguay Round at least covered a substantial fraction of it.

The coverage of the Tokyo Round agreement was evaluated at approximately SDR 22.3 billion (1989) and SDR 23.8 billion (about $33 billion) (1990). Another factor increasing the amount of procurement was of course inflation, as the thresholds were not adjusted annually. These were the sums for procurement above the threshold and they would have been much higher if procurement below the threshold had been included (an additional SDR 17.3 billion in 1989 and SDR 21.5 billion in 1990). One should not however be too optimistic about lowering the threshold by much. There comes a point in the application of the procurement agreement that makes it less economic and productive than might be expected. The reason for this is that the procedures are relatively lengthy and detailed in order to ensure transparency and that bidders on the other side of the world will have time to submit their bids. In the case of small contracts where the administration is looking for 40000 dollars worth of paper or pencils, it becomes inefficient to require it to follow the lengthier procedures of the agreement. It makes no sense for a department in Washington to procure small batches of pencils from India.

In the modern context where an attempt is being made to reinvent government and make it more flexible and efficient, the procedures of the GATT agreement are not ideal. Most tenders are now submitted electronically and in a much shorter period of time, and future versions of the agreement should take this into account. This may permit some lowering of the threshold.

The amount of procurement that was actually put out to international tender under the agreement was somewhat disappointing in the initial stages of its implementation. But the purpose of the Tokyo Round was first and foremost to establish a sound agreement that was workable and acceptable, though initially with limited scope. It is probably the case that some under reporting took place in the initial stages, and possibly even some actual cheating. However the pace of international bidding and the increase in transparency in recent years means that the agreement has begun to find its sea legs.

Indeed while the results of the Tokyo Round agreement have been mixed, even for those limited sectors that were included, this is not particularly surprising. Even within the European Union, which has rather strict rules on transparency and non-discrimination in procurement, the EU regulations have not always been honoured. National industrial policy has frequently accounted for this, but more fundamentally there is a lack of integration between the industrial sectors in the EU. In other words, in the early days of the EU, despite the existence of the common market, there were few transborder mergers and national industries remained largely national and intact.

The creation of the single market, which was given a new impetus in the period 1982–92, led to a different situation. Transborder mergers increased enormously and there developed a truly European economy and European-wide industries and firms. There was corresponding pressure to open the procurement markets of the individual member states. A situation that had previously been tolerated by an industry because it was essentially a national industry, could no longer be tolerated when that industry was operating in several markets at once. A multinational whose ownership might be French or German but which was operating in six or seven of the member states was not going to tolerate having access to government procurement in France or Germany only. It wanted access to all the markets in which it operated. Despite these developments, cross – penetration of markets has still only reached about 10 per cent. However, this may considerably underestimate the real situation, as most multinational firms bid through local subsidiaries and their bids do not show up as foreign bids.

One might draw a relatively pessimistic conclusion from the experience to date in the sense that the agreements reached in the WTO will have a certain effect, but will not necessarily achieve all their objectives in the absence of greater economic integration between the economies of the various WTO partners. It is not clear, for example, that there is a sufficient degree of integration between EU and US companies and markets to ensure the same pressure will exist with regard to the opening of the procurement markets of both parties. However this situation is probably changing as the two-way flow of investment across the Atlantic is very large and the interpenetration of firms and markets is increasingly important.

The WTO was not built in a day, and with time and practice and with increasing familiarity with foreign bidding and foreign bids, the chances are that at least the procurement markets of the main trading partners in the WTO will become more open and more reliably so.

THE URUGUAY ROUND

The new agreement on government procurement, negotiated during the Uruguay Round, contains some procedural improvements. Chief among these is the improved procedure for allowing a firm that has lost a tender bid to appeal through an accelerated judicial or administrative procedure. Administrative appeals existed under previous arrangements, but there was no obligation to have them. This will be an important weapon in ensuring transparency and respect for the rules.

As for the coverage of the new agreement, it will involve procurement of up to $350 billion a year. This is because heavy procurement sectors such as transport, electricity distribution are now at least partly included. The efficiency gains from this wider agreement should be correspondingly greater, in the order of $35 billion.

The other main development has been to include the subfederal or state and city level procurement where a lot of purchases of heavy equipment take place. Also included are public utilities involved in urban transport, ports, airports and water and electricity distribution. It was not felt possible to cover private utilities, which despite being private often apply discriminatory procurement rules. This is an unfortunate omission.

The results of the procurement negotiation are contained in detailed schedules to the procurement agreement which shows a substantial increase in the number of subfederal and local entities included. The negotiation between the EU and the United States was very difficult and protracted: the United States claimed it had submitted more procurement than the EU under the earlier agreement and that the agreement was imbalanced.

This may have been because the formal coverage of the agreement had a greater incidence in terms of procurement in the United States than in the EU or Japan, for example the size of US contracts may have put them above the threshold more frequently. But it may also be the case that contracts were published less frequently as open to international bidding than they should have been. Another distinct possibility is that there was substantial underreporting. Most major US firms have branches throughout Europe, and these establishments would normally be classified as European firms. The same would not necessarily apply for European firms in the United States. Likewise the definition of who is eligible to bid in the EU is more flexible and anyone with a formal establishment provided it meets the financial and other conditions is eligible to do so. Many firms also bid through European middlemen.

Whatever the reason, the United States claimed it was opening for international bidding two or three times more of its contracts in value than some of its partners, for instance the EU and Japan. The result was that in the Uruguay Round the United States was a somewhat reluctant partner, which was reflected in its rather limited offer at the subfederal and utilities level and its insistence on numerical balance.

In the Tokyo Round agreement, at least among the developed countries, all the central government entities and their goods procurement were covered (except the military). The exact amount of procurement was not measured, but there was a general anticipation that it would balance out. In the recent agreement the formula solution was not applied and the negotiation took place on a more request/offer and reciprocity basis, with a balance being struck at the level of estimated amounts of procurement, or the number of sectors or entities included.

The results of the agreement were nonetheless very substantial, but it remains to be seen how the agreement works out and whether both sides can find a mutually satisfactory advantage in it. It should be understood that like other WTO agreements, this agreement is subject to regular review and updating. The true balance of the agreement is a matter for continuous evaluation and it will be reviewed and improved in the light of its effectiveness.

The Uruguay Round extended the scope of the agreement in two main ways. It now covers most services (including construction but not telecommunications) as well as products, and it has been extended at the subnational level to states, *Länder* and so on, as

Table 14.1   Public procurement offers

	EU	US	Japan	Canada	Norway	Switzerland	Hong Kong	Korea	Israel
Central government	✓	✓	✓	✓	✓	✓	✓	✓	✓
Regions	✓	✓[1]	✓	✗	✓	✓	✓	✓	✓
Cities	✓	✓[2]	✓	✗	✓	✓	✓	✓	✓
Water	✓	✗	✓	✗	✓	✓	✓	✓	✓
Electricity	✓	✓[3]	✗	✗	✓	✓	✗[5]	✓	✓
Ports	✓	✓[4]	✓	✗	✓	✓	✓	✓	✓
Airports	✓	✗	✓	✗	✓	✓	✓	✗	✓
Urban transport	✓	✗	✗	✗	✓	✓	✓	✗	✗

Notes:
✓ = offer, ✗ = no offer. All sectoral offers are on a bilateral basis.
1. 37 out of 50 states.
2. Only 7 cities.
3. Only at a federal level.
4. Limited coverage.
5. Not subject to the agreement, but as privately owned with open nondiscriminatory bidding which will entitle Hong Kong to reciprocity in this sector.

well as to local authorities, for example large cities, and public utilities. Furthermore its scope has been extended to cover water distribution, ports, airports, electricity and urban transport. The latter may be managed by central, subcentral or government entities or enterprises. The basic outline of the agreement is set out in Table 14.1.

In order to interpret this table one has to leave the United States and Canada to one side for a moment. The other parties have all given reciprocity in broad terms by including central governments and subcentral entities and public utilities. They have included some minor and some not so minor exceptions for particular types of procurement by these entities, for example defence and procurement of agricultural products in furtherance of agricultural support and human feeding programmes. The general rule is that the purchasing entities at all levels remain covered. But, generally speaking, while goods and construction contracts are covered by MFN obligations, services are subject to reciprocity. At the same time MFN exemptions and reciprocity requirements are frequent in the case of subcentral entities and public utilities given the unevenness of the offers.

In the case of the United States, it was only able to make a partial offer on subcentral or public entities. This led, after great negotiating difficulty, to an agreement. The deal struck was that the United States would put in the procurement of goods, services and public works of some 37 states out of 50 (including those with the largest purchases such as California, New York, Illinois, Florida and Texas), plus two more for the EU alone. It also included seven major cities (Boston, Dallas, Indianapolis, Chicago, Detroit, Nashville and San Antonio) for the EU alone. It put in federal and other electricity authorities (Rural Electrification Administration, New York, Power and the Power Marketing Administration), and the ports of New York, New Jersey and Baltimore, and Massachusetts for the EU alone. In return for the US offer, the EU put in procurement of the goods of all its cities, regions and electrical utilities (but not procurement of services or public works, though these had been included in its offers to other parties). This package was deemed to be balanced at a level of about $103 billion on each side. The US offer was accepted by other partners, which also diluted their offers to the United States in a manner that took account of the size of that offer.

In the case of Canada, the coverage is only of central government entities and does not cover provinces, cities or utilities for the moment. Canada has committed itself to tabling an offer but has been unable to do so yet. Therefore reciprocity applies to an even greater extent here and Canadian suppliers do not have access to the contracts of other parties at those levels.

This is merely a basic outline of what the agreement contains and no substitute for a careful examination of each party's schedule, which contain sets of notes and explanations that modify the scope and coverage, sometimes quite substantially. Moreover some concessions have been made where strict reciprocity doesn't exist on the other side, for example the EU has given the United States access to its electrical utilities, despite only receiving access from the United States in regard to federal utilities. The reciprocity is struck in other elements of the bilateral EU/US agreement, or in the overall appreciation of it.

ASSESSMENT

The value of the new agreement is around $350–400 billion. If this leads to a saving of 10 per cent it will mean an annual saving of $35–40 billion. This is a very substantial sum, and if it works properly the procurement agreement may be one of the agreements contributing most directly and concretely to trade and increased prosperity. The agreement's limitation, however, is that it has only been signed by developed countries and some of the Asian 'dragons'. Even among the developed countries there are some notable exceptions, for example Australia and New Zealand.

There are other important limitations with regard to coverage. Telecommunications has been left out for the moment as this sector was controlled by monopolies in many parties to the agreement at the time of signing, though this situation is rapidly changing under the impetus of the negotiations on telecoms (see Chapter 22.) In the United States only 37 of 50 states have been included and only seven major cities (for the benefit of the EU alone). The United States has also left out all the generally included sectors other than electricity (and that has only been included at the federal level) and ports have only been included with a very limited coverage. Canada has only included central government entities.

We have seen that the United States was unable to put more into the agreement given its inability to reduce many of the Buy America limitations at state and local level. The EU on the other hand has covered procurement by all cities and regional authorities. The evolution of the agreement will have to be closely watched to see if a better balance can be struck in real terms between the various parties.

The other big issue is of course that this agreement was a plurilateral one with conditional MFN, that is, a party to the WTO can only benefit from the agreement if it joins and makes a contribution. Few developing countries did. At the ministerial meeting in Singapore it was agreed to begin discussions on possible instruments to improve transparency and due process in this sector. This was a US proposal but was supported by the EU and others.

It is not fully clear what the United States' intentions are in this field, but at the very least it will lead to discussions about how to develop a multilateral instrument in the WTO. Whether a full instrument with MFN and national treatment obligations can be developed will probably depend on the degree of reciprocity available. Something less could emerge as a compromise, which would involve a standstill of existing obligations with improved transparency, appeals procedures and so on to ensure that these obligations are performed.

Part IV

Sectors

15 Textiles

INTRODUCTION

The textile sector in most countries is a major employer. In the United States alone it employs about two million people, in the EU it employs 1.33 million and in Japan it employs 1.44 million. The sector is highly competitive and works on relatively low margins. It is probably more vulnerable to fads and fashions than any other sector. It is also sensitive because employment tends to be concentrated in certain regions.

It is also a sector in which the developed countries do not have a natural competitive advantage as substantial parts of it are highly labour intensive. This means that the developing countries, with their abundant supplies of cheap labour, have an edge. This is not true however for the textile sector as a whole. In the case of yarn and cloth, production is very capital intensive. This gives an advantage to the developed countries, where capital is in greater supply.

In the case of apparel or clothing however, the labour component is still very important (40 per cent of costs compared with 7–12 per cent in other sectors). There has been a good deal of progress in the mechanisation of clothing production in recent years, but it is far from complete and many obstacles still remain.

These differences in the underlying economic and technological situation are reflected in different degrees of success in the market. Developed countries have managed to hold their own in the yarn and cloth end of the market and indeed are still running trade surpluses in these areas. They are however vulnerable at the clothing end of the market, and it is in this area that the developing countries have made the most inroads.

Many up-market firms in developed countries are now increasingly carrying out their manufacturing in Asia and elsewhere, and there is a corresponding loss of employment in the developed world. This is also a trend one can see among such recently developing economies as Hong Kong and South Korea, which have had to move their production to low labour cost areas, for example Hong Kong's move into southern China. These countries have also managed to maintain their competitive position by a more intensive marketing effort and through their links with international textile companies and designers. This provides additional competition for developed economies in the more sophisticated product.

THE HISTORY OF TRADE ARRANGEMENTS

The textile sector has been characterised by a high degree of protectionism, starting in the early 1960s with the short-term arrangement and long-term arrangement on cotton products, agreements that were originally designed to control Japanese exports to the United States. This relatively modest beginning developed over the years into a series of global arrangements called the multifibre arrangements (MFA), which came to cover all types of fibre and apparel.[1] Four successive MFAs were negotiated in the context of GATT and as an exception to it. These arrangements allowed the developed countries to restrain imports either through the negotiation of bilateral quotas or through the application of flexible safeguard measures.

Many developed countries negotiated a series of bilateral export restraint arrangements with the largest exporters, mainly among the developing countries but also with Japan. These bilateral arrangements usually relied on a system of quotas for individual products that were creating difficulties in the home markets of the developed countries. The normal tariffs applied in the textile sector also remained at high levels and did not follow the normal GATT trend towards tariff reduction.

Apart from Japan, few arrangements were made between developed countries, which were not really considered to be much of a threat to each other. While Japan was mainly affected in the 1960s and 1970s, that country moved out of textile production and these restraints ceased to be an important factor. Tariffs however remained fairly high between developed countries. These could not be lowered without also lowering them for developing countries in accordance with the MFN principle.

The basic GATT rule was, and is now under the WTO, that under the safeguard clause measures can be taken to protect an industry when a sudden surge in the volume of imports creates serious injury. A safeguard measure must also be applied on an MFN basis (see Chapter 12).

The MFA provisions substantially relaxed this rule and allowed countries, in the absence of bilateral restraint arrangements, to take protective measures on a selective (non-MFN) basis when there is price undercutting (so-called 'market disruption'). This very substantial and rather unusual change allows a country to take measures against imports purely because they are undercutting its own; the antithesis of competition. It does not have to prove injury through, for example, a substantial loss of market share, only a risk of it.

In a sense the whole approach of the MFA is in fundamental contradiction to GATT's objective of promoting competition. It does however neatly illustrate the difficulties associated with competition in certain sensitive sectors where the developing countries have a real edge. It clearly shows the fault line that exists under any open trade system. Competition is good, but pushed beyond a certain point it would cause too much stress and the whole ideological edifice of the WTO would come tumbling down. A few points on the Richter scale are alright, but beyond that even the most imposing buildings will collapse. A lesson no doubt for the overly zealous.

The earlier versions of the MFA agreements were fairly permeable. They did not cover every product or every country. The result was that producers in the exporting countries continued to increase their exports by shifting to other products or by shifting their production to other countries. The earlier agreements also allowed for an expansion of exports under quota in the range of 6 per cent a year. The existence of the quotas also meant that in some cases exporters could charge more for their products. It was also common for them to upgrade the products within the quota, and by selling higher-quality goods to increase the value of the products exported under quota. As the years went by, however, the MFA agreements became tighter and tighter, and more effective in protecting the markets of the developed countries.

Fairly extensive adjustment was also taking place in the developed countries. This adjustment took place largely through increased mechanisation, leading to substantial drops in employment. The impact of increased productivity had a much greater effect on adjustment than any increase in imports, though of course the main impetus for this upgrading of productivity was pressure from outside. Imports do however account for an important part of the adjustment in the apparel sector. The irony is that nowadays, with the exception of the apparel sector, competitiveness in the developed countries is at least comparable to the most serious competitors in the developing countries, that is, the Asian tigers, and we have seen that the developed countries are still running a trade surplus in products other than apparel. In recent years however there has been some erosion of this competitiveness.

In the 1980s the pressure on developed country markets began to increase again. In Europe and Japan the response was to adjust, and in some cases this led to fairly radical changes, with reductions in production of up to 40 per cent in some cases. The United States was particularly hard hit by the high level of the dollar and there were some very substantial increases in imports of apparel, especially in the latter part of the 1980s. The result was increasing pressure for protection, and the United States in particular began to push for a more comprehensive system than the MFA. The MFA was still a fairly permeable arrangement that allowed for protection, but also allowed for some adjustment and development in the market.

The United States began to push for a global quota system, which would have covered imports from all sources and put a global ceiling on those imports. On the other hand it would have allowed for more flexibility in the distribution of shares within the global quota and avoided some of the rigidities of the MFA system. Needless to say it was not welcomed by the other developed countries, which would have been subjected to quota for the first time. It also displeased such countries as the Asian tigers, whose quotas were based on historical trade patterns and who saw their 'fixed' share of the US market being threatened by a global quota, whereby the market would be apportioned on a first-come, first-served basis or even directed at the least competitive.

The developing countries were keen to see some real liberalisation of the sector. For countries such as China, India, Pakistan and Bangladesh, these were essential elements of any final agreement in the Uruguay Round. Their main objective was to dismantle the MFA arrangements and return to the basic GATT rules in the sector.

The European Union, which had probably carried out more adjustment than the United States, and Japan, where textiles had fallen from 25 per cent to 3 per cent of its manufacturing base since the 1950s, were more open to the possibility of reverting to the basic GATT rules for this sector. For some major exporters in the EU, for example Italy, it was also important that the developing countries open their markets to their goods, which tended to be pitched at the higher end of the market.

The Punta del Este Declaration, which launched the Uruguay Round, included a commitment to eliminate the MFA. The discussions during the round focused on how to do this, for example over what period of time, what was to happen to quotas in the meantime and so on.

THE URUGUAY ROUND

The result of the Uruguay Round was the agreement on textiles and clothing (ATC). This provided for a return to the basic WTO rules, but over a fairly extensive transitional period: up to 1 January 2005. Two distinct mechanisms are aimed at achieving this.

The first method is for all textile products, whether under the MFA arrangements or existing outside them, to be progressively 'integrated' into the WTO. This means that all textile goods, and some goods with textile components, are being brought back under normal WTO rules over a period of time. The 'normal' rules, as we have seen, prohibit quotas and are stricter on the use of safeguards. The products are being integrated in a series of stages, and not less than 16 per cent had to be integrated by 1 January 1995. Another 17 per cent will be integrated by 1 January 1998, and a further 18 per cent by 1 January 2002. All remaining products (49 per cent) must be integrated by 1 January 2005. The calculation of percentages is based on the volume of imports in 1990.

The second method concerns the growth rates applied to quotas. Under MFA restrictions growth rates were commonly applied to the quotas. At each of the first three stages of the phaseout the growth rates of the remaining quotas will increase by 16 per cent, 25 per cent and 27 per cent, respectively, above their existing levels. This increase relates to the growth rates and not the quotas *per se*. By the fourth stage, of course, quotas will have disappeared. One estimate puts the average growth rates over the life of the agreement at 102 per cent for Canada, 64 per cent for the EU and 89 per cent for the United States.[2]

This will have a different impact on different countries, as their quotas have different growth rates built into them. Needless to say the growth rates of the quotas imposed on the most aggressive exporters are lower than for others. Those with 6–7 per cent growth rates are likely to see their quotas at least doubled, and the quotas of those with a 3 per cent growth rate will increase by about 40 per cent. Brazil and Jamaica are likely to do well as they have higher quota growth rates. Asian suppliers such as India and South Korea will do less well.

Some exporting countries have more categories of exports that are subject to restraint than others. In the case of the United States, India has 13 categories, Bangladesh 14, China 74 and Taiwan 78, while Hong Kong and South Korea are in the middle with 57 and 49 categories respectively. The EU by comparison has 20 restrained categories for China, and 22 for Taiwan, 28 for South Korea and 18 for Hong Kong. In the case of Bangladesh there are no restraints. But the US and EU categories are not exactly comparable. EU restrictions tend to focus on a limited number of products, whereas US restrictions focus more on overall textile exports from certain countries. The EU has also made important concessions in its bilateral and preferential agreements. It should be recalled, however, that in some cases countries benefit from the existence and retention of quotas: if they did not have these guaranteed market shares their lack of competitiveness would ensure that they would be losers.

EU imports of textile goods that are covered by quotas only involve about 30 per cent of its total textiles imports, or 43 per cent if China is included. However, if one makes the calculation on the basis of only those quotas that are fully utilised (over 80 per cent), these percentages fall to 13 per cent and 16.5 per cent respectively. In the case of the United States, this figure is closer to 70 per cent of imports.[3]

These arrangements also tend to reflect actual trade. In the United States in 1983 for example, trade was still dominated by Hong Kong, Taiwan and South Korea (59 per cent of imports). By the 1990s the share of these countries had fallen (for example Hong Kong from 23 per cent to 12 per cent) and China was on the way up (from 8 per cent to 18 per cent), and had become the dominant supplier.[4] The trend away from exporters such as Hong Kong, Taiwan and South Korea is because their costs have increased, and lower-cost suppliers in other developing countries have gained importance. China has acquired a considerable competitive edge and will, together with countries such as India, probably dominate in the future thanks to the economies of scale that have been achieved in the home market. China is however not yet a member of the WTO, and importers will retain considerable discretion as to how they handle imports from that country.

Table 15.1 Tariffs before and after the Uruguay Round, selected countries (percentages)

	Pre-UR tariff	Post-UR tariff	Reduction	Pre-UR bound	Post-UR bound
United States	19.6	17.5	10.9	98.9	98.9
EC	9.9	8.3	16.5	100.0	100.0
Japan	10.4	6.8	34.3	100.0	100.0
Republic of Korea	28.1	19.9	29.0	1.4	87.1
Brazil	78.5	36.7	53.2	0.3	100.0

Source: UNCTAD (1994).[5]

Tariffs that are not affected by the integration process have also been reduced, and Table 15.1 provides an indication of what has been achieved.

An MFA-type safeguard clause will remain in existence for non-integrated products for the transitional period, and some new elements in its operation allow for even more discretion than in the past (for example cumulation of imports from various sources). However the new rules also require measures to be eliminated within three years. While this MFA-type safeguard provision will not undermine liberalisation of integrated products, it could have a restrictive effect on non-integrated products despite the built-in mechanism allowing for growth of those quotas. The more flexible rules on the new safeguard mechanism were in a sense the *quid pro quo* for more free trade. The EU has not used MFA safeguards much, but others, for example the United States, are frequent users.

Safeguard measures can be taken against products that have been integrated. But in this case the level of imports must not be reduced below the level of the last three years and be progressively liberalised after one year. This is to prevent an unravelling of the progress achieved by the progressive integration of products under the WTO rules.

EVALUATION

The choice of products is important of course, and is left entirely up to the importing country. The temptation for importers, and this is only logical, is to 'reintegrate' under the WTO rules only the least protected products in the initial stages, leaving the most 'sensitive' or difficult ones to the last. This has been the approach of the United States, which has included in the initial phases only products that are subject to the least protection (zero or limited tariffs), leaving the most difficult ones (subject to quota) till the end. The EU has been more generous and has included some 18 sensitive quota-covered product categories out of 24 in its implementation of phase II, going considerably beyond its strict legal obligations.[6]

The method chosen by the United States has of course led to an outcry among developing countries, who feel cheated and are concerned that when the final phase-out arrives the United States will not be in the political position to implement the programme because it will have left too many sensitive products to the end.

Another major weakness lies on the tariff side. Tariffs of the developed countries are still high. The average tariff is still at 12.9 per cent compared with 3.9 per cent for all other industrial products, with even higher tariffs on apparel (for example an 18 per cent average in the United States, with some tariffs even above 40 per cent). There is also considerable tariff escalation. Smaller cuts have been made on exports of interest to developing countries, and tariffs in general have remained higher for imports from developing countries than from all sources.

It is not clear however whether these higher tariffs will keep out imports from the cheaper suppliers once quotas are lifted. The experience of Australia is instructive in this regard. It still has high tariffs (as high as 45 per cent on clothing, and 30 per cent on textiles) and yet import penetration has grown considerably (well above the OECD average) since the dismantling of quotas a few years ago.

Neither have the developing countries liberalised their markets sufficiently, and some exporters in developed countries could therefore consider the round to have been a failure from their point of view, though this element will remain under review in the years to come. There has however been some improvement. While starting from a lower base, imports by developing countries have been increasing more rapidly; imports by OECD countries from the developing countries have increased, but not as much (30 per cent compared with 41 per cent in the period 1989–92). Developing countries now account for 30 per cent of world imports in the textile sector. OECD exports to developing countries, however, correspond to only 50 per cent of intra-developing country trade, which is increasing much faster.[7]

The growth of imports from developing countries during the lifetime of the agreement will of course depend on some of the factors that have been outlined above. Some will be subject to more quotas than others, and these quotas will grow at different speeds. But overall there should still be substantial quota growth during the implementation phase, and it is not clear that higher tariffs will have a very negative effect on this growth – although one study suggests that growth of exports from developing countries will be only $3 billion if tariffs remain as they are, compared with $8 billion if they are reduced,[8] the Australian case would suggest otherwise. Another study estimated an increase in developing country exports of around $6.8 billion with China taking the lion's share at 69 per cent[9] (but only when it joins the WTO and ATC).

After 2004 of course there will be no quotas, and by then further tariff reductions may have taken place, though this is somewhat speculative. It should be recalled that the quota reductions that will have been achieved by then have been estimated as equivalent to a tariff reduction of 28.3 per cent on average for apparel and 21 per cent for textiles.[10]

However another factor may slow down the growth possibilities for some exporters. Markets are increasingly demand driven, and require new products much more frequently and rapidly. This will tend to favour producers who are geographically closer, for example Mexico for the United States, Turkey and Central Europe for the EU. This could take its toll on suppliers in Asia and elsewhere.

The US clothing trade deficit was $30.6 billion in 1993 ($14.9 billion in 1989), and that of the EU had reached $15.9 billion in 1994 ($4.3 billion in 1986). Import penetration in the EU could rise from 25 per cent in 1992 to 55–64 per cent by 2004.[11]

The overall trade impact of the ATC has been variously estimated. One study suggests that abolition of the MFA will lead to an increase in US imports of 5–15 per cent for textiles and 15 per cent for clothing.[12] Another study suggests that MFA importers, taken as a whole, will increase their textile imports by 10 per cent and 26 per cent for clothing.[13] Those most likely to benefit, apart from the developing countries, are consumers in the developed economies, and in particular lower-income households.

The agreement will have some serious negative consequences for employment in developed economies unless they adjust, and will create serious difficulties in certain regions. In the case of the EU, one study has projected a decline in clothing employment of up to

520000 over the next 13 years. Clothing production is also forecast to decline by 10–23 per cent up to the year 2008.[14] The WTO has forecast a decline of 23 per cent and the World Bank as much as 60 per cent.[15]

The result of all this is a substantial liberalisation of the textile sector. In future, when the agreement has run its course, the only types of protection remaining will be the traditional ones of tariffs, antidumping, or countervailing duties, or the general safeguard clause, and these can only be used with some discretion. Nor will it be possible to reintroduce an MFA-type arrangement. The agreement of course allows each country to choose which products to phase out in the first and subsequent stages. And one can anticipate that countries will phase out protection on the apparel sector only in the last stage. However ten years is a very short time in the overall scheme of things, and the agreement is a major milestone in the history of trade liberalisation in this sector.

The developing countries should benefit greatly from the agreement. One of the main criticisms of GATT, and of the trade policies of developed countries, is that they have not done enough to liberalize trade where the developing countries are strong or have an advantage. This has been a serious impediment to their development. This agreement should go a long way towards reversing this situation.

16 Civil Aircraft

THE FIRST AGREEMENT OF 1979

The Tokyo Round concluded an agreement on trade in civil aircraft in response to a bilateral initiative by the United States and the EU, egged on by Boeing and Airbus.[1] The objective for both the EU and the United States was to bring about duty free treatment for trade in aircraft, and the United States was keen to tackle some non-tariff issues as well.

Tariffs

The main purpose of the agreement[1] was to create free trade in civil aircraft, and this was substantially achieved for finished aircraft (including helicopters), engines, avionics and flight simulators, which were taxed at zero duty when the agreement was completed.[2] The agreement covered both large and small civil aircraft and parts, but not military aircraft.

What was less satisfactory was that many aircraft and engine parts were left with the existing duty rates. This had an unnecessarily protective effect as many rates were still high. Selling a plane is one thing, but a purchaser may be less keen if the spare parts carry tariffs. This will substantially increase the price of the aircraft over the course of its life. However a lot of these tariffs have since been reduced and a very substantial degree of free trade now exists in this sector. The exact product coverage is set out in the annex to the agreement.

Non-Tariff Measures

The Tokyo Round agreement also sought to tackle some of the 'unfair' trade practices deemed to exist in this sector, with a degree of success.[3] A subsequent bilateral US–EU agreement built on this further and spelt out in detail what is meant by some of these practices (see next section).

145

Undue influence in purchasing practices

The GATT Agreement sought to take government out of the business of influencing airlines to purchase aircraft from a particular source or influencing manufacturers to purchase in a manner that would discriminate against other signatories. In this respect it was aimed at preventing a government from directing the procurement activities of its own airlines and manufacturers, but it also covered governmental measures (positive or negative) aimed at inducing foreign airlines and manufacturers to buy from its firms.

Governments have frequently directed their airlines to purchase particular types of aircraft, though reports of this are sometimes exaggerated, as generally airlines will buy a mix of aircraft that suit different needs. Moreover the increasing trend towards privatisation, which means that airlines are required to stand on their own two feet and make a profit, has forced them to buy along more commercial lines than in the past.

However it is still common for heads of state to seek to promote commercial sales on their visits abroad. The fact that the United States did not make a practice of this at the time of the agreement induced it to ask for this sort of non-commercial or 'political' promotion of exports to be controlled. To judge by recent actions by the US president, for example with regard to sales of aircraft to Saudi Arabia and other contracts, it would seem that the United States has now made a virtue of this type of intervention.

In the cases just referred to, intervention or undue influence is usually difficult to prove. Any provisions to this effect therefore tend to be more symbolic than real. Though recent US declarations and inducements about sales to Saudi Arabia have been so open as to provide an abundance of proof that this provision is being violated, there seems to be no intention on the part of the Europeans to pursue this in the WTO. Both sides may now be of the view that this provision is a dead letter.

The agreement also requires that airlines and manufacturers allow access to business opportunities on competitive non-discriminatory terms. This sort of obligation is easy to operate if a signatory government has control over these firms. But if it does not, and they are private companies, it becomes more difficult to influence them directly.

Finally, the agreement also requires that products be purchased on a competitive price, quality and delivery basis. This reinforces

the other provisions referred to above, and is directed essentially
at manufacturers, but also at governments seeking to influence them.
Contracts that are subject to government influence or are not open
to competitive tender are not always going to be purchased on
competitive terms. This provision has also been interpreted to mean
that governments will not intervene to secure favourable treatment
for certain firms, for example through offsets or subcontracting, or
other considerations of an industrial compensation nature that would
involve a firm in purchases that were not necessarily competitive.
Offset requirements are frequent and visible, and therefore this
provision in principle has some real teeth.

The irony is that despite difficult negotiations on these issues,
complaints have never been raised under the dispute settlement
provisions of the agreement. The conclusion one has to draw from
this is that the provisions are being obeyed, or that governments,
airlines and manufacturers are comfortable with, for example, offset agreements, and are willing to tolerate aggressive marketing
support by other governments as they do it themselves. Finally,
the provisions may not have been invoked because of the difficulty
of proof.

Subsidies

The main thrust of the non-tariff provisions was however directed
at subsidies, which were perceived by Boeing and McDonnell Douglas
as giving a distinctly unfair advantage to Airbus Industry.

As well as confirming the application of certain provisions of
GATT and the Tokyo Round subsidies agreement to aircraft, the
agreement sought to spell out in some more detail what was meant
by certain provisions of the subsidies agreement in the context of
civil aircraft.[4]

The original Tokyo Round agreement on subsidies required governments to prohibit export subsidies and 'seek to avoid' domestic subsidies with an adverse effect on trade. This language was reaffirmed
in the aircraft agreement, and with regard to domestic subsidies it
was not strong language. Moreover there was a good deal in the
aircraft agreement to indicate that the parties should also take into
account the widespread use of subsidies and the desire of all signatories to participate in the expansion of the world market for civil
aircraft. In a sense this almost condoned the use of such subsidies.

There was also talk of signatories taking account of their

'international economic interests'. This was drawn from the clause the United States has traditionally used to describe the administration's right to use its discretion when pursuing countervail measures (the duties allowed by the WTO to counter the effect of subsidies). This discretion was steadily being whittled away in the countervail field, and this was an attempt to restore it, though without much success as it was not carried into the US implementing legislation.

The main innovation was that pricing should be based on a reasonable expectation of recoupment of all costs. This US suggestion was really directed at Airbus, where the assumption by the US side was that money invested by the partner governments of Airbus was simply being written off and not reflected in the price of the aircraft, giving them a competitive advantage. The United States no doubt hoped that if all costs were included Airbus would become uncompetitive! These costs were defined to include:

- non-recurring programme costs (including R&D);
- identifiable and pro-rated military R&D subsequently applied to the production of civil aircraft;
- average production costs;
- financial costs.

The language used in the Tokyo Round agreement was however fairly loose. It did not say, for example, over what period the recoupment should take place, or what constituted a reasonable expectation.

BILATERAL EU–US AGREEMENT OF 1992

Needless to say, the discussions and arguments did not stop there, and many more years of negotiation led to the signing of the bilateral US–EC agreement of mid 1992 concerning large civil aircraft (the Tokyo Round agreement covered all civil aircraft, large or small). The bilateral agreement does not cover engines, avionics, helicopters, and so on, which are covered by the Tokyo Round agreement.

Production Subsidies

In the area of subsidies the United States got its own way, at least in part. The agreement contains a prohibition on the use of production subsidies other than those previously committed to existing or future programmes.[5] These are the most direct type of aircraft subsidy and the ones most likely to bring down prices substantially or bring costs under control.

Previously, if an aircraft manufacturer made a huge investment in the development of an aircraft but failed to sell enough to recuperate that investment, subsidies could be used as a last resort to bring down the production costs. The prohibition on production subsidies has therefore substantially increased the risks of manufacture, and may have a more direct effect in levelling the playing field than controls on other types of subsidy.

Prior government subsidy commitments, provided they weren't modified, were exempted from the prohibitions contained in the agreement. Of course this exemption only applied to programmes where manufacturing was already under way, but could in theory at least also apply to existing commitments to future programmes. This was very important for Airbus insofar as it exempted all its start-up costs, which were heavy and probably not entirely recuperable. In any case, at that point it was somewhat meaningless to continue to dispute subsidies granted to the earliest generations of Airbus aircraft. What were important to the United States were future generations of aircraft, new projects and new commitments of money under this heading.

The bilateral agreement contains a sort of peace clause covering subsidies granted up to then. Governments undertook not to initiate actions under GATT Articles XVI and VI, but of course they could not prevent firms from seeking countervail action (Article VI) if injury could be proven.

Development Subsidies and Repayment Schedules

The agreement allows direct subsidies for the development of new aircraft, but only up to a certain level and duration.[6] Total development costs are defined as those incurred up to the point of first certification of an aircraft. If there is no reasonable expectation that these costs will be recovered within 17 years of first disbursement, the subsidies should not be given. It also limits subsidies on development costs to 33 per cent of the total programme costs (25 per cent and 8 per cent in separate tranches with different repayment conditions).

The agreement does not prohibit royalty-based subsidies, but provides a schedule for their repayment (over 17 years with repayment tied to the number of deliveries). This method of financing is frequently resorted to; the subsidiser receives a return on its money of a royalty payment on each aircraft sold. If few are sold it doesn't recoup its money, but if many are sold it enjoys very substantial returns, usually well in excess of the original subsidy.

A manufacturer will therefore be held to a set repayment period and schedule in a manner that allows little flexibility and ensures that the subsidies are built into the prices, as costs, and are recovered over a limited period of time.

Indirect Subsidies

The bilateral agreement also provides that parties shall not give indirect subsidies that confer an unfair advantage.[7] An unfair advantage is defined as subsidies, after recoupment, that exceed 3 per cent of annual turnover in the industry or 4 per cent of annual turnover of the firm in question. In other words, indirect subsidies are permitted up to a certain percentage of turnover, even when there is no recoupment.

The agreement does not clearly define what is meant by an indirect subsidy and it allows a good deal of latitude for interpretation. In addition to civilian R&D, it should be taken to include military expenditure that indirectly finds its way into civilian programmes. An example would be a subsidy given for one purpose, for example to build a new military engine, which in the end is incorporated in a new civilian airliner.

It does however specify that indirect benefits derived from government-funded R&D should be included in this definition if it is performed after the agreement came into force. This does not apply if its results are made available to all, but even in these circumstances the benefits are deemed to accrue and the provision applies if the aircraft manufacturer has actually conducted the R&D itself or has had early access to it.

These provisions were important for the Europeans given that the world's largest aeronautical R&D budgets are in the United States under various military and NASA programmes. For example while Boeing has complained bitterly and loudly about subsidies to Airbus, it has frequently been the beneficiary of very substantial funds from NASA for R&D purposes (witness the amount currently being spent by NASA on a new supersonic transport plane). It has also received substantial assistance from R&D on military planes: the Boeing 747 evolved from a prototype of a military cargo plane.

Exceptions

Exceptions are made in the agreement for certain measures:

- Loans, guarantees and so on made by manufacturers to purchasing airlines are not covered. Export credit financing is frequently given by signatory governments, but it is not included in the aircraft agreement; however it is subject to certain disciplines under an OECD understanding.
- Equity infusions are not covered unless they undermine some of the other provisions of the agreement. One has to read this in the light of the general provisions of the subsidies agreement. Governments sometimes become substantial shareholders and the money does not have to be reimbursed. The WTO subsidies agreement at least requires that such shares be treated as an individual would treat them; in other words, if shares continuously fall in value and no dividends are paid, a prudent investor would sell them. In such circumstances there is an inference that such equity holdings constitute actionable subsidies.

The bilateral agreement also provides for a very substantial amount of transparency and exchange of information as an essential underpinning of any assessment of the amount of subsidies being made available. Signatories are not always keen to release information that is going to get them into trouble, but in this case the provisions have been fairly successful.

Summary

It can be seen from the above discussion that a major effort has been made over the years to introduce some discipline in the civil aircraft sector. The agreements have moved from generally seeking to avoid domestic subsidies, to a series of rules prohibiting subsidies (production subsidies not already planned, and development or indirect subsidies beyond a certain amount), or requiring that they be recouped in accordance with a schedule (development subsidies and royalty-based subsidies).

But it is also clear that there are limits to what can be achieved. How can one measure the acceptability of equity holdings? How can one measure the impact of military research? How can one really ensure transparency? These problems are not easy to deal with and will continue to provide escape hatches from the disciplines of the agreement. However there can be no doubt that manufacturers have to think twice before they accept certain benefits, and signatories have to assess the subsidies they provide, or the pressure they exert, more carefully than in the past.

THE URUGUAY ROUND

The subsidies agreement that emerged from the Uruguay Round was substantially strengthened and the details have been set out in Chapter 11. Prohibition on export subsidies had previously existed, but domestic subsidies were made actionable for the first time while others (for example R&D subsidies) were made allowable or 'green-lighted' under certain conditions. The bilateral EU–US agreement did not quite fit this framework. Production subsidies were forbidden (more than 'actionable') but earlier programmes were 'grandfathered' or forgiven.

At the same time, under the subsidies agreement development subsidies of up to 75 per cent of the cost of industrial research or 50 per cent of precompetitive development were allowed or non-actionable. The bilateral agreement allowed subsidies for development research only up to certain lesser limits, as we have seen. Indirect subsidies are covered by the bilateral agreement but probably not by the main subsidies agreement.

The interest of the United States therefore was clearly to accept the new subsidies agreement as it was negotiated as this would penalise the Europeans more on production subsidies and royalty-based loans and there would be no grandfathering. At the same time it would have more leeway on indirect subsidies.

For the opposite reasons this was completely unacceptable to the Europeans, who would see the whole balance of the bilateral agreement evaporate. At the same time they were looking for more discipline on R&D subsidies for engines as well as aircraft, as they saw themselves increasingly disadvantaged by large NASA and military subsidies for R&D.

The outcome was that the subsidies agreement now contains footnotes at certain critical points that preserve some of the concessions of the bilateral agreement, for example royalty-based loans do not automatically become actionable if sales fall below forecasts.[8] Similarly the 5 per cent threshold above which domestic subsidies are deemed to cause serious prejudice, and are therefore actionable, do not apply to subsidies for civil aircraft. Another footnote takes indirect subsidies for aircraft out of the green-lighting arrangement. These failsafe devices were put there pending the development of multilateral rules on these matters in the aircraft sector. But these rules never materialised.

The result of all this is that the bilateral US–EU agreement will continue as it is. The subsidies agreement also applies to the civil aircraft sector, but the footnotes ensure that it is not in conflict with the bilateral agreement. It is also clear that, given the magnitude and difficulty of some of these issues, it will be some time before the two agreements can be merged, if ever.

17 Steel

INTRODUCTION

In the margins of the Uruguay Round there was a serious attempt to bring about a sectoral agreement on steel, known as the multilateral steel agreement, or MSA. Somewhat in the spirit of the aircraft agreement, it was hoped to address the multiplicity of problems associated with this sector in a balanced and comprehensive manner covering both tariff and non-tariff matters. The prize of free trade in a sector like this, which is an important part of most countries' trade balances, was an added inducement. This agreement was not concluded, but the negotiations nonetheless led to some results in the tariff field among most of the developed countries. The second section of this chapter gives an account of the negotiation.

The steel sector had been ravaged by structural adjustment problems since the early 1970s. Severe levels of overinvestment and overproduction had created enormous stress in the industry. Excessive competition and dumping occurred between developed countries, but developing countries were also getting in on the act. It had almost become *de rigueur* for every developing country to have its own steel industry, and not just for internal consumption, but as an important element in their export programme.

The industry was also hit with a series of technological developments. The production base in the United States had largely been developed during the time of the Korean War, and the more modern technologies of electric arc furnaces and continuous casting came about somewhat later. As a result US industry suffered for years from an outdated technological base, which made it very vulnerable to outside competition. Its large integrated steel mills also incorporated all the disadvantages of an outmoded management system.

In Europe the situation was much more varied, with many ultramodern mills and others that could truly be prime exhibits in a museum of nineteenth-century industrialisation. The difficulties were compounded by the fact that many firms were concentrated in certain regions and were nationalised; their governments became politically vulnerable when they shut them down, and some regional economies were devastated when they did.

The one exception was Japan, where the major steel investments occurred at the right time and because it quickly adapted to new technological developments such as continuous casting. But even in Japan the government had to assist in restructuring and merging their largest steel companies through the use of restructuring cartels and financial inducements.

Plants in developing countries tended to be more modern because technology had advanced considerably when they started their development efforts. Given the lower wages paid to workers they were also able to compete very effectively. Moreover steel production is a somewhat undifferentiated commodity where price alone counts. Competition in this sector was therefore of an interindustry rather than intraindustry type, and the pressure this put on steel industries in the developed world was intense. Another important factor was the technological shift away from steel to other materials such as composites, plastics and so on. This led to a big drop in demand and a search by the steel industry for new, more sophisticated products that were both lighter and stronger.

For the last 15 years or so, therefore, the developed countries have used innumerable devices to protect their steel industry while at the same time encouraging its adjustment (at greater or lesser speeds). The favourite technique in the United States was to negotiate voluntary restraint arrangements (backed up by the threat of antidumping actions), and in Europe great use was made of production sharing and restructuring cartels (the Davignon Plan), with floor or threshold prices applied to imports. Similar techniques were used in Japan.

This was a period of great trade tension, and matters only began to ease up in the early 1990s when the years of restructuring finally began to bear fruit. Nowadays the balance between global supply and demand is much improved. Industry in developed countries has become leaner and fitter and has moved into more specialised market niches.

This is not the place to enter into an assessment of the merits and demerits of the various adjustment programmes and whether they made economic sense. The importance of the restructuring effort has often been denigrated, but large-scale restructuring there was. This is borne out by the figures in Table 17.1.

Table 17.1   Manpower in the steel industry (average numbers
employed, thousands)

	1974	1984	1991	1992	1993	1994	1995
EU (12)	894.8	540.1	396.0	369.0	335.4	302.5	286.2
US	609.5	267.4	261.0	253.5	238.8	233.5	239.3
Japan	323.9	264.8	190.9	189.6	193.0	182.7	168.8
Other OECD	354.8	340.6	285.1	262.3	267.3	294.7	251.6
Total OECD	2183.0	1412.9	1133.0	1074.4	1034.5	1013.4	945.9

Source: OECD (1996)[1]

THE URUGUAY ROUND

In the course of the Uruguay Round an attempt was made to move
towards free trade as it was felt that the world's steel industry was
on a sufficiently sound footing to be able to handle it. There are
exceptions of course, but the dominant view in the industry is that
most can now stand on their own feet and will benefit from free
trade. The balance of opinion in industry and among governments
has tilted towards a more positive outlook, and the feeling that they
have more to gain than to lose from a more open trading system.

The draft agreement provided for a move to zero tariff duties by
the year 2005, with ten equal reductions over the 1995–2005 period.
The draft also contained a list of other provisions to deal with
measures that might block market access, such as quotas, voluntary restraint arrangements (VRAs), trigger price mechanisms, cartels
and so on. These measures, which were banned by the draft agreement, constituted the series of measures that had been used over
the years by the main protagonists.

The agreement also encouraged adherence to the GATT procurement agreement. One of the main sticking points was the desire of the EU to see the abolition of content requirements at the
national or local level, which are very common in the United States
(for example, the Buy America preferences). These provisions frequently concern steel products. While the United States is a signatory of the Agreement, the coverage of its procurement by the
agreement is still very incomplete and patchy, especially with regard to state level procurement (see Chapter 14).

The draft also contained provisions relating to subsidies, which
paralleled the provisions of the subsidies agreement but which in

some respects were more stringent than them. It required subsidies not to be granted, but allowed certain exceptions. It was more stringent than the subsidies agreement in that the prohibition covered all subsidies and not just export subsidies. The actionable subsidies set out in the subsidies agreement (that is, specific and not general subsidies) were here prohibited, and not just actionable.

The exceptions, or green-lighted subsidies, were also more extensive. Like the subsidies agreement it allowed subsidies of up to 35 per cent of research costs and 25 per cent of precompetitive development activity, and permitted subsidies for environmental measures of up to 15 per cent of their cost. In addition it allowed assistance for plant closure and redundancy, provided the closure was real. It did not allow for regional assistance. These provisions corresponded to the European Union's rules on these matters, which allowed for closure and redundancy subsidies but not regional subsidies.

To compensate for this rather rigorous regime the agreement provided for the possibility of temporary derogations, either for regimes in existence before the agreement came into force, or after. The committee of signatories would, however, have to agree these derogations. (Failure to conclude an agreement in the steel sector however meant that the normal rules of the WTO would continue to apply. In other words regional subsidies were allowable or greenlighted under certain conditions, but subsidies for closure or redundancy would be actionable.)

Also unresolved was the issue of what to do about existing anti-dumping actions. There were provisions in the draft to ensure that signatories would consult at some length before allowing such actions. A margin of discretion for governments was sought to prevent these actions being taken automatically. There was no agreement that they should be discontinued under a sort of peace clause, though this was an important and indeed fundamental point for the EU.

The main parties to the discussions (the United States and the EU) were unable to resolve their differences during the course of the Uruguay Round. The zero/zero tariff option (zero duties to be implemented for all products by all parties) was however implemented, but only by some participants in the MSA negotiation (EU, US, Japan, Canada, Norway and Switzerland, the developed countries in other words, but minus Australia and New Zealand). While participation in the zero/zero solution is limited, the coverage is very complete and covers all steel products.

It is clear that with limited participation in the tariff field and a strong desire by some to see rules on the non-tariff area as well (for example Australia stayed out of the tariff reduction exercise, citing the failure to reach agreement on non-tariff rules), it is likely that more discussions will take place in order to reach an agreement on this sector at some time in the future.

18 Information Technology

The main achievement of the Singapore ministerial meeting in 1996 was to set out the framework for an agreement on liberalising trade in the information technology (IT) sector. This information technology agreement (ITA) was finalised on 26 March 1997.

The agreement covers most IT products other than consumer electronics – the EU held out on these given that it still has, unlike the United States, a consumer electronics industry. However virtually all other IT products for professional and industrial use are included (computers and parts, carrier media, telecoms equipment, their cable and parts, electronic components, certain photocopiers and specialised scientific instruments). It also covers semiconductor manufacturing and testing equipment. All this amounts to approximately 10 per cent of overall world trade and over 90 per cent of world trade in these products, with a value of about $600 billion.

The negotiations were not without their difficulties as certain participants wanted to include consumer items (Malaysia, Singapore, Hong Kong and Japan). Others wanted to exclude certain industrial items. The United States was reluctant to include certain capacitors and optical fibre cables; in the end the raw materials, for example the optical fibre cables themselves, were left out. Canada wanted to exclude ATM machines; but only magnetic strip cards were excluded. Japan reluctantly included chemical substrates and copper cables. Korea had sought a long list of exceptions, but in last phase of the negotiations accepted most of the list of products.

The agreement provides for the elimination of tariffs over four years (by 2000) in four equal stages. These tariff reductions will be on an MFN basis. This led to some additional discussions. The United States wanted more rapid access on semiconductors in exchange for EU access to the World Semiconductor Council (set up in 1996 by the Vancouver Accords but which originally sprang out of the US–Japan bilateral semiconductor agreement). The EU conceded a more rapid elimination of tariffs on semiconductors (by 1999), and the United States also conceded an acceleration of duty elimination on some products. Other parties may also join the Semiconductor Council in the months ahead.

At the same time some other countries wanted a longer phasing-in period for certain products and a reasonable compromise was struck. Some countries, including Malaysia, Thailand, Indonesia, Costa Rica, South Korea, Taiwan and Israel, were granted a period of grace (up to 2004–5) in which to eliminate tariffs on some products. India was allowed until 2007 for tariffs on a limited number of products. The detailed concessions will be spelled out in individual tariff schedules and filed in the WTO.

The agreement was easier to implement for such partners as Singapore, Hong Kong and Japan because of their low or non-existing tariffs in the sector. It was also relatively easy for the United States and Canada, whose tariffs at the end of the Uruguay Round were low, though some tariffs reached 9 per cent. In the case of the EU, tariffs on some products were still as high as 14 per cent at the end of the round and the concessions were more difficult. To make it easier for the EU, some parallel tariff reductions were reached on spirits and an additional 400 'new' pharmaceutical products (that is, new in the sense that they were not in existence at the time of conclusion of the round, where a zero tariff effort had been made in the pharmaceutical sector).

The signatories are Australia, Canada, Chinese Taipei, Costa Rica, Czech Republic, Estonia, the European Union, Hong Kong, Iceland, India, Indonesia, Israel, Japan, Macau, Malaysia, New Zealand, Norway, Romania, Singapore, South Korea, Slovak Republic, Switzerland, Thailand, Turkey and the United States. Other countries are expected to join in the near future – in particular Poland, Panama and the Phillippines.

The discussions touched on the issue of non-tariff barriers specific to the IT sector, but there was very firm opposition to this in certain quarters, and in particular in Asia. Existing WTO agreements on non-tariff issues will apply in any case, and the agreement goes out of its way to reaffirm the general obligation not to nullify or impair the tariff concessions made even if the impairing measures are not in conflict with WTO rules (a traditional catchall obligation). The fact that the agreement was not able to go further than this was somewhat disappointing, but does not detract from the overall achievement of a free trade agreement in this sector.

Part V

Horizontal Agreements

19 Trade-Related Intellectual Property

INTRODUCTION

Intellectual property rights are those which accrue to writers or the creators of inventions, trademarks, designs, and so on who have applied for these rights. The rights are given in order to ensure that inventors and authors can benefit from the fruits of their research, invention or brand name, and that it will not be used or copied by people who have put no effort and spent no money developing the products or brands. These rights are intended to encourage creativity, investment in research and marketing, and risk taking.

The duration of these rights can sometimes be extensive, ranging from 20–25 years for patents to 50–70 years for copyright and other artistic rights, which are generally held by an individual. In the case of patents, however, a compromise is struck between the monopoly given to an individual for the development of a particular product on the one hand, and the needs of society on the other, that is, the need to have access to a product at the cheapest possible price. This is particularly important for example, in the case of pharmaceuticals. A balance therefore has to be struck between the rights of the patent holder and the rights of the consuming public.

These rights can be protected through legislation and patent offices, trademark offices and so on, which process the applications for such rights and ensure protection from other domestic producers. Patent holders can protect their inventions abroad by registering there also. These rights can be enforced through the courts or by having infringing goods seized by the customs authorities if they are brought in from abroad. However if there is no or much less protection given abroad, the only comprehensive way of ensuring patent protection is through an international agreement, either to create these rights or to bring them up to some sort of international standard.

Intellectual property rights have grown up over the years in parallel to industrial growth. In the early stages of economic development such rights were few and far between, but they became more and more common with the development of the modern industrial

163

economy. The result is that developed economies offer the most extensive protection of patents and intellectual property rights. And of course they have the greatest interest in ensuring that this protection is maintained and even extended.

The most developed economies with the most advanced products file on an annual basis for the greatest number of patents. In the case of trademarks and, for example, the luxury end of the European export effort, well-known brand names are continuously being counterfeited and sold on the streets of New York or major cities in Europe for a fraction of the price of the original. One only has to think of 'Gucci' bags or 'Rolex' watches, which roll off production lines in developing countries for a fraction of the price and with a fraction of the quality. This can only lead to a degradation of the brand name and ultimately destroy it through the use of poor-quality materials or overexposure.

The interests of developed and developing countries with regard to trade-related intellectual property are extremely divergent. Countries that are in the process of developing, are keen to have free and easy access to the results of research and development carried out in more hi-tech countries. Insofar as they do not produce hi-tech products themselves, it may not be in their interest to protect products produced by others. They may need these products in order to grow and develop, but they may not want to pay licence fees or royalties to the owners of the inventions. In the past, even developed countries have shown great reluctance to protect the intellectual property rights of others, and some have only recently signed up to major conventions or international agreements in this area, such as the Berne Union Convention on copyright.

One should not exaggerate the North–South split however. Some developing countries have major film and music industries and highly developed technology sectors, and some of the most acrimonious disputes in the negotiations were between the developed countries.

In the Uruguay Round the developed countries were keen to ensure that the foremost international agreements in the field, such as the Paris Convention for the Protection of Industrial Property (1883) and the Berne Convention for the Protection of Literary and Artistic Works (1886), and their subsequent amendments, would be implemented by all members of the WTO, and that the trade provisions of the WTO should be used to improve enforcement of those conventions. These conventions have been notoriously weak because there are no enforcement mechanisms or sanctions if the obligations are not met.

As well as basing the rules on the existing Paris and Berne conventions, the objective was to improve them in certain respects and to extend them to cover a series of other areas that have either not been covered in the past or represent new areas of intellectual property that were not in existence at the time these conventions were negotiated. With this in mind, the subject matter of the Rome Convention (neighbouring rights) and the Treaty on Intellectual Property in respect of Integrated Circuits (IPIC – protection of layout designs of integrated circuits) were also covered by the negotiations.

Bringing these agreements into the fold of the WTO will ensure a greater number of adherents to the obligations of the conventions and enforcement will become much stronger. Members of the WTO may withdraw trade concessions to punish other members that are not living up to their obligations with regard to intellectual property. This is a very effective means of ensuring that these obligations will be met.

In the initial stages of the Uruguay Round the developing countries were against the inclusion of services and intellectual property for development reasons. They were also reluctant to have any agreements in this area incorporated in the WTO precisely because of the threat of trade sanctions. In the end, however, both sectors were included under the WTO umbrella. This constituted a major concession on the part of the developing countries.

GENERAL PROVISIONS AND BASIC PRINCIPLES OF THE TRADE-RELATED INTELLECTUAL PROPERTY AGREEMENT RESULTING FROM THE URUGUAY ROUND[1]

The principle of MFN is applied here, if a WTO member has given certain rights to another, these must be extended to all other WTO members. This is a novelty in the field of intellectual property.

Another important element in ensuring that such protection will be available is the reinforcement of the principle of national treatment. It has been a fairly widespread practice to refuse patent protection or extend fewer enforcement rights to some outside firms in order to protect and promote domestic industry. This has been particularly common in pharmaceuticals with long delays in the processing of foreign patent applications, extravagant testing requirements and so on. The introduction of the national treatment principle means that foreign companies applying for various rights of protection, whether old or new, will now be on the same footing as domestic firms and, for example, should have their applications treated without discrimination as to procedures, content and so on.

The agreement also contains a section (Article 7) with a set of objectives expressed in rather grand terms. It says that the protection of intellectual property should contribute to the promotion of technological innovation and to the transfer of technology to the mutual advantage of producers and users, in a manner conducive to social and economic welfare and to a balance of rights and obligations. This is only an expression of an objective and it must of course be pursued within the obligations of the agreement.[2]

The agreement also contains the principle (Article 8) that when adopting laws the parties may take measures that are necessary not only to protect health and nutrition, but also to promote the public interest in sectors vital to their development. This section also allows members to take measures to prevent abuse, and this is defined as measures that unreasonably restrain trade or adversely affect the transfer of technology.

One fear was that these provisions would constitute a major let-out for the developing countries. However the provisions are not general let-out clauses as they have to be exercised in conformity with the main provisions of the agreement. They do however provide a means of interpreting the substantive provisions of the agreement that contain a certain margin of discretion. The public interest criterion is contained in the compulsory license provisions for patents, which is a wider definition than that used in the past by some developed countries (for example the United States). Article 8 of the agreement contains a description of this criterion.

This compromise is basically what it took to get an agreement, and as such has to be accepted. These provisions strike a balance between the interests of the developed and the developing states.

COVERAGE

In the initial stages of the Uruguay Round the developing countries were only prepared to deal with issues such as counterfeit, and then only the trade aspects of them, and indeed the EU was not much more ambitious in the early stages of the negotiations. Under pressure from the United States however, the negotiations took on the much more comprehensive task of creating substantive international standards, which effectively harmonised a wide range of different practices or created rights where none existed before. Six types of intellectual property protection are now covered and protected under the WTO.

Patents

The trade-related intellectual property agreement (commonly known as TRIPS) should be seen in the context of the international agreements on patent protection that lie behind it. These are the Paris Convention, the Patent Cooperation Treaty and, in the European context, the European Patent Convention.[3] None of these agreements provide for a universal or international patent, they only facilitate the acquisition of patents in other countries (unlike the Berne Convention on copyright – see below).

The Paris Convention (which not only covers patents but other things as well, for example trademarks and indications of origin) provides applicants from another signatory with the same protection and legal remedies as nationals (national treatment). A patent application in signatory X will also give priority in signatory Y for up to 12 months (priority is then lost if the patent is not filed in signatory Y). Moreover if applicants from signatory X obtain patents in signatory Y they are protected from forfeiture or compulsory licensing (for example for non-use) of three to five years (three or four for compulsory licensing and two more for forfeiture).

Another international agreement, the Patent Cooperation Treaty, provides the additional advantage that a filing in signatory X is automatically passed on to the other signatories. This saves multiple filings, though of course it doesn't ensure that a national patent will be granted in each case. The single filing can extend to a search of the prior art or signing a patent already in existence and a preliminary examination of the three main criteria for a patent to be granted: novelty, inventiveness and industrial applicability. Armed with these, the applicant can then proceed to the final application.

In the European context, the European Patent Convention (applicable in the 15 EU member states plus Switzerland, Monaco and Liechtenstein) takes this a step further, in that one filing in the European Patent Office or in a national patent office will ensure that all the necessary procedures will be completed in order to grant patents in those signatories of the convention designated in the original filing.

The Community Patent Convention, which is not yet in force, will allow for a single filing for a single European-wide patent, with all the cost and time savings this implies. Ratification of this convention has been fraught with problems, due mainly to issues of judicial sovereignty.

The TRIPS agreement uses the Paris Convention (Articles 1–12 and 19) as its bedrock. This means that its main focus is on applicants from one WTO country member having the same rights as nationals in another member country and on harmonising and clarifying those rights. It doesn't include the more ambitious additional steps of the other agreements just mentioned, nor improved filing procedures, nor of course any attempt to create a single form of protection. The other agreements will therefore continue to have significance and will only become less so in regard to the substantive rights and enforcement procedures.

Coverage of the TRIPS agreement[4]

The agreement extends patent protection to all inventions in all fields of technology, with the few exceptions mentioned below. At the start of the negotiation in 1986 some 50 countries provided incomplete or no patent protection for pharmaceuticals, for example. Since the agreement these important lacunae have been repaired.

Parties to the agreement may not discriminate as to the place of invention. Patent holders may import their products and therefore patents probably no longer require that they be worked, that is, manufactured locally, in order to be maintained. There is a common term of protection of 20 years accorded, from the date of filing of a patent. In the past there were many variations on the length of protection, and in the United States the rule was 17 years from the date of granting the patent rather than its filing. Protection depends on uniform conditions of eligibility, such as the requirement that the invention be new (no prior art or existing patent) involve an inventive step (not be obvious) and be capable of industrial application.

The agreement requires computer programs be given copyright protection, but there is nothing that excludes their protection through patents. As patent protection is not a requirement, patent protection may only be given by countries that have traditionally done so, for example the United States and Japan.

There are some exceptions in the agreement for patenting biotechnology products. The agreement allows parties to exclude from patentability naturally occurring breeding methods, while requiring the patentability of non-biological and microbiological processes such as biotechnological cell manipulation, gene transfers and so on. This follows the practice in many countries of not allowing the patenting of plants and animals available in nature or animals that are selectively but 'naturally' bred. Plant varieties developed through selective breeding are patentable however, either under the patent laws or specific laws on the protection of plant varieties. Under the agreement patenting of natural plant varieties is optional, but if a patent is not granted some other protection must be given.

Inventions may also be refused a patent if their exploitation would offend 'ordre public' or morality, or if they might endanger human, animal or plant life, or health, or the environment. However it is no longer possible to exclude patentability on the grounds that this would hinder economic development. As we have seen above, the agreement permits WTO members to promote the public interest in sectors of vital importance to their socioeconomic and technological development. But this does not permit measures to be taken that are contrary to the provisions of the agreement, and hence does not constitute an exception to it.

The agreement also allows parties to take appropriate measures to prevent abuses by rights holders. This is only natural and allows parties to continue to patrol anticompetitive practices on the part of rights holders, which is an integral feature of most competition policies and legal systems. It mentions some examples of abuse, such as grantback conditions, coercive package licensing and so on, but short of internationally agreed rules on competition it wasn't possible to define what was and what was not allowable under this heading.

The developing countries can attain objectives such as technology transfer through compulsory licensing. With this type of licensing a patent holder may be obliged to license the product to, for example, a series of domestic producers in a developing country.[5] In the past there were two basic rationales for this, one to promote public interest and the other to avoid abuse of the patent. An example of enforcement of the public interest criterion is a government compelling a patent holder to license a local producer in order to ensure reduced costs or build up the local industry. Examples of abuse are holders not exploiting their patents but allowing no-one else to take advantage of them, or charging excessive prices.

The doctrine of abuse was sometimes invoked to justify compulsory licensing of a patent that was not being 'worked' or the patented product was not being produced locally, even though it was being imported – but this really had more to do with industrial policy than patent abuse.

The agreement allows for continuation of the practise of compulsory licensing for both 'public interest' and 'abuse' reasons, but hedges it about with conditions to prevent unfair or unreasonable use. In the case of public interest measures, a candidate licensee should seek to obtain a licence on reasonable terms and within a reasonable period unless there is a national emergency or it is intended for public, non-commercial use. If this doesn't lead to results the compulsory licence can be granted, but reasonable compensation must be paid and an appeal must be allowed to an independent authority. In the past the fees paid were frequently low or even non-existent, without possibility of appeal. The licensee may still be subject to competition from the original holder (he or she doesn't receive an exclusive licence) and the licence is supposed to relate to the domestic market, that is, not export. One can also assume from the patent holder's right to import that compulsory licensing cannot be resorted to on the sole ground that the patent is not being 'worked' locally.

In the case of compulsory licences where there is abuse and there has been a judicial or administrative determination to that effect, the authorities can grant licences that do not respect these conditions, for example remuneration could be less than reasonable, and in general the need to correct the abusive practice may be the dominant consideration.

The extension of the compulsory licensing system goes well beyond previous US practice, which only allowed for such licences upon abuse, and the language used goes a long way towards meeting the concerns of developing countries. At the same time the 'public interest' criterion is hedged around with conditions that will at least ensure that it is not grossly abused. Moreover it limits compulsory licensing of semiconductor technology to public, non-commercial use, or to where some anticompetitive practice or abuse is occurring.

The net result is that there is likely to be more negotiation to take account of both holders' rights and the needs of developing countries, with less confiscation, less refusal to deal and genuine efforts to reach the middle ground.

Layout Designs of Integrated Circuits[6]

The agreement incorporates the most important (though not all) substantive rules and provisions of the Washington Treaty on Intellectual Property in respect of Integrated Circuits of 1989 (IPIC). The agreement requires WTO members to make it unlawful to market an integrated circuit, or a product containing one, without the authorisation of the rights holder. If importers or sellers are not aware that use of the circuit is unauthorised they have an opportunity to rectify that by paying a reasonable royalty. The protection is for at least ten years.

Many developed countries did not join IPIC because it contained an extensive compulsory licence clause. This clause has been left out of the TRIPS agreement: compulsory licences can still be used under the general compulsory licence clause for patents, though only for public, non-commercial use and for public or private use in order to correct practices determined by a court to be anti-competitive. It is not clear however if this narrower use of compulsory licences applies only to patented semiconductor technologies or whether it also applies to non-patented chip designs. If it applies to both, this is a broad exception to the compulsory licensing provisions.[7]

Utility Models[8]

Utility models are patents granted for inventions after a short search to establish that they are new and involve an inventive step. As the standards for determining these criteria are less stringent the patent can subsequently be challenged and the duration of protection is usually shorter (six years). It is also called a 'petty patent' for the above reasons.

The TRIPS agreement, unlike the Paris Convention, ignores this type of patent, though there are trends, for example in the EU, to move in that direction, and in particular towards the protection of non-obvious functional designs. One functional design that is protected is the layout of integrated circuits.

Undisclosed Information (Trade Secrets)[9]

The agreement also protects trade secrets in accordance with the rules set out in Article 10 bis of the Paris Convention. These may not be used without the owner's consent as that would be contrary to honest commercial practice. Trade secrets must not be generally known or widely accessible, the secrecy must create commercial value and reasonable steps must have been taken to keep it a secret.

The secrets covered by the TRIPS agreement are commercial ones and they do not extend to breaches of confidentiality that are protected by national intellectual property laws, such as the right of personality, state secrets, professional secrets and so on, unless there is some commercial angle to them.

Some examples of 'dishonest' commercial practices are set out, such as breach of contract or confidence, or inducement to breach. What is not clear from the text is whether the US practice of acquiring of trade secrets by reverse engineering is allowed.[10]

When producers of pharmaceuticals or agricultural chemicals have to disclose their trade secrets to a government authority to get approval for the product to be marketed, that authority must protect the secrets against unfair commercial use.

Trademarks[11]

As for patents, the Paris Convention created similar conditions for trademarks. As well as harmonising some of the conditions for eligibility, it established the principle of national treatment. A trademark holder in signatory X receives the same protection as a national of signatory Y. By registering in signatory X he can also obtain priority in signatory Y for a period of six months.

A similar arrangement to the Patent Cooperation Treaty also exists for trademarks under the Madrid Agreement. A single national registration allows for a simplified application process at the WIPO in Geneva, which then gives cover in all the signatories, subject to objection within a period of 18 months. The period of protection is 10 years and is renewable. The main weakness of the Madrid Agreement (and its Protocol) is the limited numbers of signatories (27) and the absence of major countries such as the United States and Japan.

In the EU the law has advanced considerably and applicants can obtain trademarks that are valid throughout the EU by means of a single application either in their national patent office or in the European Trademark Office. This is a major step forward and one that has not yet been taken in the patent field, as we have seen.

The TRIPS Agreement[12]

The TRIPS agreement incorporates the provisions of the Paris Convention and clarifies them somewhat. For example it sets out a clearer and more flexible definition of what is protectable and what hurdles have or do not have to be cleared in order to register a trademark.

Any sign or combination of signs that is capable of distinguishing the goods or services of one undertaking from another is eligible for registration. Where they cannot be distinguished, then registration may be granted when distinctiveness is acquired through use. A WTO member may require that signs be visually perceptible. Neither lack of use nor the nature of goods and services should be an obstacle to eligibility.

It protects against the same or similar signs resulting in confusion, and it gives similar protection to service marks as for goods. The length of protection is no less than seven years and may be renewed indefinitely.

Some limited exceptions may be made to the rights conferred, and the agreement allows for a trademark to become redundant through non-use for three years, provided this was not beyond the holder's control.

While the agreement allows for the regulation of licences, for example for antitrust reasons, it forbids compulsory licensing. It also disallows restrictions on assignment such that a trademark can not be sold without the underlying business. Nor can parties require owners of trade marks to couple their trademarks with those of local firms.

Geographical Indications[13]

The agreement ensures a high level of protection for geographical indications, including appellations of origin, which are of particular importance in the European context as a great number of such appellations exist to protect quality and the use of certain names. One only has to think of the long list of wines in France (for example champagne) and certain cheeses in Italy that base their reputation on strict adherence to standards and production in a particular area. Geographical area is extremely important in determining whether a wine will be of a certain quality and have certain properties: grapes grown in Australia do not share the same properties and qualities as grapes grown in certain parts of Burgundy, because of the nature of the soil, the climate and so on.

The agreement confers quite strong protection against misleading and other unfair uses of appellations of origin. It confers even stronger protection for wines and spirits. With these products the holder of the right doesn't have to show that there is a likelihood of confusion or that there is unfair competition; the use alone of an identical or similar indication of origin will suffice to create an infringement even if there is also an indication of the real origin, or words such as 'kind', 'style' are included. A bottle of wine from Australia bearing the words 'Australian Champagne' or 'Champagne style' would now be caught by these provisions. However existing products with such indications, indications registered in good faith and those which have acquired generic meaning in another country are exempted. Further negotiations have been scheduled to try to deal with these issues, and to dismantle such preexisting marks.

Industrial Designs[14]

The agreement builds on Article 5 quinquies of the Paris Convention. While it requires industrial designs to be afforded protection, it leaves WTO members free to give this through industrial property, design or copyright law. In the case of textile designs it should be a design or copyright law. Protection is for ten years and is against copies, or near copies being made for commercial purposes. In the case of textiles the administration of protection should not unreasonably impair the attainment of protection, that is, it should not be too complicated or difficult to acquired protection.

To be protected designs must be new and original; this stipulation probably gives more protection than the criterion for patents, which requires that an application be new and non-obvious. However designs will not be considered sufficiently original if they do not significantly differ from known designs or combinations of them. Nor is protection required if the designs are dictated essentially by technical or functional considerations. Members may also provide limited exceptions to protection if they do not unreasonably conflict with normal exploitation or the legitimate interests of the owner.

Copyright and Related Rights

The Berne Convention covers literary and artistic works (books, paintings, musical compositions, sculptures, photographs, films, lectures and so on). It does not cover live performances, sound recordings or broadcasts, which are covered by the Rome Convention and the Phonograms Convention.

The distinction between the Berne and Rome Conventions is somewhat difficult to grasp, but essentially Berne protects the copyright in the original artistic product. This is easy to understand in the case of books, paintings and sculptures as they are fixed in some way in a manuscript or other physical object. A piece of music or song is fixed in the score and a live performance (for example a ballet) is sometimes set down in choreographic notes. But many live performances are 99 per cent inspiration and there is no concrete 'fixing' of them. Nonetheless a live performance can be copyrighted if it is an original artistic work.

Recordings or broadcasts of original copyright works (for example audio books, a video of Picasso's paintings, a compact disc of a song or piece of music, a video cassette of a live show) are called secondary or neighbouring rights in that they record or reproduce original works (fixed or unfixed).

Infringement generally takes two forms: piracy, where original or secondary rights are infringed, for example when a song or the compact disc upon which it is recorded is copied without authorisation and sold; and bootlegging, for example where someone records a live performance without authorisation and sells it. Secondary infringement occurs when someone deals in copyright material or assists an infringement, for example when an individual imports a product knowing it to be unlawfully copied or provides a venue for a live performance under the same circumstances. Another aspect is the question of rental rather than copying.

The Berne Convention goes further than the patent conventions in that it gives mutual recognition of copyright. A copyright holder in signatory X can claim protection under the laws of signatory Y and under the same conditions as a national of signatory Y. There is no need to apply or register for protection in other signatories in order to obtain protection.

The Berne Convention also gives copyright protection at the moment of creation and does not require registration. One of the reasons the United States did not join the Berne Convention until 1989 was that it previously required registration before copyright could be acquired. It also had different lengths of protection than the Berne Convention, which sets the term of copyright at the author's life plus 50 years, 50 years for films and anonymous work, and 25 years for photographs.

The Universal Copyright Convention (UCC) of 1952 grew out of the need to bring the United States and others into the fold. It allows shorter terms of protection (25 years), and does not give authors the right to invoke rights in another signatory country, and only requires signatories 'to give adequate and effective protection'. This is so vague that some countries have been able to sign this convention without having copyright legislation at all. Despite this rather tepid formulation, however, the convention allows authors in signatory X to claim protection in signatory Y under the same conditions. When registration is required, as in the United States, this condition can even be fulfilled by placing the owner's name, year of publication and the symbol © on the work. While the UCC still has some use against those who are not party to the WTO, it has basically been overtaken by the TRIPS agreement, which is based on the Berne Convention.[15]

Coverage of the TRIPS Agreement[16]

The TRIPS agreement builds on the existing international situation by taking over most, though not all, of the Berne Convention rights, and works towards the development of common standards for neighbouring rights. It also addresses some of the problems that have arisen in connection with computer programmes and electronic information.

The agreement includes the main, substantive provisions of the Berne Convention, including the provisions for developing countries, with one exception: so-called 'moral rights'. These are the rights authors have to ensure their names are used correctly, that the integrity of their work is maintained, and so on. The agreement allows Berne Convention protection for life plus 50 years (25 for photographs) but doesn't require the author's life be used as a measure. Insofar as it is not, it is based on 50 years from the publication or creation of the work. This represents a compromise between those who use the artist's life as part of the yardstick and others, such as the United States which had shorter protection periods, for example 25 years.

The agreement clarifies some of the definitions of copyright and states that it shall extend to expressions, and not for example to ideas, or mathematical concepts *per se*. It also extends copyright to cover computer programmes, which are to be protected as literary works under the Berne Convention. This protection is also extended to compilations of data, which, by virtue of the selection or arrangement of their contents, are intellectual creations in their own right, irrespective of any copyright that is attached to the data itself. Some limitations are allowed insofar as they do not unreasonably prejudice the holder's rights (so-called 'fair use' – libraries, educational purposes and so on).

Copyright provisions give protection against unlawful copying for commercial purposes, but say nothing about what happens if protected material is rented, for example in video stores. The TRIPS agreement deals with this for the first time by giving rights to owners of rights computer programmes, film and sound to charge for such rentals. The agreement allows WTO members to make exceptions for film rights when the rental activity has not led to widespread copying that materially impairs the owner's rights.

As for neighbouring rights, the TRIPS agreement takes on board the provisions of the Rome Convention requiring WTO members to allow authors of sound recordings and broadcasts to acquire exclusive rights to them and to protect themselves against piracy through reproduction, retransmission and so on. It also allows the owner of the rights to prevent someone from fixing an unfixed performance, for example bootlegging by recording a live show and selling copies of the recording.

ENFORCEMENT

There is a requirement that WTO members provide for enforcement procedures,[17] such as civil court actions, including the possibility of injunctions and provisional measures to prevent infringements. The agreement also stipulates that rights holders should be able to require customs authorities to suspend the importation of infringing goods. Criminal procedures should also be available.

More importantly, WTO members can take their complaints to the dispute settlement bodies of the WTO. The Paris and Berne Conventions had no corresponding mechanism. The general improvements to WTO dispute settlement procedures mean that they are more effective, speedy and no longer require consensus for adoption of a panel decision. These are major advances. The dispute settlement procedures can lead to authorisation to suspend trade concessions and are very persuasive.

TRANSITIONAL ARRANGEMENTS

All developed parties to the agreement had one year in which to bring their laws into line with it, that is by 1 January 1996. Developing countries were given five years in all (from 1 January 1995). However, if patent protection did not exist at the time of entry into force of the Agreement for a particular sector, eg. pharmaceuticals, developing countries could take an additional five years for implementation in regard to those sectors.[18]

The agreement nonetheless requires that in the case of pharmaceuticals and agricultural chemicals, developing countries claiming a transitional period should allow sufficient time for patents to be filed. In this way the priority date and patent examination can be completed before the agreement enters into force in those countries, allowing patents to maintain some priority and take effect as fully accorded patents when implementation takes place. Economies in transition may also request a five-year respite. Least developed countries have been given ten years to conform and may request extensions of this period.

The agreement also contains a standstill clause, which forbids the lowering of existing protection and requires the application of MFN and national treatment during the transitional periods.

Whether these transitional arrangements were strictly justified or not, they were concessions the developing countries insisted on and were part of the final political compromise. Five or ten years may appear lengthy, but in fact it is a relatively short time in terms of the major adaptation being required of some countries. The compromise was also necessary to get some of the more reluctant developing countries on board. It was all the more necessary given that the developed countries had insisted on a similar transition period of ten years for the full liberalisation of textiles, which was the sector of most interest to developing countries.

RESULTS OF THE ROUND

The Uruguay Round was certainly a success from the point of view of the developed countries. A much wider range of protection is now available and patent holders and holders of other rights in developed countries are now guaranteed substantial protection in the territories of WTO members.

This is a distinct improvement over the situation before the round in that in many cases even the basic minimum protection of rights was not guaranteed let alone any remuneration for licensing of those rights. This meant that counterfeiting and patent violations were taking place on a very large scale and losses to the developed countries were substantial. To give some examples, the estimated loss to the US video industry in 1983 was about $6 billion; in 1984 the US automotive parts industry estimated its loss at $12 billion.

On the other hand, in some circumstances developing countries may find it more difficult to purchase patents and other products subject to intellectual property rights. The impact of this may create some difficulties, and the riots that took place in India prior to the signing of the round in Marrakesh indicate the degree of feeling that this seemingly dull subject can give rise to. The riots were conducted mainly by farmers, who felt they would have less access to seeds and plants or that they would cost more.

However, while there may be short-term costs, the developing countries will find that the protection of certain intellectual property rights is likely to encourage additional foreign direct investment and increased research and development by foreign firms in their markets. This will lead to more transfer of technology in the medium and long term. Foreign firms will only invest where they feel they are not going to lose all their trade secrets and the results of their research.

20 Trade-Related Investment Measures

INTRODUCTION

Governments use a number of instruments to control both foreign and domestic investment. These regulations can be precautionary (for example banks, insurance companies) and may apply equally to domestic investment, or they may be downright protectionist (for example by refusing to issue investment permits to foreign competitors). Governments can also discourage investment by confining foreign ownership within certain shareholding limits or activities, or by curtailing the repatriation of capital, profits and so on. At the other extreme governments provide substantial incentives for investment, whether in the form of direct subsidies, tax reductions, free greenfield sites, help with training and so on.

Between these extremes are measures that permit and even encourage foreign investment but set out to make it conform with, or support, an industrial strategy. In line with industrial policy objectives, governments frequently insist on a percentage of national shareholding, the establishment of a local research facility, the transfer of technology and so on.

Many of these requirements are only indirectly related to trade or are trade distorting. Others are much more direct in their approach to trade and the balance of payments. An example of a direct control is the requirement that investors buy many of their supplies or parts locally (local content requirement), which ensures they will import less or at least help build up the local industry. Others require that they export part of their production (export performance requirement) or that their imports be balanced by exports (trade balancing requirement).

These measures are commonly referred to as trade-related investment measures (TRIMs). They are most common in the car, petrochemicals and chemicals, computer/information industries, to cite but a few examples. The heaviest concentration is however in the car sector.[1]

This chapter is concerned with the third category of measures.

Incentive programmes are dealt with in the chapter on subsidies and are only touched on here. The first category of issues relating to access for investment, its regulation and the protection of assets, are dealt with in Chapters 22 and 25 (under 'future issues'). It will be seen from these chapters that these three categories of measures have been dealt with by the Uruguay Round either in a partial manner or hardly at all.

ECONOMIC DEBATE

Under classical economic theory, performance requirements are a misallocation of resources and contrary to the principle of comparative advantage; a firm should be entitled to purchase its components where it wants and should be entitled to export or not as it sees fit.

It is sometimes argued that performance requirements are among the few measures available to developing countries to organise and develop industries with economies of scale and an export vocation. Developing countries do not have the financial resources to subsidise production and economies of scale to compensate for the imperfections of the local market. They can however, by a clever balancing of import protection and export performance requirements, ensure that a foreign company will invest in its territory and will take a more strategic interest in the export performance of the local subsidiary it is setting up. In the absence of such provisions a foreign subsidiary might be set up purely to serve the local market, or a firm may prefer to sell into it from outside. These performance requirements can sometimes ensure that they invest not only for the local market but for the global market. TRIMs can also be used to control the anticompetitive practices of multilateral corporations. For example export requirements can counter a multinational firm's attempts to partition markets and prevent competition by forbidding the firm it sets up in country X from competing with another subsidiary in country Y.

There have been many studies of the scope and coverage of these measures, which have produced very varied and differing results and should therefore be treated with caution. Some suggest that TRIMs have been applied to as little as 12 per cent of foreign subsidiaries while other studies have set the application of these measures as either applying to all or at least to 75 per cent of

foreign investments. One can reconcile these figures if one under-
stands that many such programmes are on the books but are not
always applied, or are applied to firms which intend in any case to
have the degree of local activity being required.[2]

The practical impact of these measures would appear to be much
less than many have claimed. More often than not a country that
is seeking a major investment will tailor its local content or export
requirements to what is feasible and to what the firm would probably undertake in the longer term in any case. They are often backed
up with incentives, such as a protected market or direct subsidies,
which compensate for the performance requirements. Whatever the
reasons, most firms that have been questioned about the impact of
such measures have tended to say that their investment would have
taken place despite these requirements, and they have generally
indicated that they do not constitute a major nuisance. Studies of
the impact on exports from the parent country of the investor would
also suggest that the impact is minimal.[3]

Contrary to what one might expect, these measures are taken by
developed as well as developing countries. Many developed countries use such requirements and incentives, though often in a somewhat disguised form through indirect subsidies, tariff escalation and
so on.

Ironically, if one compares the amount of investment in developed countries where investment measures exist to the amount of
investment in the developing countries, one finds that the investment measures in the developed world are more frequent.[4] The
difference tends to lie in the type of investment measure used. This
is all important because the TRIMs agreement in the Uruguay Round
only covered a limited number and type of investment measures
and these tended to be of the sort used by developing countries.
Other Uruguay Round agreements, for example the subsidies agreement, are likely to have a greater impact, though only partial, on
the measures used by developed countries. The services agreement
probably went furthest in dealing with issues of access and regulation.

GOVERNMENT REGULATION

In the last century developed countries sought to ensure greater
protection for their foreign investment than was guaranteed under
many national laws. The main objective was to protect against

nationalisation or expropriation, and this aspiration was frequently backed up by gunboat diplomacy.

However, with the passage of time the general principles of international law as we know them now asserted themselves. This meant that foreign, like national, investments were subjected to national laws. International law did however guarantee that investors would be adequately compensated if expropriation took place. But there were few truly international (as opposed to plurilateral or bilateral) agreements on investment. Examples of plurilateral and bilateral agreements are referred to in the chapter on foreign direct investment (Chapter 25).

The GATT did little to change this situation, and while the Havana Charter, which preceded it, contained certain provisions, these did not survive into the GATT, and for a long time it was assumed that while the GATT dealt with measures with an indirect effect such as subsidies, tariffs, and so on, it had no provisions to deal with investment measures *per se*. However since a GATT panel's decision on Canadian investment legislation (the FIRA case), at least some trade-related investment measures have been deemed to be covered by the GATT.

The Uruguay Round started with a discussion as to whether a more ambitious approach should be adopted in order to include more general investment incentives. This did not succeed however, due to considerable opposition from developing countries, though of course subsidies and tariffs were dealt with separately (see Chapters 11 and 8). In the end, all the round managed to achieve in this respect was to confirm the interpretation of certain GATT provisions contained in the FIRA case, that is, only some narrow trade-related measures were covered. The initial Uruguay Round discussion established a list of 14 measures. A shorter list of eight measures proposed by the United States was whittled down to three categories in the final agreement, and these were only partly covered.

This slim result probably reflected an equivocal approach to the issue by certain developed partners. Many multinational firms are probably quite comfortable with performance requirements accompanied by incentives, whether in the form of subsidies or protected markets. The United States was also moving from a position of net investor abroad to the status of host country for substantial investment from others. The EU and the United States were also concerned about some of the possible negative effects of inward investment, such as a lack of local content and the spectre of investments that were no more than assembly operations of imports made abroad.

THE RESULTS OF THE URUGUAY ROUND

The Uruguay Round confirmed that Articles III (national treatment) and XI (prohibition of quotas) of GATT apply to local content and trade balancing requirements. The requirement that a firm should purchase certain quantities of products locally, or that it should only purchase or use imported goods in an amount related to the volume it exports, constitutes discrimination between foreign and local products and falls foul of the national treatment requirement (Article III of GATT) and is forbidden by the TRIMs agreement.

Governments sometimes force firms to buy locally by putting a quota on or restricting foreign exchange for imports, or they may force firms to sell locally by imposing export restrictions. The GATT (art. XI) has always prohibited import and export quotas or restrictions. These restrictions may or may not be tied to local production or purchase. But the TRIMs agreement makes clear that a restriction is still one even if a producer is only restricted until it produces a certain amount domestically. While it may only be temporarily subject to import or export restrictions, strictly speaking this is now considered to be against the WTO rules.

The result is limited. The agreement does deal with some very obvious abuses, but leaves some equally obvious ones to one side because they could not be fitted in to the straightjacket of Articles III and XI of GATT. One example is that export performance requirements are still generally permissible. An export performance requirement will not fall under Article III if it is not linked to local purchases or production, or under Article XI if it is not couched in terms of a prohibition on imports or exports. Other measures also fall outside these strict definitions.

The list of forbidden practices is only illustrative, and any other practice falling foul of Articles III and XI is condemned. But in the absence of clear examples in the agreement, the unfair aspects of these practices will be more difficult to establish. Developed countries have two years in which to phase out their restrictions, developing countries five years and the least developed seven years. Countries may introduce new restrictions in those periods in order not to disadvantage firms in their territory that are already subject to such measures. Some may find that with the lengthier periods some firms will stay away until the measures have been phased out.

As mentioned earlier, other provisions of the Uruguay Round agreement apply to other categories of investment measure. These are dealt with elsewhere in this book, but to summarise, subsidies contingent on export performance or on the use of domestic rather than imported goods are forbidden. But the subsidy is forbidden by the subsidies agreement as such and not because it is an investment measure.

One potentially far-reaching obligation in the subsidies agreement is that certain industrial subsidies that are granted domestically may now be considered actionable if they are too 'specific' or 'targeted' at certain industries or firms. This provision goes beyond the stultifying context of the TRIMs agreement, and goes to the heart of many programmes designed to encourage foreign investment. Its future development and interpretation may have a major impact on the investment issue overall.

The TRIMs agreement only covers goods. For services one has to look to the services agreement (GATS) which goes a good deal further (see Chapter 22). In services it is usually essential to gain access to a market by establishing a commercial presence, and this has been recognised. The services agreement has therefore sought to tackle some of the fundamental issues of investment by requiring that foreign investors be given MFN or national treatment and proper market access. These are extensive obligations but are not fully automatic, and an exchange of concessions has to be negotiated to bring them into effect.

THE FUTURE

It is very likely that investment will be taken more seriously in the next negotiating round. One could argue that the Uruguay Round did not make very significant breakthroughs, with the possible exception of services and subsidies. But one should recall that by eliminating local content and other trade-related requirements, investments will tend to be based more on real investment considerations. Trade restrictions are arguably more important than considerations such as shareholding requirements, the establishment of local research facilities and so on. The TRIMs agreement has at least made clear that certain measures are against GATT rules, for example local content, and at a minimum will prevent backsliding by those partners who may be having second thoughts about a liberal investment regime.

However the next round should seek to confront the issue head on, if only to reduce the cost to governments of competing investment programmes and to reduce some of the distortions to trade that are still possible. What is important is that any future negotiation should treat the issue of investment as broadly as possible, taking account not only of investors' concerns and the need to reduce barriers to investment, but also those of the host country, including its development needs if any. So far the GATT has only dealt with the issue on a piecemeal basis. For further discussion see the section on future issues in Chapter 25.

Part VI

Agriculture

21 Agriculture

JUSTIFICATION FOR FARM SUPPORT

Most economists recognise that this sector has specific characteristics that set it apart from others. The sector suffers from being
both cyclical and close to the traditional concept of a perfectly
competitive market. There is a tendency for both oversupply and
undersupply arising from crop and animal production cycles and
from farmers' lack of information or ignorance about what the
market will actually bear in a particular season. At the consumer
end, overproduction can be a good thing in that it can lead to
lower prices. However overproduction can also lead to underpro-
duction in the next season as farmers adjust their efforts, with
consequences for prices that are not so attractive.

The problem of overproduction is compounded by the fact that
lower prices do not necessarily lead to increased consumption. The
average consumer can only drink so much milk or eat so much
meat, and the demand for such products is therefore rigid or in-
elastic, unlike in the industrial sector where manufacturers can
usually dispose of surplus production by lowering their prices or
diversifying their products.

The special nature of this sector and its volatility have led governments in most developed countries, rightly or wrongly, to intervene
in the market in order to stabilise prices in the interests of both
consumer and farmer. In the interest of food security, governments
have also been concerned to ensure that adequate supplies exist
domestically. Moreover, by avoiding large-scale imports, domestic
production and a healthy balance of payments can go hand in hand.

Overall, however, governments have tended to be more keen to
protect the interests of producers than consumers. There are many
reasons why governments have intervened on the side of producers,
ranging from response to lobbying by producer interest groups to
the more sound reason of maintaining parity of income and social
stability. For some politicians, maintenance of social stability means
keeping as many farmers as possible on the land in order to maintain a conservative voting majority. By and large however the reasons
have been genuinely social in the sense that the adjustment from

189

farming to industrial or other employment has had to be carried out in a manner that would not create excessive or severe dislocation. This could only be achieved by stabilising farm incomes and maintaining some parity between farm and industrial incomes, thus easing the transition.

An important factor in this equation has been the steady increase in productivity in the sector. This has averaged up to 3 per cent a year in certain periods.[1] The result has been a long-term decline in prices, which has eroded the viability of smaller land holdings and led to a steady drift from the land.

So while in the long term farm assistance programmes have tended to speed up the productivity growth of the sector and migration off the land, in the short term they have contributed to stemming that flow by maintaining farm incomes at levels that are roughly comparable to those in other sectors.

A more positive aspect of the assistance programmes is that by providing the farm sector with more money. They have helped the more efficient and the more determined to invest and increase their productivity. Indeed some economists would argue that price stabilisation is essential to the development of a sector that is subject to perfect competition. Without price or income stabilisation, farmers would not have any profits, productivity would be poor and the sector would not grow.

They have also acted as a buffer in serious economic crises when farm incomes have been squeezed by lower prices in tandem with higher interest rates, energy prices and so on, with the threat of wholesale bankruptcy.

In the United States, the early years of the Reagan presidency were a good example of this.[2] The administration was committed to 'getting government out of agriculture', but was obliged to increase price support to a level that was substantially above mere stabilisation in order to compensate for high interest rates, high inputs, the high dollar and so on. The alternative was wholesale bankruptcy of farms and agricultural banks. Many bankruptcies did occur, but the increased price support avoided catastrophe.

Such intervention in the market is common in most developed countries. It is much less common in the developing world, where it would impose too great a burden on national budgets and consumer transfers would put too great a burden on the poor. If anything, many developing countries have kept agricultural prices low in order to subsidise urban consumers; this has had the effect of undermining the agricultural sector in these countries, with negative consequences for their development.

In the developed world such intervention has taken place in accordance with different historical circumstances. The movement of labour out of agriculture into industry took place earlier in the United States, for example, than in many other countries, and the working population involved in agriculture is much less than elsewhere (only 3 per cent).

The UK is another example of a country that adjusted and modernised its agriculture at an early stage, for example, after the passing of the Corn Laws in the mid-nineteenth century the market was opened to cheap wheat from abroad. This accounts for the modern employment structure of UK agriculture (2 per cent of the population) and continuing UK hostility to programmes such as the EU Common Agricultural Policy. It feels that, in a sense, this policy is turning the clock back, and likely at worst to create inefficiency in the sector, and at best to waste money in that it subsidises an already efficient UK sector.

Countries such as the United States are therefore in a better position to reduce subsidies and promote rapid adjustment in the sector because they face a lower political cost. Other countries, for reasons related to their historical development, are not in such a comfortable situation. Their productivity is not as high and their populations too dependent on agriculture for any quick fixes on the political front. This accounts in many cases for the conflicts that have occurred in the agricultural sector between parties to GATT, and for the different solutions that have been proposed to resolve these conflicts.

THE ECONOMIC VALIDITY OF FARM SUPPORT

The question of whether extensive government intervention in this sector is justified is hotly debated.[3] The goal of price stabilisation hinges on the idea that if a floor price is not put in place, farmers that experienced falling prices in the last season will fail to produce in the next. The resulting shortfall in supply will increase prices, seriously affect the consumer's food bill and spark inflation. With a floor price, the only situation in which there might be a supply shortfall and a rise in prices is when climatic changes destroy a harvest, in other words when nature, not man, intervenes. This happens less frequently, so some measure of stability can be achieved. This improved stability is in the consumers' interest but is also achieved at their expense, either by paying higher prices or as taxpayers.

Many economists nowadays argue that cyclical changes in price and supply do not occur in the same way, or would not do so in a properly integrated world economy. A supply shortfall in one country could easily be made up by a surplus in another, possibly in a different hemisphere or climatic zone, and the greater number of growing cycles and harvests allows for more flexibility. In any case, if the price of one product goes up consumers can switch to another, given the wide variety of produce now available.

Clearly, however, marginal farms are vulnerable to cyclical markets and they either have to adjust or go out of business. Studies show that farmers are essentially pricetakers and have little control over prices. The only way they can survive the steady reduction of prices in the market due to productivity improvements is to reduce their costs and become more productive themselves. Given the long-term trend towards lower prices, the choice is not between adjusting or not adjusting, but in the speed of that adjustment.

This leads to the second point. Adjustment in agriculture is unavoidable, but there may be political or economic reasons for wanting to slow it down, such as a high level of general unemployment. Farm support programmes can do this, while at the same time providing a breathing space and finance for productivity improvements. But these programmes are inevitably bound by the laws of economics too, and if the level of support is set too high the burden on the consumer and the national budget becomes too great.

Many developed countries have found themselves in precisely that situation in recent years, that is high general unemployment, accelerating agricultural productivity and lower prices, plus a farm support system that had become far too expensive. This led inevitably to a rethinking of the support systems themselves. They had tended to support all farmers indiscriminately, and the largest and wealthiest producers were benefiting the most. The new approach that is emerging is to reduce general farm and price supports, and to target direct income support at those most in need, that is, the marginal farmers. In the long run, this is likely to cost far less.

The next question that should be asked is whether such 'social' programmes or assistance are really necessary. One of the main arguments to justify farm support in the past has been the need to bring about parity between agricultural and other incomes. However some studies suggest that, on average, farm incomes are not only on a par with, but may well exceed industrial or other incomes. Moreover farmers often own an asset (the farm) that on the open market may well be worth a princely sum, which if properly invested could yield many times the average national income.

However if one disaggregates the figures and examines the actual incomes of certain categories of farm, their farm incomes are often highly marginal. So much so that they should not, in the words of one writer,[4] be considered farms at all, but hobbies. The real income of many of these farmers comes from off-farm sources, and the less income they earn from the farm the greater their off-farm income is likely to be. Nonetheless many are living a marginal existence, courtesy of the tax payer, though they do enjoy hidden benefits from the farm (they produce their own food, they live in the farm house and so on).

This is true of an astonishingly large number of US farmers.[5] Of the 2.14 million farms in the United States in 1992, 1.25 million produced little or no revenue and accounted for only 10 per cent of production. Essentially US farmers live off and continue to function through government support. Another 306 000 earn a low income and represent 13 per cent of production. The most prosperous 321 000 earn substantial incomes while accounting for about 77 per cent of overall production (1990 figures). Similar and worse situations exist in Europe, where the average farm size is much smaller and a large number of part-time or hobby farmers exist.

The sheer scale of adjustment is daunting, even allowing for the fact that many farmers have second incomes. To cut subsidies entirely to 1.3 or 1.6 million farms would throw large numbers of farmers (and farm labourers) on to the labour market. Many of these would be employed by the more successful farms that took over their land, and many would survive on off-farm income. But the adjustment would be a major one.

While adjustment is necessary, therefore, it will not necessarily be easy or cheap in the short or medium term, even with different types of support such as direct income. The calculation is both a political and economic one.

DEMOGRAPHIC AND SOCIAL TRENDS

The number of people working on the 2.14 million US farms is now down to about 3 per cent of the working population, compared with 13–14 million in the 1920s and 1930s and 10 million in the 1950s. The decline in the farming population has been accompanied by a trend towards greater productivity and larger farm size as smaller, more marginal farms have gone out of business or been taken over. The average farm size in the United States is now 180 hectares. There are also far more part-time farmers than in the past; the number of full-time farms is probably only 600 000.[6]

The adjustment has been slower in the EU. The farming population as a share of total employment fell from 22 per cent in the 1950s to 13.8 per cent in 1970 and 5.7 per cent in 1992. These figures mask substantial differences between individual member states, for example 2 per cent in the UK, 21 per cent in Greece, 10 per cent in Ireland and Portugal, and 5.5 per cent in France. Farm size and productivity are also lower than in the United States, the average farm size being 40 hectares. Again these figures mask substantial variations between member states and regions (farms in the vicinity of Paris are highly productive but those in the southwest of France are not).[7]

As a result it is easier for the United States to move towards liberalisation than the EU (though there are many small and inefficient farms in the US too): 3 per cent of the population is going to put up less political opposition than 7 per cent or 13 per cent. However, in the EU substantial reforms could have a stronger and more profound and beneficial impact in the medium term given the larger number of very inefficient farms. The Common Agricultural Policy (CAP) has made very substantial progress in restructuring the sector in the EU, but the task has been more difficult and started at a much later date than in the United States. This is one of the fundamental divergences between the two positions.

The situation has been made even more difficult over the years by the accession of new EU members, particularly Greece, Portugal and certain parts of Spain, where smallholdings are still very prevalent. Ironically, accession by Austria and Finland, two of the most recent entrants will also bring a fair share of problems. Though highly developed industrially, their agriculture is protected and supported to an even greater extent than in the EU as a whole (almost double the amount of EU support). This is due to the remoteness of farms in the Scandinavian countries, which are maintained for a combination of regional and security reasons. In Austria it is due to the inefficiency of hill farming, which still abounds. In Sweden, another recent entrant, the sector was reformed a few years ago, and support is mainly in the form of border measures.

The eventual expansion of the EU towards Central Europe will bring its own problems. As many of the farms in Central Europe receive no support they are relatively price competitive, and opening the EU markets will seriously undermine EU agriculture. On the other hand, if they were supported on the same scale as in the EU the cost would be staggering, given the size of some of their farming sectors. Any opening to the East will therefore have to be accompanied by very substantial reform of the CAP. This is one of the main obstacles to a speedy integration of Central European countries into the EU.

AGRICULTURAL TRADE AND SUPPORT PATTERNS

Agriculture has a different degree of economic significance for different countries. The United States has always been a major exporter and agriculture has been a very important component of its export potential. By 1950 agricultural exports had declined to 30 per cent of total exports and by 1989 they had fallen to 10 per cent. However these exports remain of vital importance to the agriculture sector, where 30–40 per cent of production is exported. The cutoff in terms of agricultural prosperity lies somewhere between 25 per cent and 30 per cent of production; if exports fall below this level the sector will be in trouble.[8]

This export potential has increased over the years, though a number of factors such as the growth of competitors or a drop in demand have tended to make this progress very uneven. The fate of exports has often depended on the level of the dollar, which has fluctuated dramatically, and the level of internal support. When internal prices have risen, the competitiveness of exports has dropped. When this has happened the US government has made strenuous efforts to rectify the situation, given the importance of agriculture for its balance of payments.

On the other hand the United States only imports up to 10 per cent of its agricultural needs. Is this a sign that it is highly competitive in agriculture? Are its exports thwarted by unfair competition and is its low import level due to the highly competitive nature of its products? The answer is not so simple. While there is no doubt that some US export markets are affected by unfair competition and import barriers, the United States itself is one of the main contributors to these 'unfair' practices. The US system of agricultural support is in itself a distortion, and US trade barriers are numerous and excessive.

There are severe trade barriers (quotas, high tariffs, VERs and so on) in areas such as sugar, dairy products, wool, tobacco, cotton and beef. The support system for other sectors is designed in such a way as to ensure that US farmers are able to compete with any world market price. The market is open, but the US government picks up the tab for domestic producers by paying the difference between world prices and what is considered to be a fair return domestically, (the so-called deficiency payments system). Exporters from other countries also have to pay transport costs. This has the effect of excluding competitors even when there are no visible barriers to entry to the US market, as US farmers can always match their prices. US exports are given additional support to enable them to go below normal world prices when competing for large export contracts (the Export Enhancement Program).

In Europe, agriculture has been in receipt of very substantial assistance throughout the history of the EU. Support was initially provided to stabilise markets and modernise the sector, but from being a net importer in certain sectors, since the early 1980s the EU has become a major exporter (7 per cent of total exports), and as such it has clashed frequently and painfully with the United States and others in the world market. On the other hand the EU imports much more than the United States – up to 40 per cent of its needs – though substantial barriers frequently exist with regard to products of most interest to countries such as the United States, Canada, Argentina, Australia and New Zealand, for example cereals, beef and dairy products. (These countries form the core of the so-called Cairns Group, a caucus formed for the purposes of the Uruguay Round negotiations.) The EU nonetheless remains the largest export market and balance of payments surplus for US exports (about $8 billion on average for 1980–94), and the second largest for Australia and New Zealand.

With time these countries came to accept the fact that penetration of the internal EU market would be difficult and more limited, though for some it meant giving up traditional export markets

(Australia and New Zealand lost substantial market share when the UK joined the EU). What they found more difficult to accept was the fact that EU exports increased and were subsidised in a way that took market share away from them throughout the world, and sometimes also broke the world market prices, rendering such markets unprofitable.

But the EU was not the only culprit in this respect, and efficient producers of beef, dairy products, cereals and so on such as Australia and Argentina had similar difficulties with the United States. They could not penetrate the US market for beef and they faced US export subsidy competition in the world market with regard to cereals and dairy products (the Export Enhancement Programme).

In the case of Japan, the problem is not its ability to export but its barriers to imports. These are most severe in such products as rice, where a very uneconomic sector has been protected for a variety of reasons, including food security, and for tradition's sake. Barriers have also been high in such areas as beef and citrus products in order to protect fairly marginal local production and more generally to protect the balance of payments.

In developing countries the situation is very varied: agricultural powerhouses such as Argentina are among the most efficient producers and exporters in the world, while some of the poorest and most overpopulated countries have to import a lot of their needs. The former have an interest in reducing subsidies and barriers to trade in their export markets. The latter have an interest in maintaining the subsidies in developed countries, as these make it cheaper for them to purchase food.

The difficulties many developing countries have had in producing enough food, apart from obvious climatic problems, have frequently stemmed from misguided development policies. The prices of agricultural goods have been kept low in order to maintain cheap food for the urban population, and the result has been stunted growth in domestic agriculture and increased import dependence. In many countries these policies have been redirected in recent years and one can expect substantial changes in trade patterns as a result.

THE INTEREST IN FREER TRADE

So what are the interests of the various parties in freer agricultural trade? Clearly the United States and the members of the Cairns group (Canada, Australia, New Zealand, Argentina and so on) feel that as the most competitive producers of certain major products (for example cereals) they stand to gain the most. Despite their competitiveness there will nonetheless be a price to pay. Those with the least subsidies – for example New Zealand, which has eliminated nearly all subsidies in the last few years, and Argentina, which never really had any – will benefit the most. Others, for instance the United States and Canada and to a lesser extent Australia, will have to go through some fairly painful adjustment, given the existing level of subsidisation and protection.

In the EU the adjustment will be even more severe, though costs will differ depending on the member state and the relative efficiency of certain sectors. One of the most painful adjustments will come in the cereals sector as EU producers are not as efficient as those elsewhere, but lower cereal prices will feed through to other sectors such as beef and dairy, and in particular to pig and poultry production, which will then become more competitive; payment for feed is after all one of the main costs of maintaining cattle. There will nonetheless be painful adjustments in the beef and dairy sectors, but increased market opportunities abroad and substantial adjustment at home will lead to a healthier and more competitive sector. But the great number of inefficient farms will require a far greater adjustment.

The EU agricultural policy, of course, has a different significance for each of the different member states. It does more to help subsidise the producers of 'northern' or temperate products, as the original policy was designed by and for them. Producers in Spain, Greece and Portugal, which acceded at a later date, found less support when they joined, though a substantial effort was nonetheless made for them too. Some member states, for example Germany and the UK, have few farmers and are large importers of food. Others such as France and to a certain extent Spain and Italy have a much greater vocation as exporters, and any reduction in export subsidies could have a substantial impact on their ability to export to the world market, and on their balance of payments. Increased market access for others would also affect their ability to export to other member states. Lower support prices favour the more efficient farmers in the EU, for example the Netherlands, Denmark and others, at the expense of some of the less efficient. Each member state therefore has a different set of interests in the outcome of a trade round.

Major export opportunities will occur for developing countries as a whole. Some will, however, have to pay higher prices for their imports. This may lead to some distress, but the more likely scenario is that this will be a temporary feature of the world market. The forces of supply will soon pick up the slack and the higher prices that will result from reduced production in the subsidising countries will soon come down again. The idea that the developing countries are going to suffer as a result of the Uruguay Round is generally an exaggerated one.

HOW ARE FARMERS SUPPORTED?

The methods of intervention used have varied from one country to another, but they can be very broadly described as falling into four main categories.

First, *price support* is the most frequently used method in the EU and consists of supporting the price of a product at a level that is likely to satisfy the requirements of the producer and produce a degree of stability that is in the consumer interest as well. The support is given by purchasing a product and storing it when the market price falls below a certain level. In order to maintain the price at a level higher than that prevailing on the world market, there must be a corresponding regime at the border to insulate the price from lower priced products on the world market. Production that is surplus to national needs must then be exported with the help of subsidies in order to meet the lower world market price.

The essence of this system is that the consumer picks up a very substantial part of the support bill. While government budgets have to be substantial to pay for intervention in the market to buy the surplus and store it, and to pay for export subsidies, it is less than might be required if the government had to pay the full measure of support itself. It is also the case that price support systems tend to be the instrument of choice where exports are low, as export support is one of the main burdens on the budget in such a system.

The system developed in the EU, for example, was designed at a time when EU exports were low. But the system was so successful in encouraging production that the EU went from being a major importer to a major exporter. This contributed in a significant way to the enormous budgetary strains in the system.

A variation of this method was the use of marketing boards in

Canada and Australia for cereals, wool and so on. The boards would buy up the stock at a certain price, then sell it abroad. This was a more centralised version of the CAP.

Price support can also be carried out by methods such as import tariffs or quotas. But these methods will only give insulation from world markets price fluctuations but will not necessarily result in stable prices on the domestic market.

Second, under a *deficiency payments system*, which is frequently used in the United States, producers receive the world market price but are compensated up to a certain level, depending on the amount produced. In other words the government intervenes to pay the difference between the world or market price and a notional higher price that it feels is appropriate to compensate farmers for their efforts. Consumers are spared higher prices, though they pay through their tax bills. Again this system operates to keep budget expenditure lower in a system that is highly export oriented.

Third, the *direct income system*, which is operated by few countries, compensates farmers for their low income, not for low market prices. This has the effect of going straight to the heart of the problem: the inadequate income of marginal farms. Unlike the other two systems it discriminates between poorer and wealthier farmers and may avoid the burden on the consumer and/or the budget that is implicit in the other systems. The budgetary burden could however be very substantial if a large number of poorer farmers have to be supported. This depends on the government's definition of 'poor' and on the cut-off level. It also has the major advantage of uncoupling income support from the amount produced. In that sense it is more market oriented and avoids direct encouragement of agricultural surpluses, which is implicit in the other two systems.

Finally, the agricultural sector is also replete with control mechanisms that are designed to rein in production, for example payments to farmers for taking land out of production (*set-asides*), *quotas* and *levies on overproduction*. The purpose of these controls is to maintain prices by reducing production. They are frequently used simply to avoid the expenses associated with overproduction, such as storage, export subsidies and so on, while continuing to support farmers.

On one side, therefore, are support measures that encourage production and others that act as a brake on overproduction, a combination of checks and balances designed to maintain the existing administrative system while at the same time avoiding its excesses.

There are many variations of these themes and different mechanisms have been designed to achieve the same purposes. They have different names and are often described in different terms. However they tend to conform, in the way they operate, to the four basic types of support set out above.

LEVELS OF SUPPORT

Whatever the justification, nowadays there is strong support for reform of the whole approach. The existing systems are a major financial burden, and even for the richest economies expenditure has escalated to the point where it is unsustainable.

In 1996 the producer subsidy equivalent (PSE) estimate for the EU was $85 billion, for the United States $23.5 billion and for Japan $49 billion. The PSE includes various elements of central and local government support to producers either through price changes, direct payments or tax concessions, and support for input costs, both specific and general. For the OECD as a whole the figure was $182 billion and has been on an upward march since the early 1980s, when the total was $88 billion (1979–81). Table 21.1 indicates a steady increase in support, particularly in the case of the EU and among others OECD countries, such as Japan and Switzerland though less so in terms of percentage of value-added. One should recall however that these increases are in part due to the movement of exchange rates. The low rate of the dollar in the 1980s meant higher PSE calculations for the EU as the world market price of many commodities is usually expressed in dollars. The EU has also expanded to include three new member states and the previous German Democratic Republic.

Table 21.1 also contains interesting information as to the percentage of agricultural production represented by subsidies. This ranges from a low percentage in 1993 in Australia and New Zealand (9 per cent and 3 per cent respectively), to much higher percentages in Japan (71 per cent), the Scandinavian countries (68–71 per cent) and Switzerland (78 per cent); the EU (48 per cent) Canada (22 per cent) and the United States (16 per cent) lie in mid range.

The figures also show that assistance is greatest where there is the greatest disparity between agricultural and industrial incomes, and where a country imports more. The probable reason in both cases is the inefficiency of the agricultural sector, as there is more

Table 21.1 OECD: producer subsidy equivalents by country, in millions of US dollars and percentage of value of production

	1986–88	*1993–95*	*1994*	*1995[1]*	*1996[2]*
Australia					
Total PSE	1033	1159	1183	1257	1191
Percentage PSE	10	10	10	9	9
Canada					
Total PSE	5839	4251	3924	4043	3837
Percentage PSE	42	26	26	23	22
EU[3]					
Total PSE	67872	84903	79788	95839	85006
Percentage PSE	48	49	49	49	43
Iceland					
Total PSE	157	128	119	134	116
Percentage PSE	82	74	73	74	68
Japan					
Total PSE	34341	43488	46554	48901	40532
Percentage PSE	73	75	75	77	71
New Zealand					
Total PSE	525	122	121	150	140
Percentage PSE	18	3	3	3	3
Norway					
Total PSE	2348	2515	2409	2535	2506
Percentage PSE	74	74	74	72	71
Switzerland					
Total PSE	4406	5516	5461	5974	5491
Percentage PSE	79	81	81	80	78
Turkey					
Total PSE	1576	3074	1913	3432	3.673
Percentage PSE	26	30	25	31	30
United States					
Total PSE	32532	23416	25213	17380	23513
Percentage PSE	30	18	19	13	16
OECD					
Total PSE	158609[4]	173908	174935	179644	166004
Percentage PSE	45	41	42	40	36

Notes:
1. Provisional.
2. Estimated.
3. EU 15 from 1995.
4. The OECD total includes the Czech Republic, Hungary, Mexico and Poland.

Source: OECD (1996).[9]

disparity in income and less ability to export if the sector is not efficient. The level of assistance is therefore quite a good measure of the relative efficiency of the sector in the various countries set out in the table.

However another factor one should keep in mind when comparing expenditure is the number of recipients. While in some cases the overall subsidy is larger than in others, the amount given per farmer is only average. The paradox is resolved if one remembers that farm support is given to rich and poor farmers indiscriminately on the basis of their production and not their income, though some countries, for example the United States, have put a ceiling on the overall amount an individual farmer can receive. It is therefore logical that large and productive farms receive the most support. This clearly illustrates the need for reform.[10]

In addition to subsidies from the taxpayer, farmers receive a consumer subsidy through higher prices, and this is often higher than the taxpayer subsidy. Taken together the two amounts are substantial.

This massive amount of assistance and its escalation led to a fundamental reappraisal of farm policies by the OECD, culminating in the OECD Ministerial Declaration of 1987. The purpose behind this declaration was to move the agriculture sector closer to the market. This could be achieved only by reducing and eventually dismantling the existing support mechanisms. Tariffs should be reduced to bring domestic prices closer to world prices, and various mechanisms used to insulate farmers from reality should be abandoned. This included mechanisms such as the variable levy, but also price supports and production subsidies, which effectively shut off farmers from the normal market price signals. If they were guaranteed a certain price or level of support, they had little incentive to become more efficient. Such supports as were still needed should be divorced from production levels, as this served to encourage unnecessary production. If they receive a payment for each one, farmers will breed as many cows as they can in order to maximise their income. This additional production may not make economic sense as there may be no demand for it.

The effect of linking subsidies to production also means that the largest farmers receive as much per item produced as small farmers. In many cases they are already wealthy and do not need public support. Ideally support should be shifted to compensate for inadequate income and be delinked from levels of production. This would also be less costly as well-off farmers would not be compensated and the money given to smaller, more inefficient producers would have a genuinely social purpose.

The OECD declaration acknowledges that set-asides, quotas and so on do help reduce production, but it generally frowns on them, either because they are administrative rather than market-based mechanisms, and therefore less efficient, or because they tend to perpetuate the link between support and production (even if, in the case of set-asides, this is non-production).

NEGOTIATING POSITIONS IN THE URUGUAY ROUND

The main difference of opinion between the EU, the United States and their various supporters during the Uruguay Round regarded the speed and amount of adjustment required to align agriculture policies. This led to some very acrimonious disputes.

The earliest US objective in the negotiation was a very ambitious one: reducing general support levels to zero over a period of ten years, with the exception of some supports that were marginal in terms of stimulating production. It is unlikely the United States could have implemented this programme itself, given the extensive nature of its agricultural support, but it made for a strong negotiating position. The EU's main objective was to reduce subsidies to the point where supply and demand on the world market would be in balance. In the end the reduction level was substantially decreased to 20 per cent over six years. This compromise was closer to what the EU could accept and represented a substantial concession on the US side.

The other main difference was about what needed to be regulated. For the EU it was sufficient to reduce the general level of support, which would then allow for flexibility in the application of that general rule, and for domestic subsidies, border measures and export subsidies to be adjusted accordingly. For its part the United States wanted to see reduction measures applied to each one of these elements. The EU saw this as an artificial method of achieving the same objective – a general reduction in support – and one that imposed artificial and unnecessary limits to the means of implementing the overall target. A reduction in domestic support would automatically lead to a corresponding reduction in border protection and export subsidies; to set definite limits on export subsidies or border protection regardless of what was permitted as domestic subsidy, was to undermine the EU price-support system of variable levies and export subsidies, the levels of which depended on each other and the world market.

The United States and its allies took the view that a reduction in domestic subsidies alone would not necessarily lead to a reduction in border restrictions or export subsidies. For them this was not necessarily a logical sequence, and indeed their views were based on previous experiences when internal EU domestic support policies did not always go in the same direction as market access or export subsidies. They were also concerned to ensure that reduction be spread evenly across all agricultural sectors; a system that only reduced the overall envelope could lead to sharp reductions in some sectors and stability or even increases in others.

Export subsidies in particular were a highly sensitive item as EU exports had increased exponentially over the last fifteen years, taking world market share away from such low-cost exporters as the United States itself but in particular its closest allies: Canada, Australia, Argentina and others in the so-called Cairns group of low-cost exporters.

The final compromise allowed for disciplines on each element, domestic and export subsidies and border measures that the United States and others wanted. While there were certain minimum requirements per tariff and product group in the case of export subsidies, the domestic support to be reduced was calculated as a global amount for the agriculture sector as a whole (aggregate measure of support). The reductions could be different for each subsector, that is greater or less, provided the overall reduction objectives were met. This corresponded more to the EU perspective.

In general all parties to the negotiation shared the objective of reducing subsidies and decoupling those that remained from production in order to bring the sector back into balance with the market. However some direct income subsidies were also excluded even though production-related. And there was no requirement that the effects of income subsidies should not outweigh production controls. This suited both the EU and the United States, but clearly it was a step back from the OECD objective of decoupling support. Like all compromises the deal was a fairly messy one.

THE GATT

The GATT agreement allowed for major exceptions to the general rules in the agricultural sector. The normal GATT prohibition on import quotas and export subsidies were either waived or drafted in such a manner as not to be enforceable.

Various exceptions were made to basic GATT rules such as the prohibition on quotas, insofar as they were part of a farm support system. Export subsidies for manufactures were generally prohibited (after 1962), but in agriculture and other primary products prohibition would only take place if the subsidies gave rise to a larger than equitable share of the world market. As no one could define what an equitable share was, this provision was virtually unenforceable.

This was a recognition of the specifity of the agricultural sector at the time of the establishment of the GATT. Even the United States felt that the question of agriculture should not fall under the full discipline of the GATT and sought a waiver from GATT rules for its own intervention system. In subsequent years the United States pursued a policy that was diametrically opposed to this early position, and fought quite hard at the Kennedy and Tokyo Rounds to have agriculture subjected to the full discipline of the GATT. These negotiations did not, however, go very far and the main effort to have agriculture properly included in GATT was left to the Uruguay Round.

The timing of the round was also propitious in that the world agricultural system and the various forms of intervention in this market were in crisis. Major trading partners such as the United States and the EU had been lurching from one major conflict and outburst to another, and one can say with a certain amount of justification that trans-Atlantic relations were being seriously poisoned by these regular confrontations. There was also a dawning realisation in the EU that the whole intervention system was in need of fundamental overhaul as the agricultural budget was increasingly difficult to control, and indeed was virtually out of control. The EU had therefore initiated a series of fundamental reforms of the CAP, starting in 1983. However these reforms were not working as well as they should and the levels of spending and overproduction were continually exceeding the objectives set.

It also became clear that the objectives of the Uruguay Round and the expectations of EU trading partners could not be met without a fundamentally different approach to the problem. This realisation occurred at the same time as the negotiations in Brussels in 1989, which sought to conclude this chapter of the Uruguay Round. These talks were a failure because positions were too far apart and it was not clear what were the implications of the negotiation for EU producers. The CAP reforms would spell out these implications, and if they were accepted by the farming community a result would be easier to obtain in the trade negotiations.[10]

Starting in 1989, therefore, the European Commission proposed a series of reforms that would shift the main centre of gravity of the CAP away from price support and towards direct income support. The price support system would be maintained but the level of prices would be severely reduced: it would only be possible to do this if farmers' incomes were subsidised by direct income support. Overproduction would be reduced by land set-asides, for which farmers would be compensated. It would be cheaper to get them to produce less than to pay for and store or dispose of excess production. Further measures along these lines were introduced in 1992.

After the EU reforms it became possible to develop a common framework for the GATT negotiations. It was generally agreed, for example, that the Uruguay Round should take a more market-based approach to agriculture. With this principle in mind, some methods of intervention would be inappropriate and should therefore be reduced. Other methods should be accepted under certain conditions, and others should be allowed and even encouraged.

After many last-minute obstacles the Uruguay Round eventually gave birth to the agreement on agriculture.

RESULTS OF THE NEGOTIATIONS

Domestic Support[11]

In the green or allowed subsidy category fell certain measures such as general government services in the areas of research, disease control, infrastructure and food security, structural adjustment assistance and direct payments under environmental or regional assistance programmes. *De minimis* subsidies of less than 5 per cent of the value of production were also included in this category (10 per cent in developing countries). No reduction in support was required.

It also included, and this is very important, the question of direct payments to producers in the form of decoupled income support. The inclusion of direct income support uncoupled from production measures was a very important indication of the direction that partners wished to see future agricultural policies take. This inclusion was not without difficulty as some felt that certain limits should be imposed. It is clear that even uncoupled direct income support would serve to keep marginal farms in existence, and indeed if direct income support were to be given without reference to income levels it would have the effect of a general subsidy, which could undermine the move towards a market-based agricultural system. But the chance of this happening is much less likely than with subsidies coupled to production. It would have been impossible to abolish coupled subsidies and put nothing in their place.

A second category of subsidies, the so-called 'blue box', concerned measures such as direct payments tied to production levels but under production-limiting programmes. These payments do not have to be tied to production set-asides or supply controls; it is sufficient if they are paid out in the context of a programme that includes a reduction of production (85 per cent of the base period). Subject to that limitation they can be production-related and even increased. In this sense they constitute a major exception to the move towards decoupling support from production. This again was an important element for the EU in that it was one of the cornerstones of the reforms that had recently been introduced into the CAP. It also had the effect of allowing the US deficiency payments if they met the conditions.

Not subject to reduction are certain government assistance measures to encourage agricultural and rural development in developing countries, investment and import subsidies for low-income producers in those countries, and measures to encourage diversification away from the growing of illicit narcotic crops.

All domestic subsidies that do not fall into the previous two categories are required to be reduced by 20 per cent over a period of six years (1995–2001) and 13.3 per cent for developing countries over ten years, and no reduction for the least developed. The base period for calculating the reduction was 1986–88. The reduction is based on a measure known as the aggregate measure of support (AMS). The AMS is arrived at by calculating the difference between a fixed external price (based on prices or estimates for 1986–88) and the institutional or administered price on a national market and multiplying this by the total amount of production. Added to it are other non-exempted domestic supports, that is, those which are outside the green and blue boxes. Not included however are subsidies covered by border measures (for example tariffs, quotas and export subsidies) where there is no domestically administered price; the difference in prices caused by these measures between the national and the fixed external price are not treated as domestic subsidies. It should be recalled however that tariffs, export subsidies, non-tariff measures and so on are dealt with under other provisions (see below).

Market Access[12]

Border measures other than tariffs are to be converted into tariff equivalents. These include items such as the variable levy used in the EU, import quotas, minimum import prices or any other protective measure. The tariff equivalent is the difference between world prices and that prevailing in the protected market as a result of the measure in question.

Existing tariffs and tariff equivalents are to be reduced by an average of 36 per cent over six years (1995–2001) with a minimum initial reduction of 15 per cent for each tariff line (24 per cent reduction for the developing countries over ten years (no reduction for the least developed) and a 10 per cent minimum initial reduction). This might lead to some anomalies. A product may be subject both to a tariff, say of 10 per cent, and to a quota. The tariff equivalent of the quota may be 25 per cent. The resulting level of protection will be based on the higher of the two – 25 per cent. This new tariff will only be reduced by 36 per cent over six years. At the end of the period, therefore, it will still be close to 16 per cent. In what sense can this be considered liberalisation?

The agreement therefore provides that where current access opportunities exist, they should be maintained. To do so a tariff quota equal to the volume of the previous import quota would have to be created, with a tariff rate of 10 per cent in the example given. (A tariff quota is a quota on which a low tariff or no tariff may be imposed but the full or normal tariff or tariff equivalent is reimposed once the quota is used up).

The agreement also states that minimum market access must be provided when the previous regime was such that market access was below 5 per cent. This is to be achieved through a tariff quota with a sufficiently low rate to ensure that a 5 per cent market opening is brought about by 2001 (2005 for developing countries).

In the case of the EU, the elimination of the variable levy means that internal EU prices can no longer be isolated from those in the world market. The levy, being variable, would simply cover the difference between world and domestic EU prices. Now the domestic price must follow the world price, with the tariff or tariff equivalent on top, and must vary in harmony with the world price.

The only exception to this is if the world price should drop by more than 10 per cent against the 1986–88 average or if volumes of imports increase by over 25 per cent compared with imports over the past three years, whereupon an additional duty may be reintroduced. This safeguard mechanism is designed to take account of excessive monetary fluctuations or major surges in imports. There are also specific exceptions for rice imports into Japan and South Korea.

Some of the calculations of tariffs to be bound, tariff equivalents (dirty tariffication) and access levels were fairly subjective and based on political trade-offs. The high level of many resulting tariff equivalents will certainly inhibit a major trade improvement. One cannot anticipate radical changes, though some of the minimum access provisions will lead to increased trade openings. But an important principle has been established in that non-tariff barriers of every hue have now been eliminated. The resulting tariffs and tariff equivalents are bound and domestic markets are firmly linked to world prices through them.

Export Subsidies[13]

On a 1986–90 base, direct export subsidy spending must be reduced, product group by product group, by 36 per cent and subsidised export volumes by 21 per cent over six years (1995–2001), 24 and 14 for developing countries over ten years and no reduction for the least developed. These commitments do not include unsubsidised exports, food aid and (with regard to volumes) processed products, but should involve, within limits, equal annual instalments.

Other Measures

Agreements were also drawn up that essentially took care of some bilateral US–EU concerns. The first related to a problem that had arisen during the Kennedy Round. At the time the EU was not a big importer of non-grain animal feed and it made a concession of zero per cent duty on this item. However, it later became a very important import item and was perceived in the EU as undermining the market for home-grown oilseed and grain for feed. The EU wanted to reintroduce a tariff in order to increase demand for these items in the framework of the CAP. The United States, as the main exporter of these products to the EU, was naturally very resistant to the idea. The result was a compromise to the effect that if imports of such products increase to the point that CAP reforms are threatened (by undermining internal production and the political acceptability of adjustment), the EU and the United States will seek a solution.

The agreement also contains a compromise solution of the long-standing dispute concerning oilseeds. In this connection the United States successfully challenged before a WTO panel EU's subsidies in the oilseeds sector, which had been designed to offset the zero duty concession made in this sector during the Kennedy Round. The agreement provides for a 10 per cent per annum reduction in acreage and the opening of a tariff quota for imports into Portugal.

Finally, the agreement contains a so-called 'peace clause' as part of the overall agriculture agreement. In accordance with this clause, internal support measures and export subsidies are exempted from claims under Article XVI of the WTO on export subsidies, though countervailing duties may be imposed in the event of injury. In effect this suspends most action under the WTO rules. Allowing such actions would undermine the delicate balance established in the agreement on how to deal with subsidies. What it means is that the WTO will try to deal with subsidies in a pragmatic manner in the foreseeable future. The best hope for subsidy reduction lies more in the exchange of concessions that has characterised this agreement than in any reliance on rules.

Sanitary and Phytosanitary Measures

Another important element of the agricultural package is the agreement on sanitary and phytosanitary measures. In the past these measures have created very substantial barriers to trade in the agricultural sector. The presence of diseases such as foot and mouth and other animal diseases in certain countries for example, in the EU has meant that exports of these products to countries such as the United States and Australia have virtually been forbidden. This accounts for the very low export level of some of these products to the US market, even at the processed foods end of the market. In countries such as Australia, for example, the insistence on quarantine measures has created a very substantial barrier to the export of live animals to that market. Another related example is the question of standards for dairy products. In the United States, for example, milk for cheese has to be pasteurised, whereas in Europe non-pasteurized milk may be used to produce certain cheeses.

It is often felt that these sanitary measures are excessive and create unnecessary obstacles to trade. The quarantine system in Australia is not strictly necessary if the animals have been vaccinated at some point in their lives. The risk of the spreading of the disease through so-called 'carriers' is often exaggerated. There has also been a strong tendency to have requirements for the slaughter of animals which apply a double standard, a higher standard for imports than domestic products.

Whatever the merits of the arguments on both sides of this rather difficult scientific and veterinary issue, the agreement seems to represent a valuable compromise. While recognising the right of governments to take such sanitary and phytosanitary measures as are necessary, the agreement nonetheless requires that they should not create unjustifiable barriers to trade. The meaning of this has been refined to ensure that standards are based on scientific principles and evidence, and take account of the effect on trade. However countries are allowed to take provisional measures when there is uncertainty about the evidence. The arguments relating to mad cow disease in the UK are a neat illustration of the two sides of this provision. The UK argues that there is insufficient scientific evidence to ban its beef exports; the rest of the EU considers there is sufficient uncertainty to justify restrictions, pending clarification. The agreement emphasises the need to harmonise such measures on as wide a basis as possible, and to seek compromises that will enable all trading partners to live with the procedures and criteria established for the assessment of risk and the appropriate levels of protection.

More importantly it is expected that the members of WTO will accept the sanitary measures of others as equivalent to theirs, if it is demonstrated that its measures achieve an equivalent level of health protection. This will not of course solve all the problems, but it has created a mechanism and a set of guidelines to resolve some of them.

It goes part of the way towards what the EU calls the doctrine of Cassis de Dijon. According to that doctrine, measures that are accepted by one EU member state must be accepted by the others unless a receiving country can demonstrate that it needs to maintain a different set of measures to protect the health of its population. This doctrine is based on the notion that all EU members have reached a similar level of health protection and that the products emanating from one member country should therefore be acceptable to the other members.

This principle has not of course been accepted in the more universal context of the WTO, where the criterion of 'equivalent level of development' clearly doesn't apply to everyone. However the principle established in the WTO is now clear, and this will allow those who have achieved an equivalent level of protection to argue that their measures should be accepted as sufficient.

CONCLUSION

One can see from the above that while the United States and its allies managed to achieve a basic structure for the reform of world agriculture that corresponded more to their idea of how this should be done, they nonetheless had to lower their sights considerably with regard to the reduction of subsidies.

The ambition of the United States at the beginning of the negotiation, was to go for total elimination of subsidies over a ten-year period, starting from 1989. However, the most it could achieve was a 36 per cent reduction in the case of export subsidies and tariffs and only 20 per cent in the case of domestic subsidies, and that over a period of six years from 1995. In addition the creation of the 'blue box' category of subsidies will cause uncertainty as to whether the overall amounts of production-related subsidy will be effectively cut back. The outcome on market access was also fairly murky given the methods of calculation used and the frequently high tariff equivalents that were adopted, though it has resulted in some degree of market opening.[14]

The results therefore were mixed, but probably the best possible deal was struck. In any case it is not at all certain that the United States would have been able to eliminate subsidies over a ten-year period. What was achieved was a very firm blueprint for reform of the world agricultural system, and future negotiations will no doubt bring about further reductions in the amounts of subsidy, and further adjustment and modernisation of the sector. Despite some of the uncertainties described, at least the rules now point fairly firmly in the right direction.

It is too early to calculate the effect the Uruguay Round will have in terms of reduction of support. But one can see from Table 21.1 above that there has been some stabilisation and reduction in the EU, Canada and Japan. While there was a substantial reduction in the case of the United States in 1995, a further substantial increase took place there in 1996.

Part VII

Services

22 Services

INTRODUCTION

From its inception, the GATT only covered trade in goods. It did not cover services, which comprise a very wide range of activities of increasing importance in modern economies. In the United States in 1994 for example, the service sector accounted for 79 per cent of the workforce and 72 per cent of GDP.[1] It also accounted for 20 per cent of exports and a balance of payments surplus of $57.5 billion (compare this with the $176.7 billion deficit in trade in goods).[2] The figures for the EU are similar, the service sector accounting for 64 per cent of the total workforce (but with variations between member states) and 66 per cent of GDP.[3] (These figures do not include government services.) In the case of Japan it is 60 per cent of the workforce and 57 per cent of GDP.[4] In the OECD as a whole services account for 60 per cent of GDP, 72 per cent if government services are included.[5]

Figure 22.1 shows the situation for the main trading partners. It can be seen that the biggest exporter of all is the EU (43 per cent), followed by the United States (16 per cent) and Japan trailing quite far behind in third place (5 per cent). The rest of the world makes up the other 36 per cent.

Trade in services grew at least 56 per cent faster than trade in goods in the period 1980–92. Globally, services now account for 25 per cent of all trade (over 40 per cent if profits, dividends and interest are included), amounting to $2160 billion in 1994. This share of world trade has increased continuously since the early 1980s from a level of about 10 per cent, and grew at least 56 per cent faster than trade in goods between 1990 and 1992.[6] What is also interesting to note is that 40–50 per cent of services are traded, and that wages tend to be higher in traded services than in the manufacturing export sector.[7]

Some of these figures contradict the commonly held view that the service sector is not very productive and that it pays poorly. This is clearly not always the case and exported services tend to be among the most productive in the economy, as borne out by the wage statistics. It is also a rapidly growing sector. While the

	1982	1987	1992	1992 (%)
EU	167 350	268 230	429 120	43
USA	48 750	83 160	162 250	16
Japan	20 430	27 660	49 560	5
Rest of world	168 470	193 500	359 070	36
World total	405 000	573 000	1 000 000	100

Figure 22.1   Service exports, 1982–92 (US$ million)[8]

manufacturing base in most industrialised countries has remained relatively stable or is declining slowly, other sectors of the economy such as agriculture are taking up an increasingly small share of the labour pool and services are the main growth area.

The developed countries were therefore very keen to have the service sector included in the Uruguay Round negotiations. The industrial sector is fraught with difficulties and has problems adjusting to changing circumstances. Some of the developed countries are running almost permanent structural deficits in trade in goods. On the other hand developed countries clearly dominate the service sector, though how long this will last is anybody's guess as the growth rate of service exports is higher in developing countries. It was therefore an important, indeed an essential element in the package from the point of view of the developed countries.

The developing countries, however, were extremely reluctant to include services in the Uruguay Round. In many cases they considered that their service industries were either in a stage of infancy or non-existent and they felt a strong need to continue protecting them. One should not exaggerate this point however. Many of the developed countries have large deficits in services and many developing countries run strong export surpluses in particular sectors. Developing countries are weaker in financial and business services (13 per cent of GDP as against 17 per cent of GDP in developed countries), but construction, distribution, tourism, transport and communications amount to about 29 per cent of GDP as in developed countries.[9]

The developing countries were also very reluctant to pay a price for substantial concessions in the industrial sector (textiles) and agriculture. They felt the rules in these sectors were an aberration in GATT terms, and in the case of textiles even an abuse of the GATT rules; they felt they should not have to pay for rectification of this situation. They were afraid that if they were given these concessions they would have to open up their service markets. They were also afraid that industrial concessions could be withdrawn if they subsequently failed to meet their obligations in the service sector.

For some of these reasons the negotiations on goods and agriculture on the one hand, and services on the other, were kept separate throughout. It was only in the closing stages that the two were pulled together under the one roof of the World Trade Organisation. This amalgamation of the two sides of the negotiation in the final agreement was more than academic, as failure to meet obligations in the service sector can now lead to retaliation in the goods sector (and *vice versa*).

The developed countries wished to extend the GATT principles directly to the whole of the service sector. This would require both developed and developing countries to exempt certain sectors that were not yet ripe for liberalisation. Exemptions would have tended to be more numerous for developing countries and they would be on the defensive trying to justify more frequent departures from these principles. It was more in their interest to sell access to individual sectors through negotiations than to have to justify exemptions from general principles.

THE URUGUAY ROUND AGREEMENT

This difference in approach between the developed and developing countries resulted in a compromise: one basic principle, namely MFN, is applied automatically and exemptions have to be made to avoid it (the so-called negative list approach). Principles such as national treatment and market access do not apply automatically and have to be negotiated (the positive list approach).

The difference is important in terms of emphasis and politics, and while one should not exaggerate its practical effect, it does have certain consequences. This stems from the fact that exemptions taken from MFN should in principle only last ten years. An MFN exemption means setting off on the slippery slope to full MFN obligation within a limited period of time. This is not true for the other obligations, and limitations placed on them, or failure to adhere to them, will not automatically be foreclosed by a requirement to adhere fully to the obligations after a certain period of time.

On the other hand, regardless of the technique used, whether negative or positive list, the Uruguay Round negotiations had to strike a balance in the obligations adhered to and concessions made. In most cases the developed countries finalised their list of concessions on the basis of a package of concessions made by other developed countries and some important developing country consumers. Each country evaluated whether the concessions made by others were adequate, if not optimal, and sometimes drew different conclusions. This clearly happened in the financial services sector, where the United States and the EU arrived at very different conclusions about the worth of the concessions made. The United States felt that the concessions were inadequate and that it was preferable to have no agreement at all.

The General Agreement on Trade in Services (GATS) also contains a series of broad definitions of the various forms of delivery of services and all measures that affect trade. MFN, national treatment and market access obligations are applied to them and the result is a sort of matrix or 'schedule'. Each party has indicated whether it has taken out exceptions to certain obligations in each sector, or it has entered a general exception or reserve of a horizontal nature, which applies to all sectors. A typical schedule is set out in Table 22.2 to illustrate how the system works.

In many cases the exceptions are so extensive that the agreements in certain sectors are not very satisfactory. Some sectors have been included in the framework agreement but important partners have not joined them because there was no possibility of agreement. In other sectors certain important parties have signed on (for example the United States in financial services, the EU in the audiovisual sector), but have taken broad exemptions on the grounds that there was insufficient reciprocity and that this substantially devalued the agreement.

But the important thing to remember is that there will be further rounds of negotiations and the content of the agreement will eventually be filled in by a progressive increase in obligations undertaken. The exercise is one of gradual liberalisation. The ultimate goal of full liberalisation is a long way down the road, but at least a mechanism now exists to ensure that there is continuous negotiation on these issues. With an agreement, no matter how skeletal in certain

Table 22.2   Illustrative schedule of specific GATT commitments

	Mode of supply	Conditions for market access	Conditions for national treatment
Horizontal commitments (applicable to all sectors in the schedule)*	1. Cross-border supply	None	None
	2. Consumption abroad	None	None
	3. Commercial presence	Incorporation required	Restrictions on purchase of real estate
	4. Presence of natural persons or individuals (non-corporate)	Bound only for intracorporate transferees	Unbound except as indicated under market access
Sectoral commitments (limitations applicable to specific service activities)	1. Cross-border supply	None	None
	2. Consumption abroad	None	None
	3. Commercial presence	None	None
	4. Presence of natural persons	Unbound, except as provided in the horizontal section	Unbound, except as provided in the horizontal section

* Most schedules do not contain horizontal limitations applying to the cross-border supply of services and consumption abroad (modes 1 and 2).

Source: GATT (1994).[10]

sectors, there is a much better chance of putting pressure on recalcitrant partners through the WTO institutions than if there were no agreement at all. The peer pressure system works quite well within the existing framework and set of institutions, and the set of exemptions or limitations clearly indicate the possible obstacles to trade. On the other hand, sectors that have been left out entirely will require a substantial political effort to bring them into the system.

DEFINITIONS AND OBLIGATIONS[11]

Definitions

Before looking in detail at the elements of the agreement it is important to understand the various forms that trade in services can take. It can be cross-border trade where only the result of the service is exported. An example of this is an architect faxing a set of blueprints to a client in another country. A stockbroker in New York advising a client in Hong Kong is also involved in cross-border trade.

In many cases, however, trade in services requires some of the factors of production to move with the service and may require either a temporary or a permanent presence in the importing country. Examples of temporary presence are a construction firm taking its own workforce with it to a project site, and an accounting firm sending employees to audit the accounts of a foreign client. Banking and insurance typically require a permanent commercial presence in the foreign market, as do law firms. A permanent presence will usually require a movement of capital and investment. Finally, services may be consumed abroad in the country of export. A clear example of this is tourism.

The GATS agreement contains a definition of trade in services that is broad enough to cover all the cases referred to above. This definition did not in itself create obligations, but set a series of wide parameters within which these negotiations could take place. A more restrictive definition could, for example, have left out cross-border trade, and would have seriously restricted the scope of the agreement. The definition also covers all types of measure taken at all governmental levels or by bodies to whom public authority has been delegated.

Obligations

The sale of goods abroad does not usually require sales personnel to be sent with the goods or a commercial presence in the importing country. Sometimes these are useful in terms of ensuring a sale, but normally they are not essential and goods can be sold through established local channels. In the case of services however, the personal skills of the service provider are usually at the heart of the contract: the very word 'service' implies a personal service. Many services cannot be rendered without the personnel in question moving to the export market, or the consumer of the service travelling to where the service is available. In both cases there is a need to allow the factors of production (or the consumer) to cross the border.

Unlike trade in goods therefore, borders have to be open to migration and/or investment and the establishment of a permanent commercial presence. As a consequence a series of problems may be encountered that do not exist with traded goods, such as laws on migration, the right to invest and the right to establish a commercial presence or do business. These are not traditionally considered as trade issues, but relate to control and regulation of the economy in general. Some of these regulations can create obstacles to trade that will exclude foreign suppliers. Others may not prevent market penetration, but nonetheless discriminate in favour of domestic suppliers.

The obligations in the agreement therefore go beyond the obligations required for goods and give a more profound meaning to such obligations as MFN and national treatment.

Most favoured nation treatment[12]

The first important obligation is most favoured nation treatment (MFN) which has been described earlier in this book. It means that where bilateral or plurilateral agreements exist, giving rights to other members of WTO, then similar rights shall be given to all members of WTO. This means different things in different sectors to different parties. To take an example, if a country has given certain banking rights to another, then those rights should be extended to all other members of WTO or the GATT.

Parties are allowed certain MFN exemptions upon joining the GATS agreement. In principle these exemptions only last ten years and are subject to five-yearly reviews. If exemptions are requested after joining, the consent of 75 per cent of the signatories is required, which is unlikely to happen. The only exception was the financial services agreement where 75 per cent consent was not required as the initial agreement was temporary.

Where such bilateral or plurilateral agreements are extensive (as they tend to be among developed countries) exemptions to the MFN obligation have been made. There are two basic reasons for this. First the MFN obligation is applied automatically, unless exemptions are made. Hence many countries have either exempted certain sectors that are not yet ready for full multilateral liberalisation, or exempted particular activities within certain sensitive sectors.

Many developed countries have made extensive agreements with others, which if subjected to the full force of MFN would oblige them to give away wide-ranging rights to third parties without receiving much in return. Mainly for this reason, while the United States signed the financial services agreement it took a full exemption for its MFN obligation because it felt it was not receiving sufficient reciprocity.

By the same logic, free trade areas or customs unions such as the EU, NAFTA and so on are not covered by the MFN clause. In this case, however, there is a formal exemption. In many cases the agreements reached among the members of these arrangements are tantamount to complete liberalisation (especially in the EU). To hand these advantages to others on a plate, solely by virtue of the MFN provision and without much reciprocity, would be too much to expect. While developing countries too have taken extensive MFN obligations, they have also taken extensive exemptions to those obligations, when they have felt that a particular industry was still weak and unable to compete. It should be recalled however that these latter exemptions only last for ten years.

In some cases parties to the agreement have taken a full MFN exemption for a whole sector (for example the United States in the financial services field). This is effectively a statement that the parties in question do not intend to open their markets without a substantial improvement in the offers of other parties. The financial sector was a special case as the agreement expired at the end of 1997. Its obligations were extended at that point as a full agreement was finally reached in 1997.

Market access[13]

The MFN obligation ensures that a supplier is treated at least as well as other foreign suppliers. But this does not guarantee access to markets where no such advantages are given to foreign suppliers. Most economies have regulations of one sort or another to restrict entry by domestic or foreign suppliers, particularly the latter.

The nature of services is such that the usual border control instruments such as tariffs are inapplicable. Even if one tried, the range of services is such that it would be impossible to list them and devise a tariff for them, and in any case unless they were incorporated in the supply of a product, they could not be monitored. Controls on imports of services take different forms and tend to relate to controls on the exercise of a particular profession or service or on the inputs or factors of production, for example capital and labour. These controls are also frequently of a regulatory nature and are there to regulate domestic firms as well.

One of the main issues that had to be dealt with was the right of establishment, whether through a branch or subsidiary or some controlling interest of a domestic firm. This is the main point of entry into a market for many services. Sometimes these are controlled in order to protect the local service industry and restrictions are placed on foreign ownership or establishment. Another way of ensuring this type of protection is to reduce the types of operation or activity that can be engaged in by foreign firms, or the degree of ownership allowed to foreigners.

In some cases the argument is based on 'economic need', for example if too many banks are allowed to operate, the market will not be able to bear it, and there will be severe competition, bankruptcies and so on, leading to a loss of confidence in the banking system. In professions such as medicine and law, the argument is usually along the lines that without strict controls, standards will drop and consumers will suffer. These latter arguments are sometimes well founded, but in many cases they are just a smokescreen for maintaining a monopolistic or oligopolistic situation.

The obligation does not apply automatically, and balanced schedules of concessions have to be negotiated. However once a concession is included in a schedule it becomes a concession to all. The Uruguay Round was therefore a negotiation to achieve a rough balance of equivalent concessions on market access.

National treatment[14]

After market access the most important obligation is national treatment. When a government makes certain rules for its own industry, it is required to extend equivalent (though not necessarily the same) treatment to suppliers from other signatories. A firm that has gained access and established a commercial presence will be unrestricted in its investment, in the range of activities it can undertake and so on. But it may still be disfavoured compared with a local firm by being obliged to pay higher taxes, or by being subjected to higher capital requirements. Hence even though it has full market access it is faced with discriminatory treatment. Discrimination against non-nationals can take many forms; the test here is whether a foreign company, once it has access to the market, is able to compete on a level playing field with local firms. As in the case of market access, the obligation doesn't apply automatically and balanced schedules of concessions have to be negotiated.

Formulation and the administration of domestic regulations[15]

As it is recognised that one of the main ways of controlling access to the market is through regulation, GATT contains obligations on transparency. It requires that the regulations be administered in a reasonable, open, objective and impartial manner, and there must be a right to challenge decisions before a tribunal.

Apart from the way they are administered, regulations must also be drafted in a way that is reasonable and creates the least obstacles. They should be based on objective and transparent criteria, should not have more requirements than necessary to ensure the quality of the service, and should not in themselves be an obstacle. If a government can show that it is adhering to international standards in this regard, it will be deemed to have discharged these obligations.

The agreement also addresses the issue of partial or full harmonisation of regulatory regimes in order to facilitate trade and avoid the problems of protectionism that such regimes can give rise to. If a bank, by virtue of its establishment and regulation in accordance with commonly accepted standards in country X, were to be allowed to do business in country Y without the problem of reapplying for a licence and the hassle and cost of operating under several different systems with different capital requirements, standards of care, supervisory regimes and so on then that would be a big step forward for trade.

The most radical solution would have been to allow for competition among regulating regimes, with each country recognising the regulatory regime of the other and accepting trade with firms subject to regulation by the other. But a country with a strong regulatory system is not likely to accept that banks from a country with fairly light supervision should be allowed to set up business in its market. Another solution would be full harmonisation of regulatory regimes, but this would be a very lengthy and complicated process.

The ideal solution for this type of problem would be a combination of the two, with mutual recognition of the regulatory regimes of the parties to the agreement, and harmonisation of minimum prudential standards. Under such a system a company wishing to export would only be subject to one regulatory regime, that of its home country. This would reduce costs and facilitate trade. This system has been adopted in the European Union in the area of banking and finance.

The solution that has been accepted as the basic regime in the services agreement allows for the maintenance of different regulatory systems and requires compliance with the system in operation in the market, but it tries to ensure that such systems are open and non-discriminatory. In other words a foreign firm should be entitled to the same treatment as a domestic firm. Harmonisation even of minimum core standards or recognition of other parties' regulatory regimes is left to the future and to the parties themselves. Moreover, it is also found that harmonisation and mutual recognition are difficult to achieve on a multilateral basis. It was felt that bilateral or plurilateral regimes were probably the best way forward at this stage and an exception to MFN and national treatment was thus allowed to encourage the development of such 'partial' agreements.

At the same time, such arrangements must be transparent and try to conform to the rules and standards of international bodies, and associations operating in the field. They are also expected to afford adequate opportunity to others to negotiate their accession to the schemes they have devised or offer comparable ones.

FACTORS OF PRODUCTION

Movement of Personnel[16]

The other difficult issue that had to be dealt with concerned the movement of personnel. The temporary movement of personnel is linked to all types of service activity, although the number of people involved can vary substantially from sector to sector. For example banking services can be provided by locally employed staff, and very often the establishment of a local banking subsidiary requires relatively few staff from the head office.

However construction contracts very often involve the movement of a large number of staff and workers of all sorts. For this reason, and because the construction industry is a key factor in national employment statistics, the tendency has been to keep the number of foreign workers to a minimum. Naturally the developing countries feel that they have a major advantage in the construction business as their workers are lower paid, and during the negotiations they pushed very hard for the temporary migration of such workers to be allowed.

The Uruguay Round, however, did not manage to arrive at more than a gesture in this regard as at that stage the developed countries felt they could not make major concessions in this area. This position was underlined by the economic recession of recent years, and the growing pressure to control emigration to the wealthier countries.

A special annex on the topic laid the ground for further negotiations. These negotiations were to relate to entry and temporary (not permanent) stay and the rules were not to be applied in such a manner as to frustrate or undermine the trade concessions made. But the language of the annex also allowed for certain controls relating to the 'orderly movement' of persons. Taken literally this could prevent any such immigration; most temporary visas do not allow the holder to take a job, and taking a job could be considered as infringing the principle of 'orderly movement' because it disrupts the local labour market.

In the ensuing negotiations, which ended in December 1995,[17] most members made concessions on 'intracorporate transferees', whereby firms may transfer key personnel that are vital to the operation of a new business they have started. Such concessions are frequently hedged about with conditions relating to number of staff, duration of stay, economic need and so on. To take the example discussed above, this provision will be interpreted as allowing a limited number of cadres to be imported; the wholesale importation of, for example, construction workers is unlikely unless there is a shortage of labour.

Somewhat fewer parties have made a firm commitment to allow individuals to operate at length outside the corporate context (called 'natural persons' in the agreement). However, permitting a short stay of up to 90 days for business visitors or those arranging to establish a firm was now fairly extensively accepted by parties to the Round. Further negotiations will be required to improve the openings made on this score.

Movement of Capital and Investment[18]

A second important issue relating to factors of production is the movement of capital. The GATS agreement places no limit on foreign direct investment, but some countries have indicated that, just as with immigration, the existing laws should apply, for example the Canadian FIRA, which imposes conditions or restrictions on investment.

A provision of the agreement requires members to allow 'international transfers and payments for current transactions related to specific commitments'. This includes payment in foreign exchange. The only exception is where restrictions are imposed for balance of payments purposes. It is clear that if this provision had not been included the whole purpose of service provision, that is, to earn money, would have been frustrated. Trade in services is unlikely to develop if payment cannot be forwarded to the home country.

While the IMF defines current transactions as including the repatriation of profits, it is not clear if it covers earnings, dividends and operating expenditure. As for capital transfers, these are only covered in the case of cross-border supply of services and supply through commercial presence. There is no such provision for individuals supplying a service in a foreign market or for someone going abroad to consume a service. The repatriation of capital is not covered due to developing countries' concern about capital flight.

GENERAL EXCEPTIONS

Subsidies[19]

The subsidies agreement does not apply to services as such and further negotiations will be required to produce specific rules on this subject. However the national treatment provision does apply, and several parties have excluded subsidies from their national treatment schedules as they are already subsidising their domestic industry. They clearly do not want to subsidise both their own and other parties' service industries which may not even be operating with any frequency in their markets and creating little domestic employment.

Safeguard Measures[20]

A provision will have to be developed for such measures as they may be required to prevent a flood of imports from threatening the survival of an industry. The normal safeguard clause is designed for goods, and will not always be appropriate in the case of services. If a country wishes to safeguard its financial sector for example, should it go as far as to withdraw the licences of foreign banks established on its territory or drastically curtail their activities? Or would it be sufficient to prevent further liberalisation of the financial sector in the country in question? Would this not be too little too late? Just to pose the questions gives an indication of the difficulties.

General Security and Balance of Payments Exceptions[21]

These provisions exist in the normal GATT and allow protectionist measures to be taken to safeguard plant, animal and human life, to counter the use of prison labour, slavery and so on, and for security purposes. It also allows for the protection of public morals. This provision also exists in the GATS agreement and has been refined to include certain other matters, such as fraud, deception, default, privacy and confidentiality. It also includes the maintenance of public order.

One can see in this clause more modern concerns such as the need to prevent fraud in the financial sector, where small investors can be particularly vulnerable. One can also see the beginnings of control of the less desirable aspects of the Internet, for example pornography and incitement to violence or hatred.

As for goods, the agreement also contains the traditional clause allowing measures to be taken to protect the balance of payments.

Taxation[22]

An obligation such as national treatment is not exactly suited to direct taxation provisions, where the field is littered with double taxation agreements and a patchwork of arrangements for mutual assistance and conflicting doctrines on how to levy taxes. This obligation is therefore exempted to ensure effective and equitable taxation. There is a list of other exempted measures, and exemptions from MFN are allowed for double taxation agreements. Indirect taxes are still covered by the national treatment provision unless a reservation is entered in the schedules.

Monopolies[23]

Monopolies are not forbidden by the GATT and foreign firms may be excluded from a market on this ground (as well as other potential domestic competitors). This may seem unfair to other states where no monopolies exist. But of course the problem can be solved by other states taking a reservation on access or by excluding the sector unless there is compensation elsewhere, for example in another sector. Sometimes this is not desirable, and the other parties have to accept this lack of access on the basis that their interests are being served by the package of concessions as a whole.

Some disciplines exist however. For example monopolists must refrain from abusing their position with regard to related services outside the scope of their monopoly, for example a telephone monopoly cannot refuse access to its lines for services falling outside the scope of its monopoly, for instance data transmission. Moreover if a monopoly is granted subsequently to the entry into force of GATS, compensation must be given to other parties for the reduction in market access that this causes.

Treatment of Developing Countries[24]

The agreement also contains certain provisions that are very favourable to the developing countries. These are drafted in broad terms and take account of the basic asymmetry that is deemed to exist between service sectors in developed and developing countries. It allows developing countries to attach conditions to their schedules of concessions, for example on transfer of technology, proportion of local staff to be employed and type of commercial presence, the idea being that they should be entitled to direct inward investment in a way that increases their development prospects. The exact interpretation of this clause remains to be established, but it comes close to allowing developing countries to impose certain conditions on FDI that could discourage rather than encourage development. While this certainly constitutes a tactical victory for the developing countries, it is not clear that it constitutes a victory for the world trading system, or indeed for their economies. It was however probably the price to be paid for a WTO agreement.

At the same time the developed countries are expected to encourage the development of the service sectors of the developing countries by improving access to their market. To take an example, tourism is a major revenue source for developing countries, but a large slice of this revenue goes to tour operators in the developed world. If the developing countries had better access to the reservation systems, some of this revenue would accrue to the developing countries as well.

Government Procurement[25]

Government procurement, which is the subject of a separate agreement based on balanced concessions between mostly developed countries, is not, by virtue of the MFN provision, extended to others who have made no similar concessions. To gain access to procurement others will have to join this agreement, which is based on 'conditional' MFN, that is, MFN is granted provided sufficient concessions are offered in return. The government procurement agreement covers most services other than telecommunications. The issue is to be reviewed in order to bring this agreement in line with GATS' full MFN, market access, and national treatment obligations.

SECTOR BY SECTOR ANALYSIS

The agreement contains a list of eleven sectors which, while not exhaustive, is generally considered to cover services known at present. Each sector is subdivided into numerous subsectors. The following sections describe the main, but not all, sectors covered by the GATS agreement. In several cases special rules have been drawn up to supplement the general framework of rules, or to derogate from them.

Telecommunications

There is a separate annex[26] to the GATS framework agreement governing this sector, which has some peculiar features. The annex clarifies the general provisions of the framework agreement while ensuring access to and use of telecom services. It also reflects the current state of play in the world telecommunications market, which is changing from a highly regulated and monopolistic one to one that is much less heavily regulated and increasingly privatised and demonopolised.

The move towards deregulation occurred initially in the equipment sector and that for new technologies that are attached to telephone lines (fax machines and so on) and went on to include so-called value added services such as data and image transmission. The old monopolies – either because they hadn't foreseen these developments in communications, because they were too slow or because the winds of change brought pressure for deregulation – found their monopolies were not extended. These monopolies have tended to fall back on their core business, mainly telephony, video conferencing, image transmission and so on.

At the same time even newer technologies and services such as mobile phones, Internet telephony, international resale and call-back, emerged to challenge even their core business. The desire to integrate all the various communications media (phones, TVs, computers) has meant that a compromise has to be struck between the suppliers of phone links, TV channels and on-line computer suppliers, each of which wants a slice of the other's business. In the United States this recently led to the ending of partition between these market segments, and of course to the end of monopolisation of international telephone business. In many countries competition already existed in the domestic telephone business, but monopolisation of the lucrative international sector has tended to be the last to fall – trade liberalisation in the context of WTO has brought about demonopolisation even in this segment.

This process, which has been described only very schematically here,[27] has of course advanced at different speeds in different countries, and very different degrees of liberalisation exist throughout the world. The United States has clearly taken the lead in this process, but highly deregulated markets exist in Canada, the UK and Hong Kong. Other countries are less advanced but are moving very rapidly in this direction. The EU has made a major effort to bring about full liberalisation and bring down costs, and 1998 should be a banner year in this regard as a series of legislative measures are to be implemented. While some developing countries, for example Chile, have been in the forefront in liberalisation, others have lagged behind.

The cost of oral communications has fallen by a factor of ten and that for data by a factor of 1000 in the last two decades, but frequently these cost advantages have not been passed on to the consumer. Some international calls enjoy a markup of 500 per cent; in the EU it was estimated that an Italian firm would pay 24 per cent less for its telephone bill if it enjoyed UK rates and 43 per cent less if it could benefit from US rates. Overall global gains in this sector could amount to $1 trillion.

While liberalisation is an extraordinarily worthwhile goal, the different speed of development in various markets has meant that the negotiators of the agreement have had to try and marry the interests of liberalised countries with the interests of those that are not. This has been compounded by the North–South divide, as many developing countries are still relying on old fashioned monopolies. It is sometimes difficult to persuade them to move towards deregulation or privatisation and at the same time open their markets to outside competition.

Some developing countries use their monopoly profits on international calling to meet general budget expenses. In Egypt, for example, these profits are financing construction of the Cairo subway; while Mexico and other countries have privatised their telecommunications authorities they have tended to leave them as monopolies. This sort of thing happens when the government is afraid that without monopoly profits there will be no buyers for the antiquated system and privatisation will fail. (Without domestic competition, however, this does not produce the best results in terms of new services, lower costs and so on.) Yet others have both privatised and broken up the monopoly, but they are still reluctant to let outsiders in until these new domestic companies have established themselves (some have been smart however and allowed foreign investors to participate in, if not control, the new companies to ensure the necessary influx of know-how, capital and so on.)

Privatisation is perceived as likely to lead to severe job losses, but the experience so far tends to indicate that while profits and jobs fall initially, they are soon compensated for (usually within 4 to 5 years) by the growth of opportunities in other services, investment in new facilities and so on. The result is usually higher growth in this sector than any other sector of the economy, especially when privatisation is combined with competition (demonopolisation). Nor are there real grounds for fearing that a national monopoly will lose out completely; in general monopolies hang on to 70–80 per cent of the market, if not more, in the face of domestic competition.

There are no clear examples of what happens when outside competition is allowed from the word go in developing economies, but there are many successful examples of outside participation being allowed in newly created domestic firms. It is a small step from that to allowing outside competition, given that such firms are often foreign competitors in all but name.

It is clear that, given the economic advantage of liberalisation, it was important for the Uruguay Round to achieve the widest possible market opening on an MFN and national treatment basis. In the case of developing countries liberalisation should aim at that too, though some interim or transitional arrangements may be necessary, allowing, at a minimum, for participation with full access after a period of four or five years. After all, even some of the most developed countries will benefit from some transitional arrangements.

It was also obvious that the agreement would have to deal with a situation where monopolies or dominant firms existed. The annex to the GATS agreement therefore reflects the hybrid state of the market and the existence of monopolies. It also reflects the fact the WTO does not prohibit monopolies. For example countries do not have to permit the construction of networks (in other words the public or monopoly supplier's network might be preserved as the main one), or allow other firms to supply telecom services. But it does require that a public or monopoly supplier to follow certain rules, such as transparency, that it does not indulge in anticompetitive behaviour, and allow access to and use by others of its network for the supply of demonopolised services. It must allow the free movement of information another supplier may want to send over that network, with the exception of radio or TV broadcasting. It also requires that even where a monopoly doesn't exist a firm may still be in possession of the main infrastructure and network which it may not be possible, at least immediately, to duplicate. It therefore provides for access to these networks and transparency in their administration.

In the later stages of the negotiation an additional set of regulatory principles was established to try to spell out in more detail what access should be afforded. These principles were considered necessary if liberalisation was to become a reality. They are aimed at anticompetitive practices or abuses that may occur when a firm has a dominant position or some degree of control, especially as owner of the main network or critical parts of it. They try to ensure proper access to the network, giving right of access to dominant suppliers, networks and by improved transparency such as giving timely disclosure of route orientation, the interconnection architecture and so on. They also deal with more general regulatory issues such as transparency and public availability of licensing criteria, cross-subsidisation, universal service, use of scarce resources (for example frequencies) and the establishment of an independent regulatory agency (to ensure that competition is really upheld).

The negotiations continued beyond the end of the Uruguay Round and concluded on 30 April 1996 on an interim basis. Further negotiations took place up to Spring 1997.

At the end of April 1996, some 44 offers were on the table, with one very notable absence: the United States. Of those 44 offers some 14 countries gave complete access to all services and facilities with full access by another 15 at various dates leading up to 2003. Three or four of these had exceptions for satellites and two for resale. This group of 29 included nearly all developed countries and five developing ones (Singapore, Argentina, Mexico, Venezuela and Peru).

Other developing countries placed a series of restrictions on their offers, with some adopting a very restrictive position and others a slightly more open approach. Most excluded international or satellite voice and other services, and most excluded local voice services also. They were more open however on value-added network services (VANS), and their offers could be considered adequate in this limited respect.

The situation with regard to investment was also less than ideal, with only 20 countries offering open investment conditions, of which five were developing countries. Here the blame can be spread a bit more widely as several developed countries imposed investment restrictions, keeping foreign participation to below a certain percentage or to certain sectors, for example broadcasting.

The draft principles, though introduced at a relatively late stage, were a brighter spot in the negotiations with 29 full adherents and about five partial adherents. However, of the developing countries only Peru committed itself fully, and approximately five other Latin American countries made a partial commitment. The developing countries in Asia were notable for their absence.

In addition to the weak offers of the developing countries, particularly those in Asia, the United States felt that some of the market access definitions should be expanded somewhat to make the commitments on sharing of frequencies, economic needs tests for licensing and so on more explicit, as well as to spell out the exact meaning of satellite services (some satellite providers have international status, for example Inmarsat, and it wasn't clear if they were covered).

The United States was also concerned about the accounting rate system. Under this system the charge on an international call is split. This means that a US supplier must provide the old monopoly rates to a country where a monopoly still exists, but has less and less money with which to pay this as the cost of its own international calls is dropping dramatically. The problem is aggravated by international resale and call-back systems.

This result was not very satisfactory and the United States felt that the offers put on the table, especially by Asian countries, were inadequate; a 'critical mass' of countries had not been achieved. The EU was more open and accepted the existing package as it included very substantial market access to the developed and some developing countries. It was better to have some agreement in place than none at all. Further negotiations led to an improvement and the United States was finally able to accept the outcome. The final package contained offers from 69 governments, some 48 of which accepted the regulatory principles, including many developing countries. The agreement covers all telecommunications services – whether (1) local, long distance or international, for public and non-public use, or (2) on a facilities basis or by resale – through all technological means (cable, wireless or satellite). Broadcasting is excluded however. These are the basic parameters and of course each schedule has to be studied to see what has actually been included by each government.

Nine MFN exemptions were taken, including an important one by the United States direct to home and direct broadcast satellite, transmission of television and digital audio services (DTH and DBS). The United States can therefore apply reciprocity in relation to those services. The EU and some other countries reserved the right to challenge this exemption, as it covers audiovisual and not telecom services and should not have been exempted in a telecoms agreement.

The accounting rate problem was not resolved and may be addressed during the next set of negotiations on services, due to start in 2000. According to a last minute understanding the dispute settlement provisions of the WTO will not be involved. For differential accounting rates, established within the framework of the International Telecommunications Union (ITU), the United States has indicated its intention to use certain benchmarks for payment, which constitutes a unilateral move on its part. It believes that those concerned will accept the lower benchmark payments if they wish to retain access to the US market. Many countries have reserved their right to challenge this measure if it leads to results that are incompatible with MFN.

The agreement will cover some 90 per cent of the world telecommunications market, worth some $660 billion. The key to US adherence was the more open position taken by the Asian Pacific countries. Ten of these (Japan, Australia, Indonesia, the Phillippines, Malaysia, Papua New Guinea, Brunei, Thailand, South Korea and Singapore) made substantially improved offers, which will ensure them full market opening by 1998. Brunei's and Thailand's markets won't be fully opened till 2020 and 2006 respectively, and the Indonesian market will be opened by 2005. Another six countries in the region, including Hong Kong and Pakistan, will only allow foreign participation in selected services. These countries were even less accommodating when it came to foreign ownership. Nine of them made offers with important qualifications. Japan, for example, will allow 100 per cent foreign ownership but will keep a 20 per cent cap on foreign ownership of its two dominant carriers. South Korea will keep a 49 per cent limit on foreign ownership.

Financial Services

The main agreement

The general negotiations proceeded on the basis of the existing GATS obligations, but two important exceptions were set out in the annex on financial services.

The GATS annex allows parties, known as 'members', to do things that are not in conformity with MFN, national treatment, or access in the interest of safety and supervision. This 'prudential carve out' was considered essential to enable authorities to ensure the safety of their domestic financial systems. They are also encouraged to recognise each other's prudential measures. Again these agreements do not have to be extended to others on an MFN basis but members are encouraged to allow others to negotiate access to their markets. The fact that prudential measures are not subject to the obligations of the agreement suggests that more difficult standards will be applied to firms from certain countries than to domestic firms, for example higher capital requirements. At the same time the agreement requires that this exception should not be used as a tool of protectionism, so it will require careful monitoring.

The financial activities of governments, government-owned and government-controlled entities (if not just commercial) and central banks, as well as activities that form part of statutory social security or public retirement plans, were not covered by the agreement.

Additional obligations

A special understanding on the financial services sector entitled 'Understanding on Commitments in Financial Services' was also agreed in the Uruguay Round.[28] The purpose of this is to provide a framework for liberalisation that will go beyond the obligations contained in the main agreement.

The understanding spells out in clearer terms what is meant by MFN, national treatment and market access for certain activities. It addresses the progressive elimination of monopolies, market access (including Glass–Steagall and McFadden Acts which reduce access to the US market for domestic as well as foreign banks), and imposes MFN and national treatment to financial services by public entities. Parties to this supplementary 'understanding' will also implement a standstill, in regard to unbound or existing non-conforming measures, that is, they will not extend them.

In the end only the OECD countries and some others accepted its obligations as between themselves. This is a 'top–down' approach establishing a broader commitment to cross sectoral liberalisation and avoids the numerous exemptions taken by others.

The results of the negotiations in 1994/95

The negotiations were completed in mid-1995, with great difficulty but the result was merely a temporary agreement that was due to expire at the end of 1997. It was temporary in the sense that offers made in mid-1995 could be modified in the light of the renewed negotiations that took place in 1997.

The main problem was that the United States did not consider that the offers put on the table by others were sufficient. It was particularly dissatisfied with the offers of some countries in Asia, for instance Malaysia, Indonesia, South Korea and India, and some in Latin America, including Brazil. It therefore took a full MFN exemption on this sector pending improvements. The EU, however, led others into the agreement available at the time. Fortunately Japan too was able to go along. The significance of all this was that at least the agreement was in place and it provided a basis for negotiating improvements.

The interim deal, which expired at the end of 1997,[29] consolidated existing access rights in the banking securities and insurance sectors of more than 90 countries. It also ensured that firms already established in these countries would receive non-discriminatory treatment. This was the bedrock of the agreement. In many countries it constituted no more than a standstill arrangement – that is, an agreement to freeze and maintain existing market access. The United

States also granted this minimum. It did not undertake any commitments for new market access, but only for national treatment of existing companies and access.

The agreement provided much less uniform access for new firms or competitors. The OECD countries, with the exception of the USA, generally offered substantial new access commitments. The EU has granted direct access to its market through the establishment of any form of commercial presence.

Japan, despite severe reservations about US withdrawal from the agreement, kept very few restrictions with regard to new market access and national treatment. It also confirmed its extension of MFN treatment for bilateral agreements it had with the United States. However, many of the problems in Japan relate to regulatory requirements which (while not discriminatory on their face) do create obstacles in practice.

The offers of the developing countries were more limited. Some Latin American countries made real concessions but the overall picture in Asia was not very satisfactory.

The EU none the less felt it was better to press ahead with the agreement as it could be improved later. The United States took a full MFN exemption in connection with new market access and the expansion of activities in all susbsectors, and was thus in a position to require reciprocity before it lifted this MFN exemption. It was not under any formal GATS obligation with regard to new access conditions or expansion of existing activities.

The OECD countries were prepared to live with this situation as the United States had obligations to them under various OECD codes on the liberalisation of capital movements and they wanted to avoid a collapse of the WTO Agreement. The United States also gave certain political undertakings to the EU and Japan that their suppliers would be granted substantially full access to the US market, on the basis of MFN and national treatment.

This account only provides a taste of the results of these negotiations, but at least the general trend of events can be gleaned from it. Individual schedules need to be examined on a case-by-case basis. What is clear is that the main obstacle to progress resided in the Asian region and among certain major players in the developing world. A successful outcome of the negotiations in 1996/7 depended on a major effort on the part of these participants.

The results of the negotiations in 1997

WTO Members agreed on 12 December 1997 to include financial services on a permanent and MFN (most-favoured nation) basis in the GATS. All major trading partners, including the USA, are now part of this agreement. Many of them have submitted significantly improved commitments as regards both market access and national treatment. The USA also showed more flexibility in what it was prepared to accept. In general terms there was a relaxation of ceilings on foreign ownership, an increase in the variety of commercial presence allowed, removal of higher capital requirements for foreign firms, and improved offers on cross-border supply. This constitutes a considerable opening of domestic banking, insurance, securities and other financial services on a non-discriminatory basis to foreign financial service suuppliers.

The overwhelming majority of the WTO members were ready to forgo the application of reciprocity measures; only very few countries have listed broad MFN exemptions for the purpose of reciprocity.

Generally improved commitments on market acces and national treatment were submitted by 70 countries, counting the EU as 15. In addition, 32 countries have maintained without changes their existing schedules of commitments, dating back either to the Uruguay Round or to the 1995 interim agreement. This is important progress not only in substance, but also as regards the total number of countries which have undertaken commitments in financial services (102 in comparison to 95 under the 1995 interim agreement).

The size of the negotiated package is substantial. The new agreement will guarantee substantially free market access and national treatment conditions for foreign financial institutions for an overwhelming portion of worldwide financial services trade, amounting to more than 95 per cent in all main sub-sectors. The volume of equity trading covered by liberalisation commitments of WTO partners in the securities sector represented US$ 14.8 trillion in 1996, or 96.3 per cent of total equity trading in WTO countries. Total banking assets in WTO countries offering a generally open banking market amounted to US$ 41.2 trillion in 1995 or 95.9 per cent of total banking assets of WTO countries. Total insurance premiums for which WTO commitments will offer open market access amounted to US$ 2.1 trillion in 1995 or 97.1 per cent of WTO countries total premiums.

The scheduling of additional commitments by Japan deserves

special attention. The substance of the bilateral measures concluded with the US on insurance in 1994 and 1996, as well as on other financial services in 1995 have been entirely reflected in the annex to Japan's GATS schedule and will thus become part of its WTO commitments. This provides an important, legally enforceable guarantee for the private sector that opening and deregulation of Japan's financial services sector will be continued. It can be considered as a first significant step to address barriers which are not purely related to market access and national treatment aspects, but which stem from the grey area of regulatory measures. The EC, as well as the USA, have both agreed to mirror the Japanese approach and to include a range of additional commitments in their schedules.

The various schedules and commitments will be consolidated in a document known as the Fifth Protocol. The Protocol will enter into force on 1 March 1999, provided there has been signature or ratification by the parties to the negotiation (at least by those considered economically significant). If this is not achieved, negotiations would probably have to resume. This is, however, unlikely to happen and one can expect a final and positive outcome in March 1999.

Construction Services

The EU and the United States hold something like 85 per cent of the world market for construction projects, 36 per cent and 49 per cent respectively. However transnational business accounts only for about 5 per cent of the EU's construction business, though this is still very substantial. The United States' main overseas market is the EU, followed by the Middle East, and the EU is strong in Africa, the Middle East and Asia. Other strong competitors for international business are South Korea and Japan.

The general rules of the GATS agreement were applied here and no special provisions were introduced. But it should be recognised that construction consists of several important strands. The fairly large-scale transfer of personnel is all important, especially at the level of cadres, consulting and design staff, and so on. The negotiation on movement of persons has probably been adequate to deal with this under the heading of intracorporate transfers, but the provision of business services (R&D, engineering consultancy, computer services, and so on) has met with a poor response in the developing countries and this may prove to be an obstacle. On the other hand countries such as South Korea would like to import their cheaper labour to carry out a construction contract abroad, but again this is not likely to happen under the rules negotiated.

The other important item is government procurement. Many large-scale construction projects are government ones. An agreement was reached during the Uruguay Round to open up this sensitive sector, whether the contracts tendered for were for goods or services, including construction. By and large only developed countries signed up for this – at least in part because it was based on reciprocity, that is, a reasonable price had to be paid to join – but three developing countries did sign.

This constitutes one of the few non-MFN agreements negotiated in the Uruguay Round and also one of the most difficult sectors to liberalise. Efforts will be made over the next few years to multilateralise this agreement, but whether it will be possible to do so without substantial offers by developing countries remains to be seen.

Audiovisual Services

This sector is of great importance to the United States as films are its second largest export. It holds some 40 per cent of the world market for films, TV programmes, videos and so on. It is also one of the largest suppliers of film and TV entertainment to the EU and has a very dominant position there, with up to 80 per cent of the films shown in cinemas and about 50 per cent of TV entertainment. The film distribution business is heavily dominated by a US export cartel and 12 US distributors; the remaining 20 per cent of the market is in the hands of 1000 distributors. Foreign penetration of the US market only amounts to 2 per cent.[30]

The United States was concerned that without a commitment in this sector, its share of future technologies and broadcasting media would be restricted to levels below those it currently had in traditional means of transmission. For the EU, complete liberalisation posed a major problem as it wanted to maintain certain exemptions to liberalisation, which would help preserve the local film industry in some of its member states.

This industry had suffered a severe decline in recent years. The problem had led to difficult discussions within the EU itself, where legislation had been sought to impose certain quotas for showing foreign films in cinemas and on TV. This had resulted in guidelines, but not hard and fast quotas, though some member states maintain the latter. Some EU member states, for instance France, as well as using quotas, levy an 11 per cent tax on box office sales. France produces 150 films per year, more per capita than the United States, but it does not export that well to the US market and to add insult to injury Hollywood frequently remakes its films in its own style. The situation was compounded by the fact that the EU is one of the fastest growing markets at 23 billion ECU in 1992. This amount is expected to double by the year 2000. Moreover the United States sold films worth some $3.6 billion to the EU while importing only $290 million's worth from it.

Other GATT members have serious problems in protecting their culture, so the issue is not confined to the EU. Canada is a good example.

The EU has responded to the problem by introducing a series of support programmes to help with the development of production and distribution. In the negotiations the EU sought an exemption that would give recognition to the special nature of audiovisual products and the importance of preserving indigenous culture. It failed to achieve this, but nonetheless joined the agreement and took an across-the-board MFN exemption. The fact that it joined the agreement meant that at the least the United States would not be able to take unilateral measures against it. The EU's MFN exemption will expire in 10 years at the latest and in the meantime there will be pressure to negotiate from the US side, which will start at the first review in 5 years time. In other words the EU has until 10 years to develop a more competitive industry.

For its part the United States went ahead with 11 other countries, no doubt feeling, as did the EU in the financial services sector, that some agreement was better than none. However it took out exemptions on foreign ownership of radio and TV transmission, and others took out MFN exemptions for coproduction agreements and some regional broadcasting, as these were generally subsidised and it was felt undesirable to be required to give these subsidies to non-domestic firms.

The United States and New Zealand offered production, distribution, exhibition, and broadcasting. Most non-EU European countries followed the EU line. Japan, Hong Kong, Israel, Korea, Nicaragua, Singapore and Thailand offered full commitments on production and distribution, but not exhibition and broadcasting. Some also included sound recording and projection services. Three other parties included either production (Mexico) or distribution

(India and Malaysia). The United States and New Zealand made commitments re new technologies for the transmission or tele-distribution of audiovisual services, but this issue has been more or less left until future negotiations, which are likely to start at the first review of the agreement in 5 years.

The development of technology has meant that there is a great multiplicity of offerings to the public, not just in the entertainment field but more generally over the internet, involving professional and other services, telecommunications and so on. Entertainment is only one aspect of this, but it is also one of the elements providing much of the revenue for the expansion of the system. The development of domestic production and distribution is perhaps the key to the development of the whole interactive system in the future and is of major significance for any economy.

Electronic Information and News Services

This is a major sector involving the provision of business data, in which both the United States and the EU have major advantages. There are few barriers, and much of the information is conveyed electronically and cannot be controlled. What is needed is better cooperation in the development of compatible infrastructure.

News agencies are also a forte of the United States, the EU and Japan. Most OECD countries made commitments on access, but the developing countries did not, and future negotiations should seek their cooperation.

Tourism

There are few if any restrictions nowadays on travelling abroad for holidays, nor on the amount of money that tourists can take with them (though restrictions still exist on the amount they can purchase and bring back duty free, and visa requirements persist). However, there are still quite important restrictions on the supply of services by travel agencies and booking systems, and of course many countries still operate investment restrictions that affect investment in their hotels, restaurants and so on. The Uruguay Round went some way towards resolving these issues, and in general the access conditions are now rather liberal.

Business and Professional Services

Business services (advertising, computer services, R&D, market research, management consultancy and so on.) are usually free of restrictions, though many developing countries maintain general restrictions on foreign investment and establishment that also affect business services.

Professional services are a much tougher nut to crack given the complexity of and extent to which the professions are regulated. Most of this is perfectly justified on the ground of consumer protection, or protection of the public interest, but some regulations are not, for example the nationality requirement for a doctor. The rules on intracorporate transfer of expert personnel go some way towards allowing the movement of professional staff. But of course they are generally confined to working for firms on an informal basis as an internal member of staff; for example lawyers often have to provide services through local law firms, or take on local partners in order to provide services direct to the public.

While a certain number of countries made commitments in this sector under the GATS agreement, in general the Uruguay Round merely scratched the surface, requiring only that professional regulations should not be more of a burden than necessary, as well as encouraging bilateral or plurilateral recognition and, eventually multilateral recognition of qualifications and the right to practise. A special group was set up to flesh out those basic rules in the GATS agreement, with priority being given to the accountancy profession.

The main problems can be divided roughly into three groups, as follows.[31]

The use of international standards

To take the accountancy profession, considerable advances have been made towards developing such standards. These standards facilitate the international provision of services insofar as all speak a common language. Progress towards developing these standards should be encouraged in the appropriate forums as the WTO is not really equipped for the task.

International standards are easier to apply in some fields than others. Legal systems are so diverse that it is unlikely that a common language can be developed, though some progress is being made in international arbitration and common principles, for example for contract disputes.

Recognition of qualifications

Most professions require high standards to protect the consumer. This means lengthy study, knowledge of a large number of subjects and so on. Requiring people to requalify from scratch in order to be able to provide a service would effectively disqualify most, and therefore many countries enter into agreements that provide for recognition of the qualifications issued in one another's countries.

The GATS agreement includes basic provisions to encourage the conclusion of such agreements, which can be based on an enumeration of basic requirements (professionals could then at least seek to fill any gaps in their qualifications), on the recognition of a list of foreign educational establishments, or a requirement that an examination be passed (as opposed to a further six years study to be allowed to sit such an exam) and so on. Supplementary tests are often required to equip professionals for local conditions. The GATS provisions seek transparency in the conclusion of such agreements and a fair opportunity for all WTO members to enter into them. Some services could be provided on a limited or temporary basis without recognition of qualifications.

These issues are probably easier to resolve for some professions, for example medicine and architecture, than others, for example the law, where a whole new legal system may need to be learned.

Regulatory requirements

The regulatory requirements are by far the most complex part of the equation as they are deeply ingrained in local history and traditions, but this should not obscure the fact that they can also constitute some of the most difficult and protectionist barriers to international trade.

Some should clearly be for the chop. Nationality requirements for practising medicine are hardly justifiable. Residence requirements come a close second, though they may have some justification to prevent fraud; on the other hand insistence on a residence requirement could effectively prevent certain cross-border activities altogether as double or triple residence is beyond the possibilities of most, unless a letter box address is sufficient.

What is more difficult to get a grip on is the way a profession organises itself. It may insist on membership of a professional organisation and possession of a licence to practice alone, in a partnership or in other corporate arrangement (the law again). Linked to this are the issues discussed above, of recognition of qualifications.

Moreover, some of the provisions requiring membership or partnership may be too burdensome for someone seeking to provide
cross-border services. The membership fees may be too high, there
may be no partnership available and so on.

The actual licence may also be too restrictive in the sense that a
foreign professional may be trained differently and not be required
to be skilled in the wide range of activities required of domestic
professionals. Is it fair to insist on qualifications for the wider range
of activities if foreign professionals intend to limit the scope of
their work? It is also true that many professional associations run
a sort of closed shop; their record on admitting new members will
have to be subjected to some scrutiny or rules to ensure more
openness.

Distribution Services

This sector is subject to the general GATS rules and there are few
overt obstacles. But one has to look at a series of more horizontal
issues to see if market access is possible, such as the local investment regime, urban planning and competition rules (in Japan the
political protection of the mom & pop store and a shortage of
land have meant that large retail stores have had difficulty gaining
access). Franchising is also important, especially for the EU, but
while commitments have been made with regard to this activity it
will need to be pursued further.

Maritime Transport[32]

Maritime transport can be divided into two fairly distinct categories: bulk transport (80 per cent of world trade) and liner traffic
(20 per cent of world trade). Oil, coal, chemicals and so on are
usually carried by special bulk cargo ships, such as oil tankers, and
ships are run according to need on a charter basis. Liner trade
consists of ships that travel at set times and in accordance with set
rates. Passenger trade is only a small fraction of this trade – most
of it is the transportation of goods, usually in containers.

The bulk trade is highly competitive, but cargo restrictions and
limitations have been attached to the liner trade. The GATS agreement has sought to eliminate these restrictions and institute a standstill where there are open markets. It has also sought to liberalise

auxiliary services such as cargo handling, storage, freight forwarding and so on.

While bulk cargo tends to travel between private specialised ports, liner traffic frequently operates through publicly owned ports with the possibility of discrimination or protectionism that might entail and might nullify existing or negotiated freedoms. While clearly it would be difficult if not impossible to achieve liberalisation through privatisation in this case, the GATS agreement at least says that these ports must be operated in a reasonable and non-discriminatory manner.

Unfortunately the negotiations on maritime transport were only able to produce results on non-discrimination in ports and the liberalisation of auxiliary services. Because of the forthcoming elections the United States was unable to move forward on this issue and failed even to put an offer on the table. Under the Jones Act, cabotage (that is, transport of cargo between US ports) is restricted to US-owned vessels. This is a very old restriction but one still supported by the maritime unions. Despite their dwindling power, they still had enough clout to prevent a deal being struck; moreover the owners and the United States government probably felt they would not receive sufficient benefits from the agreement, and in the end they didn't even try. These negotiations, which were due to end in June 1996, have been suspended until the next set of negotiations and GATS review in 1999.

Land Transport

Cross-border supply by land transport is generally of interest only to neighbouring countries and the general view was that this issue was best left to the bilateral or plurilateral agreements dealing specifically with it. MFN exemptions have generally been taken out for such agreements. There was also little demand for the opening up of railways as they are usually publicly owned monopolies.

However some negotiations in the maritime sector were aimed at allowing cross-border suppliers to have access to transport in their export market by ensuring that they could at the minimum rent or lease trucks, railway carriages and so on, on reasonable and non-discriminatory terms. There are fewer restrictions on a transporter buying into a transport company, other than rail, across the border. This was considered important to ensure that the multimodal transport companies of today can operate beyond the port of destination.

Air Transport Services[33]

The difficult and important question of air traffic rights was left out of the negotiations, including landing rights, routes, capacity, fares, and ownership and control of airlines. This major omission severely reduces the value of the agreement, but as in telecommunications, the process of deregulation and demonopolisation is slow. Many bilateral arrangements existed at the time and it was considered too difficult to introduce an MFN agreement at that stage. However, some progress is being made and every five years a review will be conducted; the hope and expectation is that with time progress can be made as a result of individual national plans for deregulation.

The negotiation did cover ancillary services such as repair and maintenance, selling and marketing (but not pricing), and computer reservations systems. Most developed countries made extensive commitments to liberalise these sectors. The EU, however, took out an MFN exemption on reservation systems as there were not enough detailed rules to ensure that commitments could in fact be complied with. This will have to be a matter for further negotiation.

THE RESULTS OF THE URUGUAY ROUND

The Uruguay Round eventually produced a very substantial agreement on services and something like 111 parties to GATT submitted schedules of concessions, running to some 2500 pages in all. Given the complexity of the agreement however, it is difficult to assess the exact proportion of the services sector that is covered. It is fair to say that the developed countries have covered most sectors, though with some major exceptions and/or reservations.

The result of the agreement is twofold: a framework has been established for a set of important obligations and principles. These fundamental obligations apply to a great number of sectors, but some of the major and economically most important sectors still have to be negotiated into the agreement and exemptions eliminated over time. Indeed many years of negotiation lie ahead to pad out the results of the Uruguay Round and ensure free trade in services. This is not surprising given the importance of the economic concerns involved, and full liberalisation cannot be achieved in a day. The round did however establish a very sound basis for trade and a series of important concessions and the promise of further negotiation (with deadlines) in areas of major importance.

Part V

Future Issues

23 The Future of the WTO

The WTO had a series of negotiations to complete after the end of the Uruguay Round. These included three service sectors where resolution of the outstanding problems had proved too intractable: financial services was subject to a temporary agreement due to expire at the end of 1997; the telecommunications negotiations were only concluded in February 1997; and the negotiations on maritime transport were abandoned and will be resumed in 1999.

The WTO was also expected to come up with solutions to outstanding horizontal issues in the services field such as the free movement of persons. This question was eventually resolved, though at a relatively low level of liberalisation. It was also supposed to come up with a model agreement on accountancy to improve liberalisation of the professions. The aim now is to complete this by the end of 1997.

The Committee on Trade and Environment was requested to work on solutions to the difficult issues in its field. A solution was not forthcoming by the WTO Singapore ministerial meeting in December 1996 and work on the issue will continue. At the same time the WTO has an agenda of work to be conducted in the following areas: agriculture, antidumping, civil aircraft, market access, regional trade agreements, rules of origin, services, technical barriers to trade, trade and environment, trade-related intellectual property rights and trade-related investment measures. These and other items of future work are sometimes described as negotiations, reviews, studies or examinations. A review or study may or may not lead to further negotiations. Some committees have been asked to come up with solutions to particular issues by a particular time, for example accountancy, while others have a looser mandate, for example trade and the environment.

The Singapore meeting also authorised the further examination of some new issues, such as investment and trade (already partially covered). A group was set up to examine the relationship between competition policies and the WTO, and another to develop an interim agreement to improve transparency and due process in procurement procedures. It may at some time also examine the possibility of a social clause in the WTO, it being understood that the main focus of discussion and responsibility for this should lie with the International Labour Organisation.

The results of the Uruguay Round have been dealt with in earlier chapters, with references to future activities and the built-in agenda where useful. The following chapters refer to some of the main issues with which the WTO has to come to grips in the coming years. One of these, trade and environment, is not new, and investment and trade has already been dealt with by the WTO, albeit in a partial manner. But the link between competition and trade and the difficult question of a social clause are new. They have been given special treatment in the chapters that follow as they represent some of the biggest intellectual challenges the WTO has to face in the years to come.

It should be borne in mind that the various strands of future WTO activity may be brought together in another negotiating round. This round could well start in the year 2000 and this has indeed been proposed informally.[1] The advantage of such an initiative is that it could permit real progress and negotiations (as opposed to just studies) on a wider range of issues than presently foreseen. By enlarging the package all parties are likely to find some advantage in it. The package may or may not include all the elements in the built-in agenda or new topics. The developing countries, for example, are unlikely to be happy about negotiations on a social clause.

But one can see from the disparate nature of the elements in the agenda, and the difficulty of making progress on individual parts of it, that the best home for many of these discussions is likely to be in a new round.

24 Trade and the Environment

INTRODUCTION

The debate on trade and the environment is partly based on fact and partly on assumptions that do not stand up to rigorous scrutiny. The perception held by the environment lobby is loosely as follows.

The rate of growth and development of the world's economy has put increasing pressure on the world's environment. This pressure has come from industrialisation and intensive agricultural production, which has involved degradation and pollution of our surroundings. Industrialisation and agricultural productivity have also increased pressure on raw materials.

This has been accompanied by a major increase in world trade, which has underpinned faster economic growth. The increase in trade has been perceived as enabling some firms to transfer their environmental problems elsewhere as the markets in some other countries are not as heavily regulated as their home market. Countries with lower environmental standards often allow them to despoil natural resources such as forests, to run polluting factories or dump waste in a manner forbidden at home. At the same time they can export the resulting products from these new manufacturing bases more cheaply than if they had been produced at home.

So while trade *per se* is clearly not the main cause of environmental degradation, in the eyes of some it has facilitated environmental damage. There is also an increasing focus on trade because, while national regulations can control abuses of the environment that take place nationally or locally, they cannot control events taking place in other countries that have spillover effects and global or regional consequences for the environment.

It is also obvious that failure to develop an international consensus on environmental standards will eventually result in global degradation that is so bad that major problems may arise. Tropical forests, for example, are the best and cheapest means we have to regulate and absorb the gases that create climate change. It is easy to understand the frustration of environmentalists who have to stand

257

by while authorities continue to allow the importation of tropical timber that has been cut down to feed the developed world's endless appetite for wood, paper napkins, disposable nappies, chopsticks and so on. And one can also understand their natural desire to halt the environmental degradation that is taking place in increasingly severe proportions throughout the globe.

There is therefore a good deal of pressure to utilise trade policy as a means of controlling environmental destruction outside national limits with regard to issues of increasing global concern. The instruments of trade policy could be very effective in controlling environmental degradation in other countries by preventing the importation of their products into important markets. Trade instruments could ensure that countries wishing to export adopt environmental standards that are similar to those in countries with tighter regulations or at least ensure some degree of environmental protection and sustainable development.

One may well ask why trade controls are considered such a bad thing and why have they not been used more frequently. Why does the WTO have the reputation of being somewhat hostile to the environment and the use of trade measures to protect it? Is the picture just described an accurate one, or is it flawed?

ECONOMIC CONSIDERATIONS

Growth and the Environment

It is obvious that the increase in economic growth and trade are creating problems for the environment. However it would be wrong to draw the conclusion from this that one should hold back growth or trade. In any case to do so would be unrealistic.

In most developing countries the low level of environmental protection is due to the low level of economic development. Indeed as a country's economic development proceeds it can better afford to protect its environment. There is a tendency to decry growth and trade as negative for the environment. While this may be true in the early stages of development, trade can play an important role in growth and in the long run it can lead to increased environmental protection as countries generate enough wealth and resources to achieve this.

Nor is it correct to assume the opposite, namely that more

environmental protection means less development, or at least a deceleration of it. Developing countries tend to argue that they are being required to slow their economic development by spending more than they can afford on the environment.

Sustainable Growth

In some respects this is still the choice facing societies, but insofar as development comes at an environmental price, more and more countries have come to the conclusion that growth and the environment must go hand in hand. There's not much point in growth that completely lays waste to the environment.

It is enough to think of the severe environmental damage caused by poverty – for example the felling of forests for firewood, one of the main reasons for environmental degradation and desertification in Subsaharan Africa – to realise the truth of this statement.

The damage done in some parts of Eastern Europe can only lead one to wonder what was the point of paying such a high price for development; it would have been better to pay in the initial stages for cleaner growth, than to destroy the environment so completely and pay ten times as much in the long run to clean up the mess, if that is still possible (sometimes the damage is permanent).

At the same time the development of environmentally clean technology can be a business in itself and a major export. Moreover the market for environmentally clean and acceptable goods is increasing. A country's development may be stunted if it is not in a position to produce and sell such products.

Limits to Sustainable Growth

While most developing countries support the notion of sustainable development, they are still very much constrained by lack of economic resources. Though they will no doubt pay more and more attention to the environment in their development programmes, there is sometimes a limit to what they can achieve if they are to grow at the speed they desire.

Likewise there are many parts of the developed world where environmental standards are not what they should be. Are developed countries going to allow their exports to be countervailed or refused entry to certain countries where the standards are higher or where the means they have employed to produce the particular goods are considered environmentally unsound? Environmental protection even in developed countries is often patchy and inadequate, or quite simply reflects a different view about how to go about things.

Protectionist Pressure

The issue is not clearcut. It is true that if the world were a perfect place, countries would have only sustainable, environmentally friendly development programmes. Trade could not be seen as exacerbating a problem that did not exist. In these circumstances the use of trade policies to advance environmental protection would not be an issue. But perfect sustainability is not around the corner for either the developed or developing countries and trade policies will continue to remain an issue for the foreseeable future. As long as countries do not have sustainable development policies, there will always be calls for the use of trade measures to counter them.

There is a strong tendency nowadays for developed countries that fear competition from low-wage countries to try to insist that they apply higher environmental standards. (This tendency was very clearly present in the build-up to the NAFTA agreement.) Protectionist reflexes are very strong in these circumstances, and environmental protection can be a convenient excuse for giving it a free rein. But no systematic relationship between existing environmental policies and the impact of competition has been identified. Nor is there evidence of countries deliberately resorting to low environmental standards to gain competitive advantage or attract investment.[1]

There is also a strong tendency to seek to penalise those firms that have gone abroad to produce under laxer environmental laws and re-export to the country of origin. These firms are however relatively few and far between, as the savings attached to this sort of delocalisation tend to represent only 1–2 per cent of costs and are insufficient to prompt such a move.[2]

It would be extremely difficult for the WTO or any other body to determine whether a proper environmental standard or level of expenditure on the environment were being applied in an exporting developing country in the absence of clear and internationally agreed standards. Nor are these standards likely to be developed by the WTO. It is not a standardising body, nor one that is competent to develop international agreements in this field. A unilateral determination by an importing party to the GATT would be even more dubious. Moreover trade measures that have been taken have not always worked as expected. A tariff or quota can lead to higher prices and encourage smuggling (for example ivory), or it may simply be misdirected (tropical forests are being destroyed not for export purposes, but because local people want land).

One can see that the whole issue is a can of worms and that opening up an environmental exception in the GATT to allow trade measures to be taken could be tantamount to allowing the protectionists to take it over. At the same time one cannot continue to allow the world's environment to be seriously damaged by irresponsible actions on the scale that has been happening to date, and sooner or later the pressure to use trade sanctions will become overwhelming. It is important to strike the right balance between environmental and development needs.

THE ROLE OF THE WTO

The problem for those who wish to pursue environmental improvement through trade policies is that the WTO does not provide enough support. One can prevent entry into a national market provided the importer is treated in accordance with the non-discrimination principle of the MFN and national treatment provisions. That is, an importer can be prevented from selling in the market, but only if domestic producers are also prevented from doing so. For example a model of car can be denied entry if it pollutes too much and falls short of the standard applied to domestic cars.

The exceptions that are allowed to the MFN or national treatment provisions of the WTO (Article XX) allow measures that are necessary to protect human and animal health and plant life, and measures relating to the conservation of exhaustible natural resources, but do not include the broader idea of environmental protection. Not only must the objective be legitimate (protection of health, resources and so on) but trade actions in pursuit of the objective must be either necessary to achieve it or related to it in the case of conservation of natural resources. Nor can it constitute an arbitrary or disguised restriction.

A standard may be challenged as illegitimate if it is based on an objective whose scientific grounds are considered shaky. For example, the debate on global warming is still very much alive, although substantial reports by UN-sponsored scientists would lead one to believe that the matter had been put to rest. This illustrates the sorts of difficulty these 'scientific' discussions can give rise to. While the need to prevent global warming may be accepted by most, some would argue that the world is not in danger from this phenomenon.

In the dispute between the EU and the United States over US vehicle emission standards, the Panel was reluctant to challenge the right of the United States to introduce such standards on scientific grounds. This concerned the so-called corporate average fuel economy standards (CAFE standards for short).[3] This follows a similar line taken in the EU, which has opened the door to higher levels of protection in individual member states than exist in EU regulations.

As for the methods used to pursue an Art. XX objective, a common practice is the quarantine of beef imports to control disease, for example. This could be challenged on the grounds that it is unnecessary or unscientific, in that vaccination rather than quarantine is sufficient. A similar logic would apply to measures designed to protect the environment; they must not exceed what is 'necessary' to achieve the objective. However the CAFE panel gave fairly short shrift to the issue of proportion, and said that if the measures were designed to meet a clear environmental objective, they did not have to be the least trade restrictive measure possible. It is not clear whether this line will continue to be applied by the WTO, as the CAFE decision was contested and in some respects obscure. A measure introduced to ban the importation of cigarettes into Thailand but which did not ban their consumption locally, was considered a disguised restriction of trade, as the protection of health would have required action against domestic consumption as well to achieve the health objective.

Measures to promote conservation through import or export controls are similarly constrained and they must be linked to a domestic conservation programme. For example US import controls on tuna from Canada aimed at protecting the US tuna-processing industry were not allowed; it was determined that they should have been tied to a domestic programme to conserve tuna fisheries.[4] Similarly a Canadian ban on herring and salmon exports,[5] deemed improperly caught from a conservation point of view, was not held to be legal under GATT as it was not combined with restrictions on the sale of all the fish in question, nor with restrictions on sales on the domestic market.

The WTO also allows restrictions that relate to the conservation of natural resources (Article XX g). In this case the measures do not have to be necessary to achieve the objective, but only 'related to' conservation (the Canadian salmon and herring, and the 1996 reformulated gasoline cases).[6] This is interpreted to mean that they must be primarily aimed at conservation. This gives a somewhat wider and more environmentally friendly connotation than a 'necessary' measure.

The WTO also allows subsidies for environmental purposes and there are provisions in other agreements that allow for some environmental control, for example refusal to grant a patent when a product is likely to damage the environment.

So in general terms, while the WTO allows considerable freedom in the policies adopted domestically, it attaches certain conditions to ensure that importers are not penalised by the way the policy is devised, that is, if it is scientifically unsound, discriminatory, an unnecessary obstacle to trade and so on. But as we have just seen, there has been some movement towards a more accommodating stance on how these provisions are interpreted with regard to the environment.

Another issue that has caused considerable debate is the use of ecolabelling. These labels or certificates indicate that the product has been manufactured in a sound environmental manner. If they apply to domestic and imported products alike they do not infringe the WTO rules. They are usually voluntary in application, but despite this they can have a very profound impact on consumer choice and on trade, and there has been considerable discussion in the WTO as to how they should be handled.

Another example is the use of domestic taxes to protect the environment. A good illustration is the attempt to introduce carbon or energy taxes, which will affect producers, refiners and consumers alike. No border measures are involved and the national treatment provision is respected, but this sort of tax can have a major effect on demand and imports.

Some countries have stopped giving preferential access to their markets when the goods in question are made in ways that are environmentally unsound. Preferential tariff treatment for developing countries is granted autonomously and is not bound in GATT. It is therefore free of MFN constraints and GATT members may reduce or eliminate the tariff preference on a particular product from a particular source in order to protect the environment. The

EU uses this technique in its GSP system. This is a fairly limited option that is not effective in all circumstances, though it can be quite potent in certain conditions.

The WTO is less receptive to any attempt to take trade action against the environmental policies of other countries, or to anything that smacks of an extraterritorial exercise of jurisdiction.

While a product that is polluting in itself may be refused entry, what is not allowed is banning a product because the production process used in the exporting country does not meet the environmental standards of the importing country. The tuna–dolphin case brought before a GATT panel was the main decision in this area.[7] The United States had decided that tuna caught in an environmentally unsound way – that is, a lot of dolphins were caught at the same time – should not be allowed into the United States. The GATT panel said that this was a unilateral attempt to tell Mexico how it should catch fish and was therefore an attempt to control the environmental practices of another country. It was disallowed.

The fisheries cases described earlier, which were struck down because there was no corresponding domestic conservation programme, could have been interpreted to mean, *a contrario*, that the domestic programme would allow measures to be taken against imports from countries with no such programme. However any hope that this type of interpretation could be adopted was eliminated by the tuna–dolphin case.

There has been some discussion as to whether the situation has changed by virtue of inclusion in the Agreement on Technical Barriers to Trade of standards drafted in terms of process and production methods (PPMs). In other words, does this inclusion mean that a country can control imports that fail to meet a standard drafted in terms of PPMs, as the United States tried to suggest in the tuna case. A panel is likely to give this inclusion a narrow interpretation, and only PPMs that have an impact on the final characteristics of a product, for example by leaving traces of chemicals used in the process in the final product, are likely to be covered by the TBT agreement.

On the export side, however, the WTO is more strict. Many countries now control the exportation of dangerous and toxic substances, and there have been no complaints to the WTO, despite the fact that for some importing countries waste disposal is a lucrative business. As we have seen, however, the situation might be different for export controls that were ostensibly designed for conservation but were in fact aimed at preventing the exportation of raw materials in short supply on the world market.

One can see from the above that a country is free to adopt whatever environmental laws it pleases inside its territory provided the objective and means are legitimate and it applies the same rules to its own firms. A country can forbid the importation of goods that are defective and banned domestically, but not on the basis that their method of production is considered unacceptable. The WTO draws a firm line on the use of trade or border measures on imports solely because their method of production is different, unless that is essential to ensure the safety or other characteristics of the product.

HOW TO PROCEED?

It is clear that the WTO does not favour the exercise of jurisdiction by one set of states over another, and indeed it has always severely circumscribed any exercise of unilateral action. What solutions might be envisaged?

One solution might be to extend the exceptions in Article XX to include the environment in general as an exception to MFN. This would open up an environmental window in the WTO. The interpretation of the existing exceptions has been so limited by the tuna–dolphin case as not to be very useful. Nor have other cases established a strong environmental thrust. It is unlikely that the developing countries in particular would agree to any broadly based or general right to take trade measures for environmental purposes, and particularly not any reversal of the tuna–dolphin case. They would strenuously object to measures taken in accordance with the standards of developed countries, as they are not in a position to equal those standards at this stage.

It might be possible, however, to reach international agreement on certain sectors or objectives. Indeed, the main way of ensuring that environmental standards are protected throughout the globe has been to negotiate international conventions or agreements: 180 such agreements exist, 18 of which contain the possibility of trade measures. The trouble with many of these agreements is that the number of signatories is limited. Nonetheless there are agreements with a large number of signatories, and the parties concerned regularly apply import controls to pursue the objectives of the agreements. One such is CITES, an agreement designed to protect endangered species, another is the Montreal Protocol on the protection of the ozone layer. In the case of the latter there is even an element of discrimination in that imports can be forbidden altogether, while domestic producers have a transition period in which to adjust. Moreover parties to these agreements sometimes take measures against non-parties. This creates a degree of legal uncertainty and implies the imposition of certain international standards on parties who may be reluctant to accept them.

This may require some mechanism in the WTO either to approve them by giving them a waiver, or to ensure their WTO compatibility or acceptability to other parties to the WTO (non-parties to the agreements) through some other means. It only requires 69 votes out of 130 in the WTO (a majority of 75 per cent) to ensure a waiver is passed. This in itself implies fairly widespread acceptance and this may be the sort of solution that is eventually adopted. The urgency of some environmental causes may ensure tacit acceptance at least that the will of the majority should be respected.

Probably the most acceptable approach, however, is through international agreements with as wide a basis of acceptance as possible. If international standards can be endorsed or international agreements adopted with a wide coverage and a large number of signatories, then the problem of unilateral imposition will be largely resolved.

In recent years there have been major successes in negotiating such agreements and ensuring widespread support for them. For example the conventions that came out of the Rio Conference on Environment and Development (UNCED) and the UN Environment Protection Agency (UNEP) on climate change, biodiversity, desertification and so on received a large number of signatures. This was due in part to the negotiating forum chosen. By negotiating these measures in the UN there was more or less universal participation in the negotiations and more ready acceptance of the results.

However this sort of agreement can not be properly implemented without financial assistance from the developed to the developing countries. This indeed was the approach undertaken at the Rio Conference, in accordance with which a very wide programme of action was adopted. The *quid pro quo* of this process was the financial contribution that the developed countries were supposed to make to it.

The whole basis of the Agenda 21 process of the UNCED was that all countries should be *responsible* for sustainable development. For the first time it was fully accepted that the process of development had to involve environmental protection if it was to be sustainable. In other words, the headlong style of development of the past had to be adjusted to prevent massive deterioration of the environment. Development had to be accompanied by, or take the form of, development that did not damage the environment.

The second main principle of the UNCED process was that all countries should be responsible for *ensuring* that development is sustainable. The developing countries just as much as the developed countries should try to ensure, through their economic policies, that their development is environmentally sound. But clearly the developing countries will not be able to afford to protect the environment to the extent desired without substantial assistance from the developed world. Assistance was therefore the key to ensuring that the agreements will be adhered to and implemented.

The amount of assistance granted for environmental purposes has increased a great deal over the years, however this money has tended to be drawn from existing development funds that have been redeployed to the environment, or by injecting a green dimension into an existing development programme. The additional finance that the developing countries sought vociferously and at great length during the course of the UNCED process has been forthcoming to a certain extent, and is administered through the Global Environmental Facility. But it has not been made available on the scale anticipated at the time of the UNCED conference. This essentially means that while some improvement will be made to the environment through more sustainable development policies, this improvement is not likely to be as great as it would have been with more adequate financial support.

The WTO should also look at issues such as ecolabelling, as well as the use of domestic as opposed to border taxes to control environmental damage. These issues are not properly dealt with by current WTO rules. Any serious investigation of trade and the environment should also look at some of the WTO jurisprudence to see if it is on the right track and if it can be improved, including the matter of process and production methods but also the more general aspect of what standards can be applied and what measures can reasonably be used to implement them. Some institutional issues should also be addressed, such as the need for a notification system in the WTO (for dangerous substances and so on) and improving the dispute settlement process.

So there are ways of moving forward based on a consensual

approach. This will not still the voices of those looking for an environmental window in the WTO, but at this stage this does not seem to be particularly feasible given the suspicions of the developing countries as to what this would imply.

The Singapore ministerial meeting was a disappointment in this regard. The working group on trade and the environment, which had been dealing with this issue for some years, was not able to come up with agreed solutions, and neither were the ministers. The meeting could only conclude that the working group should continue its activities and resume discussion of the issues. This result fell far short of the aspiration of the developed countries to obtain WTO acknowledgement of existing international agreements, and for the developing countries to control such practices as ecolabelling. No doubt the time is not yet ripe for a deal, but it is to be hoped that this will come about in a few years time.

25 Foreign Direct Investment

INTRODUCTION

Until relatively recently there was a fair amount of suspicion of foreign investment. One only has to think of the sensitivity in Europe in the 1960s after the initial wave of US investment, which gave rise to J.J. Servan-Schreiber's book *The American Challenge*.[1] As a young student at the time, to me there seemed little difference between the Cold War and the economic war; both appeared to be life and death struggles.

A similar panic appeared to set in in the United States in the 1980s with the wave of Japanese investment of that period, culminating in the 'national affront' of the Japanese purchase of the Rockefeller Centre (which subsequently became a financial albatross!)

As for the developing countries, more often than not they appeared to view foreign investment as likely to undermine their development and independence and that somehow because of it they would lose control of their economy. This was not surprising in countries just emerging from colonialism, where indeed they had had no control over their economy, or where they had been systematically exploited by a few foreign firms. They tended, however, to go overboard insofar as they discouraged all or most foreign investment or regulated it in such a way that foreign investment was discouraged; in that sense they were only damaging themselves. Eastern European and other state-run economies hardly allowed any foreign investment at all, not that there were many queuing up to invest.

The 1980s however saw a change in perspective. The deregulation of financial markets and the relaxation of exchange controls inevitably increased the supply of capital in circulation and available for investment abroad. This was partly because of a change in policy, but also because changes in technology, for example computerisation, meant it was increasingly difficult to control capital flows. This also led to the clear understanding that if this capital was not encouraged to stay at home or made to feel comfortable, it would go elsewhere. Far from Japanese investment being a negative factor, it was realised that if the money that arose out of the US deficits was not attracted back in the form of direct investment, there would be further damage to the economy.

The debt crisis spelled the end of investment through debt creation. Much of the foreign debt incurred by governments had not been spent on investment, or if it had been, not wisely so, and in any case the sources of such funds had dried up. The result was a much keener interest in attracting private direct investment from abroad. Likewise development assistance was decreasing with the onset of donor fatigue. There was a dawning realisation that governments were not well equipped to manage their economies, and that much greater emphasis should be placed on the private sector and private investment.

The pace of this conversion was accelerated by the thaw that took place in Eastern Europe and the dismantling of the communist system. Developing countries found themselves competing with a number of ex communist countries for a dwindling supply of public funds and private investment.

The result has been increased attention in both developed and developing economies to sound economic management and to the underlying conditions needed to attract private capital from abroad as well as generating it at home. These new trends have not taken place without considerable debate, especially in the United States with regard to Japanese investment. In the EU the debate took place in the 1960s at the time of greatest inflow of US investment and had largely been resolved in a positive sense as hostility to such investment soon died away. For the United States the debate was still relatively new in the 1990s as the earlier level of FDI had not been so large or so unexpected.

The US debate centred on such issues as the impact of FDI on employment and its quality, that is, whether foreign investment would involve higher quality activity such as R&D or only assembly operations. Underlying this concern were such questions as whether FDI would mean more sourcing abroad, thus undermining the balance of payments, or whether it would improve employment and bring high quality jobs. In general terms there was concern about overall strategic independence and national security. The evidence tends to suggest that the overall impact has been positive, as it was in Europe, that good jobs have been provided, that high-quality activities have been maintained and that the strategic impact has been limited. The impact on trade due to greater sourcing by FDI firms abroad has tended to resolve itself over time. And of course any society's industrial base can be substantially revitalised by new money and technology.[2]

INVESTMENT TRENDS

The level of mutual investment between developed countries has always been high, with investment between Europe and the United States standing at $460 billion, with a further $35 billion being added every year.

During the 1980s partly as a result of deregulation, direct investment flows increased by around 30 per cent annually, more than three times the growth rate of world exports and four times as fast as world GDP (Table 25.1). This underlines the fact that investment is not just ancillary to trade, but that it is a major factor in the creation of it. More recent signs show an even bigger increase of between 40 and 50 per cent.[3]

The sources of this investment are changing and there are many new players on the stage, including small and medium-sized businesses and newly industrialising countries such as the Asian tigers, which are among the largest investors in China. Nor is the destination of the finance the same as in the past. The share of global foreign investment going to OECD countries dropped from about 80 per cent in the late 1980s and early 1990s to about 60 per cent in 1995. The share of developing countries went from 20 per cent to 30 per cent in the same period. The bulk of investment in developing countries has gone to South and East Asia ($65 billion in 1995) with a large part going to China ($37.5 billion). The investment is increasingly in services rather than goods (50–60 per cent of flows and about 50 per cent of FDI stocks).

Inward stocks of investment in 1995 were as follows: world, $2657 billion; developed countries, $1932 billion; EU, $1028 billion; US, $564 billion; Japan, $17 billion; developing countries, $693 billion; South and East Asia, $360 billion; China, $128 billion.[5]

Table 25.1   FDI inflows and outflows ($ billion)

	Developed countries		Developing countries		Central/Eastern Europe		All countries	
	In	Out	In	Out	In	Out	In	Out
1983–87	58	72	18	4	0.02	0.01	77	76
1988–92	139	193	36	15	1.36	0.04	177	208
1993	129	192	73	33	5.59	0.20	207	225
1994	132	190	87	38	5.89	0.55	225	230
1995	203	270	99	47	12.08	0.30	314	317

Source: United Nations (1996).[4]

INTERNATIONAL REGULATIONS

Governments have sought to protect their investments abroad through a large number of bilateral treaties with many and diverse provisions, though there are many common elements.

The OECD has a set of codes[6] that provide for the liberalisation of capital movements and current transactions in accordance with the MFN and national treatment principles. It uses the negative list system, that is, the principles apply unless countries that are not ready for their application lodge a series of exemptions. The OECD then tries to convince them, through peer pressure, to lift their exemptions. This is a long and laborious process as it is largely voluntary, though it has borne a certain amount of fruit over the years.

Other regional agreements exist, such as the EU (a full obligation to liberalise investment and grant national treatment)[7], NAFTA and APEC, to cite but three examples. NAFTA is less demanding than the EU, though it is one of the most comprehensive multilateral instruments. The APEC provisions are really only in the form of good intentions or best efforts.

We saw in Chapter 20 what GATT has sought to do, and the relatively limited nature of it (though in the case of subsidies and services there were some real breakthroughs). The question is what should be the next step, if any?

HOW TO MOVE FORWARD

At the time of the Uruguay Round it was clear that there was no real constituency for a broad-based negotiation on investment measures. The trade-related investment measures agreement dealt very narrowly with local content and trade balancing requirements, and failed even to deal with export performance requirements *per se*. The subsidies agreement outlaws subsidies that are tied to export performance and goes some distance towards making domestic investment subsidies actionable, that is, if they are specific.

The services agreement went much further on liberalisation of investment in that it made the right of establishment or to invest one of its guiding principles, but the actual content of the agreement has to be negotiated as the obligations do not apply automatically. The irony is that the framework services agreement is now much more progressive than anything that has been achieved with regard to goods.

The Uruguay Round singled out investment as an issue that would require further negotiation. A constituency exists for greater freedom in the investment field, especially among the developed countries. Negotiations are currently taking place, in the OECD, with an expected completion date of June/July 1997. The European Union and some developing countries would like to see a parallel effort taking place in the WTO.

The United States was more reluctant about an early start in the WTO as it felt it could get a better agreement in the OECD, which could then be opened for signature to all interested parties. It felt that a parallel negotiation in the WTO would undermine the OECD negotiations, or at least lead to fewer signatories to an OECD agreement. This was clearly not a procedure that found favour with many developing countries, which were keen to be involved in the negotiations but could not as they were neither members of the OECD nor invited to participate. In the WTO at least they could have some influence.

The discussions in Singapore proved very difficult however, as important developing countries such as India, Malaysia and Indonesia were very opposed to controls on inward investment.

An agreement was finally reached[9] to discuss the issue in the WTO, with one qualifier, that the discussion would concern 'trade-related' investment. This sounds a bit like the trade-related investment measures, and was no doubt intended by the negotiators from the developing countries to limit the discussions in the way it had in the Uruguay Round. However it is arguable that nowadays all investment issues are trade related; if one can't invest in the country to which one wants to export, very often trade is not possible. We have seen how true this is in the context of services, and it is also true for merchandise trade.

The main result, and it is a positive one, is that the WTO now has some sort of mandate to discuss this issue. The exact content of these discussions will depend on the parties to it, but like all such discussions it is likely to evolve over time. It is very unlikely that it will have the narrower focus of the TRIMS discussion in the Uruguay Round.

WHAT WOULD SUCH AN AGREEMENT CONTAIN?

It should seek to establish as wide a definition as possible. In this perspective it should cover both goods and services and all investment measures. It will have to tackle some difficult issues such as territory (offshore as well?), type of investments (whether just in companies or other things too, such as portfolios, patents and so on), domicile of investors (based in the territory of a member, or not), government entities (federal and subfederal?), capital flows (inward obviously, but also outward, which may create more anxiety from a balance of payments point of view), and so on.

The agreement will need provisions on transparency to enable investors to apply for investment licences and to ensure that there is a minimum of due process. The obligations of the agreement should contain the usual MFN, national treatment and market access provisions. It may have to go further to cover cases where the granting of formal national treatment is not enough, that is, where there are limitations not only on foreign but also on domestic investments. Regulations will have to be fair and reasonable.

These provisions will probably be structured along the lines of the recent GATS agreement, with a set of obligations and the possibility of entering reservations. There will be a substantial effort in the OECD at least to maintain strong obligations and as few reservations as possible, but it would be unrealistic to expect full liberalisation in the WTO from the word go. Like the GATS agreement therefore, the real content of the agreement will have to be negotiated over time.

The issue of MFN will come up against some problems due to bilateral tax or investment treaties, where parties will not be ready to grant the same concessions worldwide. Regional arrangements may also have very liberal provisions and the parties to them may not be ready to grant them in the absence of reciprocity. Inward investment and a lack of barriers to it are more likely to benefit an economy than free trade as there will be few short-term adjustments to be made, but it is hard to imagine the EU, for example, offering up its complete free movement principle in the absence of reciprocity by the United States, which still has important national security and R&D restrictions.

Access discussions will of course have to concentrate on ensuring that there are no obstacles to foreign investment and ownership. This covers a multitude of provisions.[10] Several countries still operate a general screening system, but this has become of much less significance, while screening for more specific purposes has come more to the fore. Some countries insist on domestic ownership of broadcasting authorities for security and political reasons, but also to preserve the cultural heritage. Moreover there is an increasing trend to focus less on the investment than on what is done with it. Though some still have ownership requirements for broadcasting authorities, the emphasis tends to be on a percentage of local production being broadcast.

Some sectoral investment restrictions exist, for example on maritime transport in the United States to preserve the ship building, on air and land transportation, telecommunications and so on. Some of these are being outflanked by new technology, for example in telecommunications, and others are simply relics from the past that will be phased out with time. The recent telecommunications negotiations under GATS have resolved many of the issues related to this sector.

More serious are the restrictions on foreign investment in R&D programmes. There has been a revival of interest in these given the unequal access to them in various countries. The value of these restrictions is somewhat dubious given that the technology may ultimately have to be sold to make it pay, and others will enjoy the benefits without the initial expense and risk. The exclusion of powerful competitors can also lead to underfunding of a programme and less input of expertise. At most it can give an initial competitive edge. These provisions may have a value in extracting reciprocity from others, and are frequently considered as important elements of a strategic trade or industrial policy.

More intractable perhaps are the national security exceptions operated by many countries. It is easy enough to draw the line between investments with a security element and those without, for example a semiconductor plant versus a hotel. But it is more difficult is to separate the myriad investments with potential military or security significance from those that really count. It may be important to preserve your manufacturer of fighter planes, but is it really wise to avoid foreign investment in a semiconductor facility? The US national security exemptions are very extensive and are directed at foreign nationals seeking to purchase US firms.

A national treatment provision will be essential to ensure that regulations applied to foreign investors are no less favourable than for domestic firms. It will also have to tackle the problem of monopolies, and while it will probably not be possible to abolish them, it will have to ensure that other investors, foreign or domestic, will not be abused by the monopoly, for example by refusing access to transmission lines for telecom activities outside the monopoly.

It might also have to touch on the issue of corporate governance. Some systems of corporate ownership (for example Japanese *Keiretsu*) are so opaque and impenetrable that it is virtually impossible to invest in them. Some of these mechanisms are arguably in the interest of the economy in that firms can take a longer-term view and do not have to face hostile takeovers every day of the week. However if international investment is to become widespread some of these forms of corporate control may have to be relaxed. Privatisation is also an issue in this context. Many countries still require that a portion of shares be maintained in local hands in the course of privatisation exercises.

Unlike the services agreement, it will have to tackle a series of other issues, such as unfair trade practices (for which trade-related investment measures are sometimes designed as a counter measure), transfer of technology matters (though the recent TRIPS agreement may be adequate initially). Many of these issues are important for striking a balance between the interests of the investor and those of the host country.

It may have to tackle subsidies, including tax incentives, in a more detailed manner, as well as government procurement, safeguards, movement of key personnel, performance requirements and so on. Many of these issues are either covered by the GATS agreement or are due for further negotiation in the WTO anyway, but some questions specific to the investment field may need to be addressed. Subsidies and performance requirements have been discussed in Chapters 11 and 20.

It will be important to have solid provisions on the right to repatriate capital or profits and their convertibility, or expropriation and compensation rights. Without clear and liberal obligations on these issues, investment will be substantially discouraged.

A series of institutional issues will have to be considered, in particular dispute settlement. The usual WTO dispute settlement provisions may be invoked, but the question will also arise of whether private firms can settle disputes with government through access to a settlement mechanism such as compulsory arbitration. The question will also arise as to what remedies should be available. Under the normal WTO rules a policy may be condemned if it is in violation of the rules, and trade sanctions may be imposed, but different remedies will probably have to be devised for individual firms whose interests have been affected.

To avoid conflict between host government treatment of an individual firm, and that of the firm's country of origin, in the longer term it may be necessary to develop additional agreements or codes on issues such as taxation, transfer pricing, accounting standards, environment and labour standards and so on.

Many of the above suggestions relate to host government obligations, but others also concern the behaviour of firms, for example antitrust rules and taxation. While it might be possible to deal with the behaviour of firms under certain headings where the problems are most acute, it would be difficult to establish a more general charter of obligations for multinational firms. This was tried by the UN and basically failed.

Another consideration is that the world is changing rapidly, and what may appear reasonable concerns today may not appear as such in the future. It is not wise to set everything in concrete. One only has to look at the evolution of antitrust laws in the last 15 years, as these have regularly blown hot and cold. Interfirm accords, which a few years ago were jumped on by any self-respecting competition authority, are encouraged nowadays as they correspond to a general move towards greater complexity in the process of manufacturing and research.

CONCLUSION

While this is an ambitious programme, certain progress was achieved during the Uruguay Round and some of the elements of a future agreement are at least foreshadowed in the GATS agreement. The existence of this agreement moreover sets a useful precedent as to how to proceed, and sets out the sort of firm framework within which a gradual evolution can take place.

However a series of ancillary issues are not dealt with satisfactorily in the GATS agreement, for example unfair trade practices, free movement of persons, equity control issues and so on, and these will require very substantial political concessions.

The work being done in the OECD gives a clear indication of the sort of agreement that can be achieved. No doubt a WTO agreement will fall somewhat short of this, but the OECD work should nonetheless be an inspiration for a WTO agreement.

26 Trade and Labour Standards

INTRODUCTION

The NAFTA discussions brought to the fore the question of low social conditions and standards in most developing countries. The fear was that with complete free trade between the United States and Mexico, US industry would invest heavily south of the border to take advantage of lower social costs, and that this would cost many US jobs and force a lowering of labour standards in the United States.

This was a reiteration of the more general discussion touched upon at the beginning of this book. Globalisation and free trade have now reached the point where the benefits of free trade are being questioned. It was all right when only the developed countries were the major trade players as their wages and costs were more or less comparable. But once developing countries became active participants in the world trading system and capital flows were liberalised, there was a perceived risk of instability developing in the trading system, and the threat of a low-skilled underclass emerging in the developed countries.

However the cost of labour in many developing countries generally reflects their productivity. If the wages are low this doesn't necessarily mean that prices are low, because their productivity may be poor. In such cases, developed countries with high wages and high productivity can compete without difficulty on price. The problem of low-wage competition may arise where wages are lower than productivity and competitive prices can thus be charged. This might occur where no trade union rights exist, for example, or where child labour or slavery of one sort or another is common.

In the view of this author the developed countries can only do well out of these developments, though clearly much adaptation and restructuring will be needed. The real problem for the developed countries is whether they can adapt quickly enough.

Instability is more likely to occur in the developing countries, where rapid growth is going to create its own problems. It has recently become clear just how precarious the situation is in Mexico, while so far the United States has generally benefited from membership of NAFTA.

Nonetheless these issues have caused trade union and other political movements in some developed countries to review the need for a social clause in GATT–Ross Perot and Pat Buchanan spring to mind in this respect. The idea is to find some way of dealing with the perceived threat of imports from developing countries where social benefits are low or non-existent and where an 'unfair' advantage is allegedly being taken. This is sometimes called 'social dumping'.

A FRAMEWORK FOR DISCUSSION

This move will clearly have a strong protectionist flavour if applied in a comprehensive manner. Most developing countries cannot afford the sort of social protection given in the developed world and certain rules would clearly be unfair to them. The question is how to deal with some of the worst aspects of this issue without spilling over into protectionism.

While some see the issue as a trade matter, others simply see these differences in developing economies as normal differences in competitive conditions and not something to worry about. Yet others see the competitive threat as marginal at best, and some groups are more concerned by the human rights dimension than the economic impact. A convenient way of looking at these issues is to divide them into fundamental or 'core' rights and other social rights.

Fundamental Economic or 'Core' Rights

One can distinguish two types of social right. The minimum definition would cover the sort of things that are already covered by the International Labour Organisation's (ILO) conventions on trade unions, such as rights of assembly, collective bargaining, non-discrimination rights, and bans on slavery, child labour and so on. These are generally referred to as fundamental or 'core' human rights to distinguish them from rights that are more social or economic in nature. The latter are described in the next section.

The ILO conventions have been in place for a long time but have not always been well respected. There are also some notable absentees from their lists of signatories, even among developed countries. To date the United States, has not ratified the ILO Forced Labour Convention of 1930 (because of prison labour), the Freedom of Association Convention of 1948 and the Right to Organise and Collective Bargaining Convention of 1949. There are other notable exceptions too.[1]

Some UN conventions have wider adherence because of the slightly more modulated way in which they are drafted. The United States and others have found these easier to accept because there is no outright ban on, for example, prison labour which is allowed under certain conditions, and freedom of association clauses are drafted in less absolute terms and allow for more controls, including on the right to strike.

The advantage of bringing these under the purview of WTO is that they would then be applicable to all GATT members and could be made much more effective through the use of trade sanctions or peer pressure (the trade policy review process – see Chapter 5), or simply through discussion and negotiation.

Trade union rights do not directly increase costs, but make for a redistribution of the profits and revenues. They do not increase costs *per se*, though initially they may, if these rights are exercised in an irresponsible way by the trade unions. With time however this should stabilise. They should allow for gradual adaptation and adjustment based on what the market will bear.

One of the accusations made in the NAFTA discussions was that Mexican trade union rights were severely and unnecessarily constrained. The result was that wages were kept low and profits maximised. Mexican industry was being run for the benefit of the few, who did not always invest their profits in Mexico. Apart from being socially unjust, this was bad economics. Whether or not this led to lower Mexican prices (the gap between wages and productivity may be filled by higher profits than usual) but it emphasised another point: low wages meant lower overall demand, including for imports from the United States.

Issues such as slavery, child labour, unremunerated prison labour and so on are to a certain extent economic issues, but are above all important moral issues. Slavery is clearly repugnant and should be banned. Child labour is also repugnant to those of us in developed countries with memories that do not stretch back to the child labour of our own industrial revolutions. In India and Pakistan it is common to see children at work (making carpets and so on),

and sometimes they are the only breadwinner in a poor family, or
at least what they earn is essential to the family's survival and to
their own. In the absence of such jobs children are often forced
into worse situations, for example begging or prostitution. So the
issue is not always clearcut. Nonetheless action should be taken,
because children are all too easy to exploit and are more in need
of protection than most. Their lives are blighted by this sort of
exploitation, often with long-term health consequences, and their
condition is often just another form of slavery. A proper approach
might be to ban certain types of child labour and to regulate others
– working hours, conditions, school attendance and so on.

Non-discrimination is also an important element in ensuring that
women and religious and other minorities are properly treated. There
is no good economic reason why women should not be paid as
much as men, though of course there will be problems of adjustment. However this problem has not been fully resolved even in
the most developed economies.

A lot of the rights just described are close to protection of human rights and there is a strong case to be made that they should
be protected as such for moral reasons. This argument is reinforced
by the fact that there isn't a strong economic argument to be made
against this type of protection.

The suggestion that an absence of core rights makes some sort
of economic difference and has an impact on trade has not been
proven. Indeed an OECD[2] study suggests that there is little or no
causality. Even in countries with the poorest record on core rights
there is no clear link with improved economic or export performance; exports do not noticeably increase. It is also the case that in
countries with special economic zones, where unions and the right
to strike have been banned, wage and price levels in the zones are
generally higher than in the country as a whole; this tends to show
that the absence of trade union rights doesn't necessarily lead to
low wages. The increase in democratisation and the associated right
to strike in countries such as South Korea and Taiwan have taken
place against a background of a rising market, tight labour supply
and so on, and it has been difficult to attribute any wage rise to
the improvement of democratic rights.

So while the significance of these matters for trade does not appear
important, for economic and moral reasons there is general interest
in seeing such rights applied in countries that do not have them.
The abolition of slavery, child exploitation, discrimination and so

on could lead to economic distortions and the misallocation of resources within a country. Freedom of association could also lead to more productive and healthy labour relations and a better economy. The moral issues are also clear. These core rights are increasingly seen as fundamental human rights in the labour field.

Other Economic Rights

The second category of social rights, however (including minimum wage legislation, workplace conditions and so on), if imposed by the WTO could certainly have a direct impact on costs – costs that more often than not the developing countries will not be able to afford. Insofar as these measures are negotiated between trade unions and employers, it must be supposed they can be borne by the economy; it is imposition of these conditions from the outside that will create difficulty.

It is probably wrong and counterproductive to even try to impose such measures on developing countries. Developed countries would also have difficulty with them. One only has to think of UK opposition to the EU 'Social Chapter' or the opposition of the United States and others to 'rigidities' in the labour market. The chance of getting such measures through the WTO is slim to non-existent.

CONCLUSION

The discussions in the run-up to the Singapore WTO ministerial meeting at the end of 1996 sought to meet some of the main concerns of the developing countries. The EU, itself rather badly divided, took the middle ground.[3] Its main proposal was that the WTO should at least discuss the issue, but it reduced the scope to 'core rights' and said that trade sanctions should not be available.

The developing countries faced the prospect that other non-WTO measures would be taken as a result of internal pressures in the developed countries.

Other more 'voluntary' ways exist to achieve the same ends. The EU, for example, attaches conditions to its GSP provisions, extending preferential treatment to those that have established core rights. Labelling that indicates whether a product has been produced by prisoners, child labour and so on would also have a real effect. Some US producers of textiles suffered severe repercussions recently when US trade unions published the fact that they were producing goods in sweatshops in developing countries, where factory conditions bordered on slavery. Guidelines and codes of conduct for multinational enterprises can also have an impact. In the GATT some provisions exist to permit measures against imports resulting from prison labour (Article XXe).

The developing countries were very hostile however, as they saw any type of social clause or discussion thereon as thinly veiled protectionism. However some of those with experience in the field of textiles had begun to understand the difficulties they would increasingly face if their manufacturing methods were not up to scratch. It is in their long-term interest to ensure that autonomous measures such as those just described are brought within a multilateral framework. The WTO would be an appropriate body to ensure that such measures do not become protectionist and impede trade.

The result of the Singapore meeting was fairly positive insofar as it was agreed that the issue should be further discussed,[4] albeit hedged around with conditions. The focus will be on core rights, and the discussions will be just that, and not negotiations. The primary locus for labour rights issues is to be the ILO and not the WTO; the implication here is that an examination of these issues should initially be undertaken in the ILO context. This does not exclude discussion or even negotiation in the WTO over the longer term.

This result was about the best that could have been hoped for, given the difficulty of the discussions and the extreme hostility of the developing countries. However it is to be hoped that in the future there will be a better understanding of the need for some multilateral solutions in this context.

27 International Rules on Competition

INTRODUCTION

For years the world's governments have been battling against obvious barriers to trade such as tariffs, non-tariff barriers and so on, which for the most part are government, or government-inspired actions. As the tide of these measures has receded, other issues have made their appearance and stand out like rocks around which wary (and weary!) trade mariners have to navigate.

One issue is anticompetitive or abusive behaviour by firms. This normally takes the form of trying to restrict competition by fixing prices or sharing out markets. The consumer suffers, but so too do competing firms as they are cut off from supplies or excluded from retail outlets.

These are largely private abuses that are regulated by the government. However the level of regulation varies from country to country, and while some are highly regulated others are less so or not at all. Again, though the necessary legislation may exist, the level or degree of enforcement may be very different among countries. What is permitted or tolerated in one country, may be considered an outright abuse in another.

The importance for trade is that different rules and different enforcement practices can hamper market access or create a non-level playing field. For example if a government tolerates the presence of monopolies, a monopoly firm can refuse to import foreign goods or those of a foreign competitor. The same can occur if it tolerates or has no rules on import cartels. Likewise, strong vertical integration, in which a firm controls most retail outlets for a particular product, can have the same effect. Export cartels have also been treated leniently in the past as the anticompetitive effect was taking place outside the jurisdiction.

One of the reasons for the renewed interest in competition matters is the situation that exists in Japan. While Japan has had fairly complete and stringent, US-inspired antitrust legislation since the end of the Second World War, it has not been vigorously applied, and in practice the prewar *zaibatsu* or conglomerates have been allowed to continue and even encouraged to flourish. The result is an economy that is difficult to penetrate, as the tentacles of these large firms reach out into a vast array of activities, both vertically and horizontally. It is very difficult, for example, to break into certain distribution networks.

This has led to the realisation that reducing tariff and non-tariff barriers is only half the story, and that for a successful penetration of some markets the competition rules may have to be made more effective and perhaps even changed. At the same time firms have trouble complying with the multiplicity of existing rules and legal systems, and sometimes they simply cannot comply as some systems contradict each other. Governments are embarrassed because, in the absence of common rules and international cooperation, they are often confronted with the unilateral and extraterritorial exercise of jurisdiction by other governments against their firms.

These conflicts and tensions are bound to increase with time and the further integration and globalisation of markets. It is therefore not too soon to initiate discussion, on a more coherent international system and a set of rules to deal with these issues. The problem facing such negotiations will be twofold: the substantive rules are frequently different between countries, and the manner and type of enforcement also diverge. Substantial concessions will therefore be needed on all sides to find a solution to these rather wide disparities.

DIFFERENCES IN SUBSTANTIVE RULES[1]

In very broad terms, antitrust rules fall into three categories: horizontal agreements, vertical agreements, and monopolies/mergers.

Horizontal Agreements

Horizontal agreements between competing firms that are at the same level of business are usually designed to reduce or eliminate the competition between them by fixing prices and conditions of sale, limiting production or sharing out markets. All this operates to the detriment of the consumer.

They have various effects on trade. A price-fixing arrangement that increases prices will not survive if foreign competitors can come into the market, provided of course that they are not coopted into the scheme. However an arrangement that lowers prices below costs will probably be a form of predation and will affect entry by foreign competitors. Market-sharing arrangements also give firms a financial advantage in that, for example, they incur lower advertising and distribution costs. This makes them better able to compete with foreign entrants and they may even be in a position to predate. These arrangements can have similar predatory effects on the global market if the parties to them are powerful enough.

Forms of horizontal agreement falling short of merger are usually frowned upon. An arrangement between firms to increase domestic prices, or to carve up and share out certain markets to reduce competition are considered a violation of the basic rules and are generally forbidden. There is therefore a good prospect of arriving at some common understanding with regard to these practices.

There have, however, been exceptions to this type of prohibition in the past. Cartels formed by governments – for example OPEC, voluntary export restraint arrangements and many types of crisis cartel – have been considered untouchable. Yet other practices have been authorised by legislation (for example the US Webb Pomerene legislation, which allows certain types of export association for sharing marketing costs), and their indirect effect on foreign markets has been seen as improving the prospects of national competitors on international markets. However voluntary export restraints were banned by the Uruguay Round (see Chapter 12) and any agreement in this area would clearly have to eliminate Webb Pomerene type arrangements.

Private arrangements between firms have tended to get much shorter shrift though some practices have been tolerated, as made evident by non-enforcement or even encouragement by the authorities. However private arrangements such as agreements to share R&D, production specialisation agreements and so on have tended to be accepted on their merits as their effect on trade is much less noticeable, with R&D arrangements being more favoured than production specialisation.

If the firms adhering to the agreement are powerful enough, they are able to affect prices at other levels of the business by, for example, joint purchasing or joint selling practices. Joint purchases can ensure that suppliers are prevented from competing on price or charging what they feel the market will bear, and joint selling can ensure that the group's distributors charge a collective and no doubt higher price. These arrangements have an obvious impact on firms trying to get into the market.

Another issue of some importance is the question of interlocking relationships and arrangements between firms that are little short of mergers. Many firms in the high tech sector have developed networks of complex interlocking arrangements to develop certain products, and it is difficult to determine their effect on competition. (The United States has laws on interlocking relationships among officers of competing firms.) These questions will need some consideration as they are an increasingly common feature of the international economy – one only has to think of semiconductors and telecommunications.

Vertical Agreements

Vertical agreements, whereby a firm ties up its suppliers or distributors in a contract that makes them its sole supplier or the sole distributor of its goods, and at the same time the supplier agrees not to sell to anyone else and the distributor agrees not to sell anyone else's goods, can lead to a situation where the consumer suffers through higher prices, especially if there's an element of resale price maintenance, and competing firms are put at a disadvantage because they cannot get supplies or cannot sell through the distribution chain.

The treatment of such restraints differs from country to country. The EU tends to be tougher on the question of territorial restraints as being tough on this type of restraint is part and parcel of the business of creating a common market. In the EU for example, while non-collective exclusive dealing arrangements are tolerated when they help the distribution of goods by increasing the distributor's commitment and increasing competition, the exclusivity is limited in that parallel imports from or exports to another member state must be allowed and territorial restrictions are nearly always forbidden. However the United States is less strict and is quite tolerant of vertical restraints as long as there is sufficient competition between brands.

Japan's lenient treatment of this behaviour has been one of the main reasons for the difficulty of penetrating the Japanese market. In important sectors a lot of the distribution channels are effectively controlled by large conglomerates and the only solution is to invest in a distribution network of one's own or to purchase one.

This is a major additional cost but one that the Japanese themselves did not shrink from when entering the US car market. No doubt they also had difficulty persuading existing dealer networks in the United States to sell their products, given the relatively tolerant US attitude towards restrictive dealership arrangements.

Resale price maintenance (RPM) has been used in the past to support the continued existence of smaller non-discount stores in the face of competition by large supermarkets. Smaller stores also tend to import less, and this is considered an important factor in Japan, where mom and pop stores are still well protected. This is unlikely to last however, and RPM is likely to disappear in the future. The most recent and publicly debated example was the abolition of RPM for books in the UK; this was felt necessary to preserve specialised books and stores, but recent evidence tends to suggest that fear about their disappearance was exaggerated.

A firm can also use intellectual property rights to carve up markets and reduce competition. A patent right held in several countries allows a firm to license the manufacture in certain locations, and a trademark enables a firm to license the mark for sale only in certain markets.

The EU tends to be more strict about such cases than the United States, because arrangements of this sort could be used to partition the single market. While practices of this sort are more easily tolerated in a market that is already well established, for example the United States, they cannot be tolerated when a market is in the process of being established.

The WTO is likely to have difficulty coming to an agreement on substantive rules in this context. There is a good deal of common ground insofar as most countries tolerate vertical arrangements. But it will be more difficult to establish rules that will improve the prospects for trade. It is unlikely that the WTO will agree to abolish exclusive dealerships as such, but it might be possible to go halfway, as in the EU which allows exclusivity but not territorial divisions. This may turn out to be a reasonable compromise that will improve trade prospects. While clear rules might be difficult to establish, it might be possible to establish factors that should be considered by competition authorities to avoid territorial foreclosure.

Monopolies and Mergers

In the case of monopolies, the problem is whether monopoly power is being abused, for example by raising prices or eliminating competitors by refusing access to the system owned by the monopoly (as in telecommunications) or by predatory pricing.

Monopolies in the United States used to be forbidden, but recently a more lenient attitude has been taken with the development of the doctrine of contestability; most monopolies nowadays are considered to be open to challenge.

In Europe a different tradition has meant that abuses of dominant positions are attacked rather than monopolies *per se*. The abuser does not have to have a monopoly, merely to be in a sufficiently dominant position to have some price or marketing independence. If this position is used in a way that is considered unreasonable it is condemned by the competition rules. This is easier to prove if the abusing firm has a natural monopoly, for example a privatised telecommunications authority that refuses to allow competitors to interconnect with its lines, but would be more difficult to demonstrate, for example, should companies such as IBM abuse their computer architecture dominance or Microsoft its dominance of the software market.

The approaches of the United States and the EU to mergers and monopolies have grown closer over time, and both admit the existence of monopolies but condemn abuse. The United States position on contestability however means that it is perhaps less likely to identify abuse. Mergers are examined to see if they are unduly reducing competition. If mergers result in a monopoly, or a dominant position that could lead to abuse, it may be better to forbid them in the first place in order to prevent such abuses occurring.

But in the EU and the United States mergers tend to be treated with more leniency nowadays. In the United States markets are now generally considered contestable, and as a general rule, mergers are thought likely to promote efficiency rather than reduce competition. In the EU, mergers that might be forbidden as they would take too great a market share in certain member states, will now tend to be judged in the context of the EU as a whole and the effort to create a single market. They will also increasingly be judged in the context of the firms' ability to compete on the global market and decisions will probably have a certain industry policy content. Paradoxically there is a lingering tendency in the United States and the EU to treat national or EU-wide mergers with more suspicion than international mergers.

Antidumping

The issue of price discrimination and antidumping has been dealt with in Chapter 10. Suffice it to say here that the antidumping provisions are designed to deal, in a fairly simplified way, with foreign competitors who charge lower prices than in their home market, or who sell below cost. This leans towards protection of the producer at the expense of the consumer. There is a certain pressure to ensure that such actions are examined more closely by the standard of competition laws which attach more importance to the consumer than to producers. This has been one of the objectives of the countries most affected by antidumping actions. However they have sought to remove antidumping rules without taking account of the fact that this can only be achieved in the context of a 'single', non-segregated market where dumping is not usually possible. Solving the problem at the international level will require much more genuinely free trade, and global competition rules that take proper account of the possibility of non-competitive practices that are similar to dumping (predatory pricing, price discrimination and so on).

The Way Forward

The question is, what can future negotiations achieve with regard to competition rules? While the discussion above does not provide anything like a complete analysis of the difficulties, there seems to be room for some harmonisation of standards and for the alignment of substantive rules. The prospects for this are good in the case of horizontal agreements, and fairly good in the case of vertical restraints. In the case of monopolies, while the rules are somewhat different a compromise doesn't appear impossible. Mergers are more problematic, but it is fairly unlikely that the WTO will be able to deal with this in the near future given the intense national rivalry of firms and the intimate relationship between mergers and forms of industrial and strategic trade policy.

In many cases it may not be possible to apply hard and fast rules, and there may have to be a rule of reason to allow for the great variety of situations and practices that will arise. However the aim of the negotiators should be to develop common rules. This will not only make an agreement easier to enforce, but will increase certainty for the economic operators.

A more difficult issue is that many developing countries do not even have competition laws on their books. However this is not an insurmountable problem given that, as in the TRIPS agreement in the Uruguay Round, it will be possible to give them a grace period to develop such legislation. While it is the case that many of their economies are not sufficiently developed or sophisticated to warrant the introduction of competition legislation, in the more developed of them anticompetitive behaviour may be quite a factor. Many of these countries have developed behind barriers of one sort or another, and have practised an import substitution policy and protected infant industries for many years, and there may be many informal obstacles to competition. It will be important to tackle such remaining cartels or monopoly franchises with some vigour.

ENFORCEMENT

The more difficult questions lie with the issue of jurisdiction and who will enforce the rules. The rules applied by one country cannot usually be applied to acts committed by a firm in another country as this is considered an extraterritorial application of jurisdiction, and as such is unjustified. Moreover if a cartel has been approved or encouraged by government, it is considered immune under the principle of international law known as the 'state acts' doctrine (though this is no defence under EU law). These rules are however being gradually eroded in accordance with a series of interpretations such as the 'effects doctrine', operated by some countries, which provide for action where the anticompetitive effects are being felt by firms in the domestic market, or where the exports of local firms are being affected by unfair competition elsewhere. The EU uses competition law against conduct implemented in the EU, while the US also uses the law against conduct affecting US exports.

In the absence of common rules, common procedures and institutions for enforcing them, with increasing globalisation the tendency, has been towards unilateral and extraterritorial application of national laws. This is of course far from ideal, and has sometimes led to extreme results. An individual firm can find itself condemned in one country but unable to respond to that judgement because it would then be in violation of the laws of its own or another jurisdiction. Various bilateral and plurilateral agreements have been drawn up to avoid this sort of clash and to encourage cooperation between antitrust authorities. Instead of trespassing on each other's turf, they are encouraged to take a stroll across the lawn together.

These agreements have generally managed to avoid the more glaring examples of conflict just mentioned (so-called negative comity – agreement to avoid the most negative clashes) and have even moved towards more full blooded cooperation (so-called positive comity) between antitrust authorities; a country can request another to institute antitrust proceedings against a firm in its jurisdiction that is deemed to be committing an offence. This sort of agreement has been quite successful and has lowered the pressure on antitrust authorities to take unilateral action with questionable extraterritorial effects. The EU has several plurilateral agreements, in particular with EFTA and Central European countries. The EU and the United States were also able to reach an important bilateral agreement along these lines.

The problem with these agreements is that they do not usually allow for exchange of confidential information. Most antitrust authorities are under strict business confidentiality rules and cannot disclose information domestically let alone to the authorities of another state. This seriously hampers an outside antitrust authority being called on to prosecute a firm in its jurisdiction as it may not have access to the necessary information. It has to generate the information itself.

Exchange of information is easier when both parties are keen to deal with a particular firm or practice, but less so when they are not. One way to sidestep this dilemma is to give each other investigating rights in each other's territory. This type of information gathering already exists in the antidumping field. By allowing others to exercise these powers, a country can avoid having to take a positive action itself, that is, to hand over the evidence.

Increasingly however, governments are being authorised to negotiate cooperation agreements that provide for exchange of confidential information (true for the United States and the EU) and one can expect more powerful agreements along these lines to be negotiated in the near future.

At the same time it will be necessary to look beyond these bilateral or plurilateral agreements. While they will remain useful building blocks in any new international system, it will be increasingly important to develop common rules and a set of common institutions or procedures for settling disputes. Enforcement will of course have to be left to the national authorities, but the new institutions will have to be able to condemn any failure to enforce the common rules.

One viewpoint is that it is probably too early for international jurisdiction in antitrust cases, though there could be some sort of international system for advisory opinion.[2] While the main enforcement authority would probably have to reside at the national level for some time to come, foreign plaintiffs should at least have some standing under national systems and be entitled to claim that they have been affected by actions taken outside the jurisdiction. Some refinement of the effects doctrine, and possibly some limitations on the state acts doctrine may also be required. It may not be possible to bring competition rules under the WTO, at this stage, but the WTO should be able to use its consultation procedures to resolve disputes amicably. It should be possible to seek arbitration by the WTO if both sides agree, and some possibility might exist for some system for giving advisory opinions.

This is, however, a fairly tame approach and one that was heard in connection with intellectual property rights before the Uruguay Round. There seemed to be a feeling that a matter that was so intrinsically legal or had always been dealt with by courts, could not be confided to a mere trade policy body such as GATT. The snobbery of lawyers (like myself) knows no bounds. But there is no reason why a WTO panel, properly constructed, should not be able to pass judgement on whether an antitrust decision conforms to international rules and whether trade has been hampered. However, this touches on the central and most difficult issue of enforcement. Some authorities, for example the EU, operate by administrative fiat, though there is a system of appeal to the European courts. Others, for example the United States, have to go through the courts to attain their goal.

While it may seem natural for someone in the EU to have a second administrative institution at the level of the WTO to act as an appellate body, it is much more difficult for those used to a court-based system to accept that appeal could lie from a judicial body to an administrative one like the WTO. Quite apart from the question of separation of powers, the evidentiary and other procedures in a court and in an administrative body are quite different and can therefore lead to substantially different results. One may, in certain countries, be confronted with constitutional problems, as there is usually no appeal from the supreme court of the land.

It will be very difficult to square this circle. Either court-based systems will have to live with the anomaly, or the body set up in the WTO will have to develop procedures similar to those of a court. But some may have reservations about setting up a court in the WTO, and about its constitutional implications. The statement of the issue shows, I think, where the difficulties lie.

CONCLUSION

Something ambitious could probably be achieved in the area of competition and trade, given the political will. The situation in Japan is such that an international agreement on competition rules may be seen as the last remaining tool with which to pry open that market if matters haven't substantially improved in a few years. In that sense such a negotiation may be Japan-driven.

It may also be that a little action will go a long way. It may be enough – in order to ensure that trade with Japan improves – for Japan to open up its distribution systems and abolish import cartels. It may be possible to take a fairly piecemeal approach and initially tackle, only the sort of antitrust behaviour that has a clear and obvious effect on trade, and at least try to eliminate state-sponsored practices. It may be found, however, that a lot of anticompetitive practices are interrelated and that if one is abolished another will take its place, or suddenly appear to be just as important.

There is also a danger that overemphasis on one aspect, such as antidumping, will spoil the whole exercise, given its entrenched nature. Proponents of the abolition of antidumping provisions have made the mistake of asking for their abolition without proposing a set of common rules to put in their place.

It pays to be ambitious when tackling a subject like this. Partial solutions tend to create more problems and inequities than they solve. It is in any case increasingly necessary to try to find global solutions to what has become a global problem of competition and enforcement.

Notes and References

1 Introduction

1. World Trade Organisation, *Regionalism and the World Trading System* (Geneva: WTO, 1995); A. Maddison, *Economic Growth in the West, The Twentieth Century Fund* (London: George Allen and Unwin, 1964); A. Maddison, *The World Economy in the Twentieth Century* (Paris: OECD, 1989).
2. World Bank, *World Development Report* (New York: Oxford University Press, 1987), pp. 46–57.
3. Ibid., pp. 84, 85.
4. World Bank, *World Development Report* (New York: Oxford University Press, 1991), p. 97, box 5.2.
5. World Bank (1987), op. cit., p. 86, fig. 5.3.
6. The literature on the Japanese economic and trade model is very extensive. For a good account of the difference between the Japanese and Western systems see J. Fallows, *Looking at the Sun, the rise of the new East Asian Economic and Political System* (New York: Vintage Books, Ch. 4. See also *The East Asian Miracle, Economic Growth and Public Policy,* World Bank (New York: Oxford University Press, 1993). There are those who consider that the Japanese economy is open, but even the Japanese have more or less acknowledged the fairly closed nature of their economic system. In this context see the Maekawa report entitled 'Report of the Advisory Group on Economic Structural Adjustment for International Harmony' (Tokyo: Government Publications, April 1986) which discusses at length the structural impediments to trade in the Japanese economy. A more recent report (so-called 'new Maekawa Report' of the Economic Council to the Prime Minister is called *Policy Recommendations of the Economic Council-Action for Economic Restructuring* (Tokyo: Government Publications, 1987). See also I. Ozawa, *Blueprint for a New Japan, the rethinking of a Nation* (Tokyo: Kodansha International, 1994) and E. Sakakibara, *Beyond Capitalism: the Japanese Model of Market Economics* (Lanham: University Press of America for the Economic Strategy Institute, 1993).
7. R.Z. Lawrence, 'Imports in Japan: Closed Markets or Minds?', *Brookings Papers on Economic Activity*, vol. 2 (1987), p. 520; E.J. Lincoln, *Japan's Unequal Trade* (Washington D.C.: The Brookings Institution, 1990), pp. 39, 43–44, 55.
8. W. Greider, *One World Ready or Not* (New York: Simon and Schuster, 1997); E. Luttwak, *The Endangered American Dream* (New York: Simon and Schuster, 1993); J. Goldsmith, *The Trap* (London: Macmillan, 1994).
9. P. Krugman, *Pop Internationalism* (Cambridge, Mass: MIT Press, 1997).
10. OECD, *Trade and Employment* (Paris: OECD, 1994).
11. Ibid.

12. R. Batra, *The Great American Deception* (Chichester: John Wiley, 1996).
13. W. Greider, *One World*, op. cit., pp. 317, 318.

2 Trade Theory

1. See P. Krugman, 'Is Free Trade Passé?', in P. King (ed.), *International Economics and International Economic Policy, a Reader* (New York: McGraw Hill, 1995), for a good account of the economic basis for strategic trade policy.
2. See ibid., pp. 28–32.

3 Trade Policy

1. This school of thought is based on David Ricardo's theory of comparative advantage.
2. Some seminal essays and comments on strategic trade policy are to be found in R.M. Stern (ed.), *US Trade Policies in a Changing World* (Cambridge, Mass.: Massachusetts Institute of Technology, 1988); P. King (ed.), *International Economics and International Economic Policy* (New York: McGraw-Hill, 1995). See in particular the contributions by Krugman, D'Andrea Tyson and Saxonhouse.
3. P. King, *International Economics*, op. cit., ch. 2.

4 The Role of GATT and the Nature of GATT Negotiations

1. J. Jackson, *The World Trading System* (Cambridge, Mass.: MIT Press, 1994), p. 53.

5 Institutional Issues

1. One of the best general analyses of the institutional issues is to be found in J. Jackson, *Restructuring the GATT System* (New York: Council on Foreign Relations Press, 1990); J. Schott (ed.), *Completing the Uruguay Round* (Washington D.C.: Institute for International Economics, 1990), see ch. 11 by Jackson, adapted from the book just referred to.

6 Developing Countries

1. World Trade Organisation, *International Trade, Trends and Statistics* (Geneva: WTO, 1995), p. 6, chart 1.4.
2. World Bank, *World Development Report 1987* (Washington D.C.: World Bank, 1987), p. 47, tables 3.1, 3.2.
3. Ibid., p. 47, table 3.3.
4. Ibid., p. 46; UNCTAD, *Trade and Development Report, 1994*, pp. 51 to 52.
5. World Trade Organisation, *International Trade*, op. cit., pp. 15–19.
6. World Bank, *World Development Report*, op. cit., p. 81.
7. Ibid., p. 159, box 9.2.

7 Regional Arrangements

1. World Trade Organisation, *Regionalism and the World Trading System* (Geneva: WTO, 1995), p. 41, box 4.
2. European Commission, 'The Impact and Effectiveness of the Single Market', Communication from the Commission, COM(96) 520 final, 30 October 1996.
3. World Trade Organisation, *International Trade, Trends and Statistics* (Geneva: WTO, 1995), pp. 13, 14, tables 1.7, 1.8.
4. World Bank, A. Yeats, *Does Mercosur's Trade Performance justify concerns about the effects of Regional Trade Arrangements?* (Washington D.C.: World Bank, 1996).
5. Carnegie Endowment for International Peace, *Reflections on Regionalism* (Washington D.C.: Brookings Institution, 1997).

8 Tariffs

1. GATT, *The Results of the Uruguay Round of Multilateral Trade Negotiations, Market Access for Goods and Services: Overview of the Results* (Geneva: GATT, 1994), p. 69, appendix, table 5.
2. The European Commission, Final Report of European Commission Services on the results of the Uruguay Round 1994 (unpublished).
3. Ibid.
4. Ibid.
5. GATT (1994), op. cit., pp. 69 and 70, appendix tables 5 and 6.
6. GATT (1994), op. cit., p. 11, Table II. 2.
7. Ibid., p. 13, table II. 4.
8. Ibid., p. 78, appendix, table 14. The European Commission, *The Uruguay Round, Global Agreement, Global Benefits* (Luxembourg: The European Commission, 1994).
9. GATT, *An Analysis of the Uruguay Round Agreement with Particular Emphasis on Aspects of Interest to Developing Economies* (Geneva: GATT, 1993), p. 29. See also GATT, *The Results of the Uruguay Round*, op. cit., p. 15, table II.5, which gives slightly different and presmably more up-to-date figures, but does not give a comparison between bindings on imports from developing countries and all sources.

9 Tariff-Related Issues

1. World Trade Organisation, *Understanding on the Interpretation of Art. II.1(b) of the General Agreement on Tariffs and Trade* contained in 'The Results of the Uruguay Round of Multilateral Trade Negotiations: The Legal Texts' (Geneva: GATT, 1994), pp. 23–24.

10 Antidumping

1. There is a lively debate nowadays about the justification for antidumping actions, and the criticism is generally levelled at the fact that under normal antitrust laws these actions would not be condemned in national

markets. The author's view is that this argument does not take account of the segmentation of international markets, which permits a great deal of uncompetitive behaviour not normally to be found within the confines of a national market. In the absence of more open markets and enforceable international competition rules, antidumping rules will continue to play an essential role. This section tries to make this case taking account of and attempting to answer the contrary arguments.
2. World Trade Organisation, 'Ministerial Declaration', Singapore, December 1996 (Geneva: WTO, 1996). doc. ref. WT/MIN/(96) Dec.
3. World Trade Organisation, Agreement on Implementation of Article VI of the General Agreement on Tariffs and Trade (Geneva: WTO hereafter, ADA (Antidumping Agreement)). Contained in 'The Results of the Uruguay Round of Multilateral Trade Negotiations: The Legal Texts' (Geneva: GATT, 1994), pp. 168–196.
4. See R. Boltuck and R. Litan (eds), *Down in the Dumps* (Washington D.C.: The Brookings Institution, 1991), for various examples of the difficulty of measurement and other matters relating to the administration of antidumping laws in the United States.
5. WTO, ADA, op. cit., Articles 2.2.1 and 2.4.
6. Ibid., Article 2.2.1.
7. Ibid., Article 2.4.2.
8. Ibid., Article 2.4.1.
9. Ibid., Article 2.4.
10. Ibid., Article 3.
11. Ibid., Article 3.4.
12. Ibid., Article 3.5.
13. Ibid., Article 3.2.
14. Ibid., Article 3.3.
15. Ibid., Articles 3.3 and 5.8.
16. Ibid., Article 7.
17. Ibid., Article 8.
18. Ibid., Articles 9 and 10.
19. Ibid., Article 11.
20. Ibid., Articles 5.2 to 5.8.
21. Ibid., Article 5.4.
22. Ibid., Article 17.
23. Ibid., Article 17.6.
24. 'Gatt Activities 1994–1995' (Geneva: WTO, 1996), p. 78.
25. WTO, 'Ministerial Declaration', op. cit.

11 Subsidies

1. OECD, *Public Support to Industry* (Paris: OECD, 1996).
2. European Commission, *Fourth Survey on State Aid in the European Union in the Manufacturing and Certain Other Sectors* (Luxembourg: EC, 1995).
3. OECD, *National Accounts, Main Aggregates*, vol. 1 (Paris: OECD, 1960–1994).
4. OECD, *Public Support to Industry* (Paris: OECD, 1996), p. 16, graph 1.

5. European Commission, *Fourth Survey on State Aid* (Luxembourg: EC, 1995), p. 7.
6. OECD, *Public Support to Industry*, op. cit., p. 18, table 1.
7. European Commission, *Fourth Survey on State Aid*, op. cit., p. 24, table 6.
8. OECD, *Public Support to Industry*, op. cit., pp. 33–5.
9. Ibid., pp. 55, 56.
10. G.C. Hufbauer and J.S. Erb, *Subsidies in International Trade* (Washington D.C.: Institute for International Economics, 1984) provides a good account of the development of the laws on subsidies.
11. World Trade Organisation, 'Agreement on Subsidies and Countervailing Measures' contained in 'The Results of the Uruguay Round of Multilateral Trade Negotiations: The Legal Texts' (Geneva: GATT, 1994) pp. 264–314, Articles 1 and 2, hereafter ASC.
12. Ibid., Article 3.
13. GATT documents L/4422–4425, (2 Nov. 1976) (Geneva: GATT).
14. WTO, ASC, op. cit., Articles 1, 2, 5 and 6.
15. Ibid., Article 8.
16. Ibid., Article 11.
17. Ibid., Articles 27, 28 and 29.

12   Safeguards and Countervailing Duties

1. UNCTAD, *The Outcome of the Uruguay Round: an initial assessment* (Geneva: UNCTAD, 1994), p. 51, box 8.
2. Ibid., p. 58, table 3.
3. World Trade Organisation, 'Agreement on Safeguards' contained in 'The Results of the Uruguay Round of Multilateral Trade Negotiations: The Legal Texts' (Geneva: GATT, 1994), pp. 315 to 324, Article 11.
4. Ibid., Article 11.2.
5. Ibid.
6. Ibid., Article 10.
7. Ibid., Article 7.
8. Ibid., Article 6.
9. Ibid., Article 5.
10. Ibid., Article 8.3.
11. UNCTAD, *The Outcome of the Uruguay Round*, op. cit., p. 58, table 3.
12. Ibid., p. 61.

13   Technical Barriers to Trade

1. World Trade Organisation, 'Agreement on Technical Barriers to Trade' contained in 'The Results of the Uruguay Round of Multilateral Trade Negotiations: The Legal Text' (Geneva: GATT, 1994), pp. 138–162, Articles 2.1–2.3, 2.8.
2. Ibid., Articles 2.5, 2.9–2.12, 10, 11.
3. Ibid., Articles 2.4 and 2.6.
4. Ibid., Article 2.7.
5. Ibid., Articles 5 and 6.
6. Ibid., Articles 3 and 7.

7. Ibid., Articles 7 and 8.
8. Ibid., Article 8.

14 Government Procurement

1. Canada, 15 EU member states, Israel, Japan, Korea, Netherlands on behalf of Aruba, Norway, Switzerland and the United States. The new agreement negotiated at the time of the Uruguay Round has for the moment 26 signatories and came into force on 1 January 1996. The accession of Hong Kong, Singapore and Liechtenstein have been approved but the instruments of accession have not yet been deposited. Taiwan has also submitted an offer.

15 Textiles

1. See W. Cline, *The Future of World Trade in Textiles and Apparel* (Washington D.C.: Institute for International Economics, 1987), for a good outline of the development of the MFA and the industry. See also World Bank, *World Development Report* (New York: Oxford University Press, 1987), p. 136, box 8.3.
2. 'Estimates of the International Textile and Clothing Bureau (ITCB)', quoted in UNCTAD 'Preliminary Analysis of Opportunities and Challenges resulting from the Uruguay Round Agreement on Textiles and Clothing' (Geneva: UNCTAD, 1995), p. 15, para. 58.
3. European Commission, 'The Impact of International Developments on the Community's Textile and Clothing Sector', communication from the Commission, COM(95)447 final, 11 October (Luxembourg: EC, 1995).
4. Quoted in M. Majmudar, 'Trade Liberalisation in Clothing: the MFA Phaseout and the Developing Countries, in Development Policy Review, vol. 14, no. 1, March 1996, p. 12.
5. UNCTAD, *Outcome of the Uruguay Round: an Initial Assessment* (Geneva: UNCTAD, 1994), p. 128, table 11.
6. Council Regulation (EC) No. 2315/96, *Official Journal of the European Communities*, no. L314/1, Dec. 1996.
7. UNCTAD, *Preliminary Analysis*, op. cit., p. 19, para 75.
8. I. Trela and J. Whalley, 'Unravelling the Threads of the MFA' (1990), in C. Hamilton (ed.) (1990) *Textile Trade and the Developing Countries: Eliminating the Multifibre Arrangement in the 1990s* (Washington D.C.: World Bank).
9. Y. Yang, *The Impact of the MFA Phasing Out on World Clothing and Textile Markets* (Canberra: National Centre for Development Studies, Australian National University, 1993).
10. United States International Trade Commission, *The Economic Effects of Significant U.S. Import Restraints*, Publication 2222 (Washington: USITC, 1989), pp. 4–6.
11. M. Majmudar, *Trade Liberalisation*, op. cit., pp. 12, 25; M. Majmudar, The MFA Phase-out and EU Clothing Sourcing: Forecasts to 2005, Textile Outlook International, March 1996, pp. 33, 44, 57.
12. United States International Trade Commission, *Potential Impact on*

the US Economy and Industries of the GATT Uruguay Round Agreements, Publication 2790 (Washington D.C.: USITC, June 1994), pp. IV–3.
13. Y. Yang, *The Impact*, op. cit.
14. European Commission, *The Impact*, op. cit. see Reference to Mercer Report estimates.
15. See OECD, *The Uruguay Round and The Future Multilateral Trading System* (Paris: OECD, 1994), pp. 114 and 115 for the economic implications of the agreement.

16 Civil Aircraft

1. GATT, 'Agreement on Trade in Civil Aircraft' (Geneva: GATT, 1979, B15DZ6S/162) Article 2. The parties to the agreement are Canada, Egypt, the EU, Japan, Macau, Norway, Rumania, Switzerland and the United States.
2. It eliminated duties and all other charges on goods imported for sale, manufacture, repair, maintenance, rebuilding, modification or conversion.
3. GATT, 'Agreement', op. cit., Article 4.
4. Ibid., Article 6.
5. Agreement between the European Economic Community and the government of the United States of America concerning the application of the GATT Agreement on Trade in Civil Aircraft on trade in large civil aircraft, 1992, *Official Journal of the European Communities No. L301/ 31 of 17/10/92, Article 3*.
6. Ibid., Article 4.
7. Ibid., Article 5.
8. 'Agreement on Subsidies and Countervailing Measures' (Geneva: GATT, 1994), footnotes 15, 16, 24.

17 Steel

1. OECD, *The Steel Market in 1995 and the Outlook for 1996 and 1997*, (Paris: OECD, 1996).

19 Trade-Related Intellectual Property

1. Articles 1–8 of the 'Agreement on Trade Related Aspects of Intellectual Property Rights' contained in 'The Results of the Uruguay Round of Multilateral Trade Negotiations: The Legal Texts' (Geneva: GATT, 1994), pp. 365–403.
2. J.H. Reichman, 'Universal Minimum Standards of Intellectual Property Protection Under the TRIPS Component of the WTO Agreement', *The International Lawyer*, vol. 29, no. 2, 1995, p. 357, for a discussion of this.
3. See P. Marett, *Intellectual Property Law* (London: Sweet & Maxwell, 1996), for a general account of the various treaties and conventions. See also M. Blakeney, *Trade Related Aspects of Intellectual Property Rights: a concise guide to the TRIPS Agreement* (London: Sweet and Maxwell, 1996).

4. TRIPS, Articles 27–34.
5. TRIPS, Articles 30, 31, 40.
6. TRIPS, Articles 35–38.
7. J.H. Reichman, 'Universal Minimum', op. cit., p. 356.
8. TRIPS, Articles 25, 26.
9. TRIPS, Article 39.
10. Reichman, Universal Minimum', op. cit., p. 378.
11. See Marett, *Intellectual Property Law*, op. cit., for a general account of the treaties and conventions.
12. TRIPS, Articles 15–21.
13. TRIPS, Articles 22–24.
14. TRIPS, Articles 25, 26.
15. See Marrett, *Intellectual Property Law*, op. cit.
16. TRIPS, Articles 9–14.
17. TRIPS, Articles 41–64.
18. TRIPS, Articles 65–67, 70.

20 Trade-Related Investment Measures

1. United Nations, *The Impact of Trade Related Investment Measures on Trade and Development* (New York: UN, 1991), p. 3.
2. Ibid., p. 3.
3. Ibid., p. 54–55.
4. Ibid., p. 3.

21 Agriculture

1. W. Cochrane, *The Development of American Agriculture, a Historical Analysis* (Minneapolis: University of Minnesota Press, 1992). In the United States, productivity varied from 2.2 per cent in the 1950s to close to 3 per cent in the 1980s.
2. Ibid., p. 166.
3. See J. Bovard, *The Farm Fiasco* (San Francisco: Institute for Contemporary Studies, 1991), ch. 3.
4. Cochrane, *The Development*, op. cit., p. 162.
5. Ibid., p. 160, table 8.4, extract from 'National Financial Summary, 1990', U.S. Department of Agriculture, Economic Research Service, ECIFS 10–1, November 1991, pp. 53, 55; J. Bovard, *The Farm Fiasco*, op. cit., pp. 44–48.
6. Cochrane, *The Development*, op. cit., p. 162.
7. Ibid.
8. Ibid., p. 151.
9. OECD, *Agricultural Policies, Markets and Trade* in OECD countries, (Paris: OECD, 1997) Table III.1, p. 31.
10. European Commission, *Uruguay Round, a Turning Point for Agricultural Trade* (Brussels: EC, 1992).
11. WTO, 'Agreement on Agriculture' contained in 'The Results of the Uruguay Round of Multilateral Trade Negotiations: The Legal Texts' (Geneva: GATT, 1994), pp. 39 to 84, Articles 6 and 7, annexes 2, 3 and 4.

12. Ibid., Articles 4 and 5, annex 5.
13. Ibid., Articles 8–12.
14. See T.E. Josling, S. Tangermann and T.K. Warley, *Agriculture in the GATT* (London: Macmillan, 1996), for the best account of the history of the negotiation, its results and weaknesses.

22 Services

1. OECD, *OECD in Figures: Statistics on the Member Countries* (Paris: OECD, 1996) pp. 8 and 30.
2. World Trade Organisation, *International Trade, Trends and Statistics* (Geneva: WTO, 1995), p. 14, table 1.8.
3. Eurostat, *1996 Facts through Figures: a statistical portrait of the European Union* (Luxembourg: EC, 1996).
4. OECD, OECD in Figures, op. cit., pp. 8 and 30.
5. European Commission, *The General Agreement on Trade in Services, a Guide for Business* (Luxembourg: EC, 1995), pp. 9, 12, graph 2.
6. WTO, *International Trade*, op. cit., p. 14, table 1.8.
7. Ibid
8. European Commission, *The General Agreement*, op. cit., p. 11, graph 1.
9. Ibid., p. 12, table 2.
10. GATT, *The Results of the Uruguay Round of Multilateral Trade Negotiations – Market Access for Goods and Services: Overview of the Results* (Geneva: GATT, 1994).
11. World Trade Organisation, 'General Agreement on Trade in Services', contained in 'The Results of the Uruguay Round of Multilateral Trade Negotiations: The Legal Texts' (Geneva: GATT, 1994), Article I, hereafter WTO, GATS.
12. Ibid., Article II.
13. Ibid., Article XVI.
14. Ibid., Article XVII.
15. Ibid., Articles VI and VII.
16. Ibid., Annex on 'Movement of Natural Persons Supplying Services under the Agreement'.
17. World Trade Organisation, 'Decision on Movement of Natural Persons Commitment' S/L/10 (Geneva: WTO 24 July 1995); *Decision on Acceptance of the Second and Third Protocols to the GATS*, S/L/28930 July 1996 (Geneva: WTO, 1996).
18. WTO, GATS, op. cit., Article XI.
19. Ibid., Article XV.
20. Ibid., Article X.
21. Ibid., Articles XIV, XIV bis, XII.
22. Ibid., Article XX.
23. Ibid., Article VIII.
24. Ibid., Article IV.
25. Ibid., Article XIII.
26. Decision on Negotiations on Basic Telecommunications, contained in 'The Results of the Uruguay Round of Multilateral Trade Negotiations: The Legal Texts' (Geneva: GATT, 1994), p. 461.

27. See B. Petrazzini, *Global Telecom Talks: a Trillion Dollar Deal* (Washington D.C.: Institute for International Economics, 1996), for a more detailed account.
28. Understanding on Commitments on Financial Services, 'The Results of the Uruguay Round of Multilateral Trade Negotiations: The Legal Texts' (Geneva: GATT, 1994) p. 478.
29. See R. Kampf, 'A Step in the Right Direction: The Interim Deal on Financial Services in the GATS', *International Trade Law and Regulation*, vol. 1, issue 5 Nov. 1995.
30. UNCTAD, *The Outcome of the Uruguay Round: an initial assessment* (Geneva: UNCTAD, 1994), p. 162, box 16.
31. Charles P. Haeter Jr., 'Professional Services Domestic Regulation and the WTO Working Party', 12th Progress Seminar, Services and the Trade Liberalisation Agenda of the WTO, Geneva, 1996.
32. WTO, GATS, op. cit., Decision on Negotiations on Maritime Transport Services. Contained in 'The Results of the Uruguay Round of Multilateral Trade Negotiations: The Legal Texts' (Geneva: GATT, 1994), p. 459.
33. Ibid., Annex on Air Transport Services, contained in 'The Results of the Uruguay Round of Multilateral Trade Negotiations: The Legal Texts' (Geneva: GATT, 1994), pp. 353–354.

23 The Future of the World Trade Organisation

1. Sir Leon Brittan, vice president of the European Commission, has called informally for a 'Millennium Round'.

24 Trade and the Environment

1. OECD, 'Report to the Ministers on Trade and Environment' (Paris: OECD, 1996).
2. European Commission, 'Communication to the Council and the Parliament on Trade and Environment', COM(96)54 final (Luxembourg: EC, 1996), p. 5,
3. European Union vs United States, 1994. Challenge to US vehicle emission (CAFE) standards, Gas Guzzler Tax and Luxury Tax on the ground they discriminated against foreign cars in fact if not in intent. Report of the Panel, doc. Ref. DS 31/R (Geneva: GATT, 1994).
4. Canada vs US, 1982. Challenge concerned a US prohibition of tuna imports from Canada. Report of the Panel, doc. ref. DS21/R (Geneva: GATT, 1991).
5. United States vs Canada, 1988. Challenge concerned Canadian ban on exports of herring and salmon. Report of the Panel, doc. ref. L/6268 (Geneva: GATT, 1987).
6. Venezuela and Brazil vs United States, 1996. Challenge to US requirement that foreign gasoline producers use US industry average baseline to improve environmental standards. Report of the Panel, doc. ref. WT/DS2/R (Geneva: WTO, 1996).
7. Mexico vs United States, 1991. Challenge to US restrictions on tuna imports under the US Marine Mammal Protection Act. Report of the Panel doc. ref. DS29/R (Geneva: GATT, 1991).

25 Foreign Direct Investment

1. J.J. Servan, Schreiber, *The American Challenge* (Harmondsworth: Penguin, 1968).
2. E.M. Graham and P.R. Krugman, *Foreign Direct Investment in the United States* (Washington D.C.: Institute for International Economics, 1995).
3. United Nations, *World Investment Report* (Geneva: UN, 1996).
4. Ibid.
5. Ibid.
6. Code of Liberalisation of Capital Movements, Code of Liberalisation of Invisible Operations, and the National Treatment Instrument, OECD.
7. Treaty establishing the European Economic Community, 1957, Articles 67–73.
8. North Atlantic Free Trade Association, ch. 11.
9. World Trade Organisation 'Ministerial Declaration', Singapore, December 1996 (Geneva: WTO, 1997), doc. ref. WT/MIN/96/Dec.
10. See OECD; Market Access after the Uruguay Round, Investment, Competition and Technology Perspectives (Paris: OECD, 1996). See in particular in chapter 2. E. Graham, 'Investment and the New Multilateral Trade Context', for a good summary of the type of investment restrictions that exist, and issues that need to be addressed in negotiations on a multilateral agreement on investment. See also in Chapter 23 E. Graham, *Global Corporations and National Governments* (Washington D.C.: Institute for International Economics, 1996).

26 Trade and Labour Standards

1. OECD, 'Trade and Labour Standards', study carried out jointly by Trade and Education, Employment, Labour and Social Affairs Directorate (Paris: OECD, 1996).
2. Ibid.
3. European Commission, 'The Trading System and Internationally Recognised Labour Standards', Communication to the Council, Brussels (COM C96) 402, final (Luxembourg: EC, 24 July 1996).
4. World Trade Organisation, 'Ministerial Declaration', Singapore, December 1996 (Geneva: WTO, 1997), doc. ref. WT/MIN/(96)/Dec.

27 International Rules on Competition

1. OECD, 'Market Access after the Uruguay Round, Investment, Competition and Technology Perspective' (Paris: OECD, 1996). See in particular in ch. 6 M. Warner, 'Private and Public Restraints on Trade: Effects on Investment Decisions and Policy Approaches to Them', which gives a good brief account of the main issues. See also OECD, *New Dimensions of Market Access in a Globalising World Economy* (Paris: OECD, 1995).
2. F.M. Scherer, *Competition Policies for an Integrated World Economy* (Washington D.C.: The Brookings Institution Press, 1994).

Index